*Che Guevara: Economics and Politics
in the Transition to Socialism*

To Elena Gil Izquierdo
To Haydée Santamaría Cuadrado
To Celia Sánchez Manduley

Carlos Tablada

CHE GUEVARA:
ECONOMICS
AND POLITICS
IN THE TRANSITION
TO SOCIALISM

PATHFINDER

NEW YORK   LONDON   MONTREAL   SYDNEY

Cover photograph: Elliott Erwitt/Magnum
Cover and book design: Toni Gorton
Original title in Spanish: *El pensamiento económico de Ernesto Che Guevara* (The economic thought of Ernesto Che Guevara)

Manufactured in the United States of America
First edition, 1989
Second edition, 1990
Third edition, 1998
Third printing, 2000

Pathfinder
410 West Street, New York, NY 10014, U.S.A.
Fax: (212) 727-0150
E-mail: pathfinderpress@compuserve.com

PATHFINDER DISTRIBUTORS AROUND THE WORLD:
Australia (and Asia and the Pacific):
    Pathfinder, 176 Redfern St., 1st floor, Redfern, NSW 2016
    Postal address: P.O. Box K879, Haymarket, NSW 1240
Canada:
    Pathfinder, 2761 Dundas St. West, Toronto, ON, M6P 1Y4
Iceland:
    Pathfinder, Klapparstíg 26, 2d floor, 101 Reykjavík
    Postal address: P. Box 0233, 121 Reykjavík
New Zealand:
    Pathfinder, La Gonda Arcade, 203 Karangahape Road, Auckland
    Postal address: P.O. Box 8730, Auckland
Sweden:
    Pathfinder, Vikingagatan 10, S-113 42, Stockholm
United Kingdom (and Europe, Africa except South Africa, and Middle East):
    Pathfinder, 47 The Cut, London, SE1 8LL
United States (and Caribbean, Latin America, and South Africa):
    Pathfinder, 410 West Street, New York, NY 10014

CONTENTS

5   Ernesto Che Guevara

7   Carlos Tablada

9   Preface

25   *Fidel Castro*
Che's ideas are absolutely
relevant today

PART ONE
The economic management system under
socialism: Theoretical and methodological
questions discussed by Che

55   CHAPTER 1 The economic management
system and its categories

77   CHAPTER 2 The Marxist conception of
politics as concentrated economics and its
importance in economic management
under socialism

83   CHAPTER 3 The relationship between the
budgetary finance system and the
economic accounting system in the
management of the socialist economy

PART TWO
The economic management system in the
first stage of building socialism
in Cuba

97 CHAPTER 4 Emergence of the budgetary finance system

109 CHAPTER 5 Economic planning: its function as principal organizer of the socialist economy

127 CHAPTER 6 The role of money, the banking system, and prices

149 CHAPTER 7 Unequal exchange

163 CHAPTER 8 Che and voluntary work

167 CHAPTER 9 Incentive systems

197 CHAPTER 10 Problems of leadership, organization, and management of social production in the budgetary finance system

203 CHAPTER 11 Cadre policy: political leadership and the development of administrative and technical personnel

211 CHAPTER 12 Conclusions

223 Appendix: Manual for administrators

229 Notes

257 For further reading

259 Bibliography

287 Index

ERNESTO CHE GUEVARA

ERNESTO CHE GUEVARA was born in Rosario, Argentina on June 14, 1928. Both before and after graduating from medical school in 1953, he traveled extensively throughout Latin America. While living in Guatemala in 1954, he became involved in political struggle, opposing the CIA's attempts to overthrow the government of Jacobo Arbenz. Following the ouster of Arbenz, Guevara escaped to Mexico. There, in the summer of 1955, he was selected by Fidel Castro as the third confirmed member of the expeditionary force being organized by the Cuban July 26 Movement to overthrow dictator Fulgencio Batista.

In late November 1956 the eighty-two expeditionaries, including Castro and Guevara, set sail from Tuxpan, Mexico, aboard the yacht *Granma*. The rebel forces landed on Cuba's southeastern coast in Oriente province on December 2 to begin the revolutionary war from the Sierra Maestra mountains in the eastern part of the island. Originally the troop doctor, Guevara was named commander of the second Rebel Army column (Column no. 4) in July 1957. At the end of August 1958 he led Column no. 8 toward Las Villas province in central Cuba. The Las Villas campaign culminated in the capture of Santa Clara, Cuba's third-largest city, and helped seal the fate of the dictatorship.

Following Batista's fall on January 1, 1959, Guevara carried a number of responsibilities in the new revolutionary government, including president of the National Bank and minister of industry, while continuing his duties as an officer in the armed forces. He frequently represented Cuba internationally, including at the United Nations and in other world forums. As a leader of the July 26 Movement, he helped bring about the political regroupment that led to the founding of the Communist Party of Cuba in October 1965.

Guevara resigned his government and party posts, including his military commission and responsibilities, in early 1965 and left Cuba in order to return to South America to help advance the anti-imperialist and anticapitalist struggles that were sharpening in several countries. Along with a number of volunteers who would later join him in Bolivia, Guevara went first to the Congo where he aided the anti-imperialist movement founded by Patrice Lumumba. From November 1966 to October 1967 he led a guerrilla movement in Bolivia against that country's military dictatorship. Wounded and captured by the Bolivian army in a CIA-organized operation on October 8, 1967, he was murdered the following day.

CARLOS TABLADA

Carlos Tablada, born in Havana in 1948, is a researcher for the Havana-based Center for the Study of the World Economy and an associate professor at the University of Havana. From 1967 to 1971 he studied and taught in the Philosophy Department of the University of Havana. From 1973 to 1990 he worked as an economic director of Cuban state enterprises while also earning a degree as doctor of economic sciences in 1986.

The manuscript for this book, begun in 1969 and completed in 1984, received the Ernesto Che Guevara Special Award in the 1987 literary contest sponsored by the Havana-based cultural institution Casa de las Américas. The first edition of the book was published in Cuba in 1987 in two limited printings under the title *The Economic Thought of Ernesto Che Guevara.* When Casa de las Américas publishing house came out with a second edition in early 1988 the initial printing of 250,000 sold out in Cuba within a few weeks. Since then twenty-four editions of the book have been published in eight languages and thirteen countries.

Over the last decade, Tablada has traveled extensively, speaking about the political and theoretical contributions of Che Guevara and their relevance today, defending Cuba's socialist revolution, and affirming the right of the Cuban people to chart their own political and economic course independent of imperialist interests. He has given talks and participated in academic conferences and numerous other public forums in some 30 countries in Central and South America, Western Europe, the United States, and Canada.

PREFACE

The struggle against imperialism, for liberation from colonial or neocolonial shackles, which is being carried out by means of political weapons, firearms, or a combination of the two, is not separate from the struggle against backwardness and poverty. Both are stages on the same road leading toward the creation of a new society of justice and plenty.

It is imperative to take political power and to get rid of the oppressor classes. But then the second stage of the struggle, which may be even more difficult than the first, must be faced.[1]

—*Che Guevara*
Algiers, February 1965

Che believed in man. And if we don't believe in man, if we think that man is an incorrigible little animal, capable of advancing only if you feed him grass or tempt him with a carrot or whip him with a stick— anybody who believes this, anybody convinced of this will never be a revolutionary, never be a socialist, never be a communist.[2]

—*Fidel Castro*
Havana, October 1987

The questions that Ernesto Che Guevara, acting as part of the central leadership of the Cuban revolution, sought to help the vanguard of the working class answer more than three decades ago remain the most pressing of our epoch.

Guevara charted a course to rid the world of the capitalist

system, with all its horrors, and open the way for working men and women to begin a transition toward a more just and human socialist society, transforming themselves in the process. That course determined his every deed as a conscious political person.

Like the young founders of the modern communist movement, Che deeply believed, and acted on his conviction, that "revolution is necessary . . . not only because the *ruling* class cannot be overthrown in any other way, but also because the class *overthrowing* it can only in a revolution succeed in ridding itself of all the muck of ages and become fit to found society anew."[3]

Che died thirty years ago in the mountains of Bolivia, fighting to create the conditions out of which could emerge the leadership of a Latin America-wide movement of workers and peasants capable of winning the battles for land reform and independence from imperialist domination and opening the socialist revolution. Today's world would not be alien to him, however. The sharpening interimperialist trade and financial conflicts and looming economic crises, the deteriorating wages and living conditions facing working people everywhere, the depression levels of unemployment and poverty endemic throughout much of Latin America, the growing political polarization and incipient fascist movements rearing their heads in the imperialist countries, the social disintegration threatening large parts of Africa, and the booming cannons of imperialist powers firing the first salvos of World War III in Iraq and Yugoslavia—the deadly historic logic of capitalism continues to unfold. Details have changed since the 1960s, but the fundamentals of the world Guevara sought to lead working people to transform have not.

With one important qualification: Imperialism is weaker than it was thirty years ago, more vulnerable, and the working class is a larger percentage of the world's population. The stakes have gone up.

The shattering of the bureaucratic regimes and parties of Eastern Europe and the Soviet Union, culminating in 1989–91, would likewise not have been unthinkable to Che. Guevara was among the most conscious of the Cuban leaders that, despite the welcome aid Cuba received from the Soviet bloc, the political, economic, and social policies of the leaders of those countries were alien to the proletarian and internationalist course being charted in Cuba. Cuban President Fidel Castro addressed this fact, speaking to a gathering of Cuba's Union of Young Communists in April 1997. Referring to the events that unfolded in the Soviet bloc countries at the beginning of the decade, he noted that nearly forty years ago "no one could have imagined" what later transpired there. But "we did have one who could see into the future among us, and that person was Che," Castro said.[4]

For decades the methods employed in the organization of production, distribution, labor, and planning in each of the Soviet bloc countries, with this or that variation, were promoted by the big majority of those the world over who called themselves communists as the only road from capitalism to socialism. But the verdict on the so-called Soviet model has now been rendered by history: the planning and management systems in the USSR and Eastern European countries—and the organization of labor underlying them—were pushing these peoples *away from* socialism, not toward it.

The alternative course, advanced in Cuba by the central leadership in the opening years of the socialist revolution, and placed on its soundest theoretical foundations by Ernesto Che Guevara, is the subject of this book. It will be studied by revolutionary fighters the world over with even greater interest today because of the verdict of history that Guevara himself did not live to witness.

*   *   *

After Fidel Castro—the historic leader of the Cuban revolutionary forces from 1953 to today—Ernesto Che Guevara was the best-known leader of the revolution during its early years, when "we were used to making the impossible possible," as Castro said in paying tribute to Guevara in October 1987.[5]

Guevara was Argentine by birth. Having graduated from medical school in Buenos Aires in 1953, he met Fidel Castro in Mexico in July 1955 and immediately agreed to join the

July 26 Movement and to sign on to the expeditionary force
Castro was organizing to launch a revolutionary war against
the U.S.-backed Batista dictatorship in Cuba. Guevara—soon
nicknamed "Che" (a popular form of address in Argentina)
by his Cuban comrades—was initially recruited as troop
doctor, but he rapidly proved himself to be an outstanding
combat leader and educator. In 1957 he became the first combatant promoted by Fidel to command a separate column of
the Rebel Army. Guevara led the December 1958 campaign
that culminated in the capture of the city of Santa Clara in
central Cuba, effectively sealing the fate of the Batista dictatorship.

But Guevara's most important contributions to the Cuban
revolution were not military. In paying tribute to Che in October 1967, a few days after his death, Castro called attention to
this fact, saying:

> Che was an extraordinarily able military leader. But
> when we remember Che, when we think of Che, we do
> not think fundamentally of his military virtues. No!
> Warfare is a means and not an end. Warfare is a tool of
> revolutionaries. The important thing is the revolution.
> The important thing is the revolutionary cause,
> revolutionary ideas, revolutionary objectives,
> revolutionary sentiments, revolutionary virtues!
>
> And it is in that field, in the field of ideas, in the field
> of sentiments, in the field of revolutionary virtues, in
> the field of intelligence, that—apart from his military
> virtues—we feel the tremendous loss that his death
> means to the revolutionary movement. . . .
>
> Che was not only an unsurpassed man of action—he
> was a man of visionary intelligence and broad culture,
> a profound thinker. That is, in his person the man of
> ideas and the man of action were combined.[6]

During the opening years of the revolution, Guevara took
on some of the most challenging, and heaviest, responsibilities. He helped draft the 1959 agrarian reform law, the measure that, in Castro's words, more than any other single act,
"defined the Cuban Revolution."[7] Che headed the depart-

ment of industrialization established by INRA, the National Institute of Agrarian Reform. He was president of the National Bank during the tumultuous year 1960, before the end of which virtually all foreign- and domestic-owned banks and major industries were nationalized, and the economic foundations were laid for socialized production and planning. He became minister of industry in 1961, assuming responsibility for reorganizing on new working-class foundations some 70 percent of industry in Cuba, while maintaining production as former owners and most management personnel, both foreign and Cuban, left the country. He represented the revolutionary government of Cuba on trips to dozens of countries, and spoke with a memorable and clarion communist voice at important international forums and conferences, from the United Nations General Assembly to the Organization of American States. He worked with revolutionists from around the world who were drawn to the example of the Cuban revolution and sought guidance in learning and applying the lessons of that struggle in their own countries. He helped bring about the revolutionary regroupment within Cuba that led in 1965 to the formation of the Communist Party of Cuba.

Amid all this intense practical work helping lay the foundations of a new society, Guevara also organized time to write a prodigious number of articles and letters. He made hundreds of speeches, many of which were published in Cuba and translated and distributed by supporters of the revolution around the world. He gave countless interviews.

In April 1965 Che left Cuba to lead a mission of internationalist Cuban fighters aiding the anti-imperialist struggle in the Congo. His longer-term aim was to return to Latin America to help advance revolutionary struggles that were building from Tierra del Fuego to the Río Bravo. Resigning his leadership posts and responsibilities in the Cuban government, party, and armed forces in order to take on these new revolutionary duties, Guevara left behind a rich written legacy of his political and theoretical contributions to the economics and politics of the transition to socialism. This product of Che's years of work as part of the communist leadership of Cuba's working class has been carefully mined by Carlos Tablada in crafting this book. Among Guevara's works cited in these pages are writings and transcripts that have not been published in full, and are as yet not available to the public to study or use. Many other works cited here have long been out of print.

The author of this book, Fidel Castro remarked in his October 1987 speech commemorating the twentieth anniversary of the death of Che, "compiled, studied, and presented in a book the essence of Che's economic ideas, retrieved from many of his speeches and writings—articles and speeches dealing with a subject so decisive in the building of socialism."[8]

*   *   *

The socialist revolution opened by Cuba's working people in the early 1960s did not fall from the sky. Their long emancipation struggle dates back to the first war of independence against Spanish colonialism, which began in 1868 and was closely intertwined with the revolutionary struggle by slaves to abolish the right to hold human beings as chattels. From the crucible of these and subsequent battles emerged leaders such as Antonio Maceo, Máximo Gómez, and José Martí, whose words and revolutionary deeds left a heritage of anti-imperialist intransigence, internationalism, political integrity, selflessness, and courage.

The leadership that launched the assault on the Moncada and Bayamo army garrisons of the Batista dictatorship on July 26, 1953, and later led the Rebel Army and working people of Cuba to victory, drew strength from this revolutionary heritage and enriched it. This legacy helped prepare these revolutionary leaders to uncompromisingly guide the transition from Cuba's national democratic revolution—that in the fall of 1959 brought a workers and farmers government to power—to the socialist revolution that accelerated in late 1960 and early 1961 in fearless response to the hostile actions of domestic and foreign reaction, above all U.S. imperialism.

The socialist road Cuban working people set out on in those years had been opened some four decades earlier by the October 1917 revolution in Russia. The Bolshevik Party leadership headed by V.I. Lenin directed the first efforts in history by workers and peasants to chart a course towards socialism as an integral component of the fight to advance the world revolution. These efforts, from the Bolshevik insurrection in late 1917 through the end of Lenin's active political life in March 1923, left an invaluable legacy to revolutionists who later sought to advance along a similar path. The record of the Soviet government, Communist Party, and Communist International in Lenin's time is rich in lessons in the economics and politics of the transition from capitalism to socialism that Guevara plumbed in such a disciplined manner some forty years later.

Che "advocated something that I have often insisted on," Fidel Castro emphasized in his 1987 speech. "Building socialism and communism is not just a matter of producing and distributing wealth but is also a matter of education and consciousness."[9]

The socialist revolution, as Guevara explains repeatedly in the works cited in these pages, marks the first time in history that expanding political participation and revolutionary self-consciousness of the toiling majority becomes necessary to the economic organization of society. The door is opened for working people to cease being the blind objects of economic laws that determine humanity's living and working conditions and social relations, and instead to begin placing society's productive forces, and thus their lives, under their own conscious control. As Che said in 1964:

> With the revolution of October 1917, the revolution of Lenin, man acquired a new consciousness. The men of the French revolution, who told humanity so many beautiful things, who set so many examples, and whose tradition is still preserved, were nevertheless simple instruments of history. Economic forces were in motion, and the French revolutionaries sought to interpret popular sentiments, the sentiments of the men of that era. Some of them saw farther than others, but none were capable of taking history into their own

hands, of consciously making their own history.
This became possible after the October revolution.[10]

As events in the twentieth century have amply confirmed, such a course—the Bolshevik course—is not optional; it is not just one way among others following a successful popular revolution for vanguard workers to advance the transition to socialism. The most committed and self-sacrificing vanguard of the working people, organized in a communist party, *must* lead growing layers of their class in taking more and more control over the political direction and administration of the state and economy. This is the *only* way workers can transform themselves as they collectively transform the social relations under which they work, produce, and live. It is the only way they can make these social relations among human beings more and more open and direct, tearing away the veils and fetishes behind which the capitalist system hides the reality and the brutal consequences of its exploitation of all toilers and obscures the unique contribution of labor to social and cultural progress. Along any other road, society will not advance toward socialism and communism, but instead—mired in bureaucratic planning and management—will regress toward capitalism.

"Socialism is not a welfare society," Che explained in one of the speeches cited in these pages, "nor is it a utopian society based on the goodness of man as man. Socialism is a system that arises historically, and that has as its pillar the socialization of the means of production along with equitable distribution of all of society's wealth, in a framework of social production."[11]

The fundamentally *political* character of economic questions and decisions during the transition to socialism is central to everything Guevara wrote on the subject, as well as to everything he did in practice. His contributions in this regard, like those of Lenin, extend well beyond what is normally, and narrowly, thought of as "economics." Che stressed the inseparable interrelationship and mutual dependence between the transformation of the social relations of production and the transformation of the political and social consciousness of the working people carrying out this revolutionary process. "In our view," Che emphasized in another speech cited by the author,

> communism is a phenomenon of consciousness and not solely a phenomenon of production. We cannot arrive at communism through the simple mechanical accumulation of quantities of goods made available to the people. By doing that we would get somewhere, to be sure, to some peculiar form of socialism. But what Marx defined as communism, what is aspired to in general as communism, cannot be attained if man is not conscious. That is, if he does not have a new consciousness toward society.[12]

Such references to works by Marx, Engels, and Lenin occur throughout Guevara's speeches and writings, as Che reached back time and again to the lessons drawn by communist leaders from the experiences and struggles of previous generations of working people. He worked ceaselessly to deepen his understanding of the writings of the great historical leaders of Marxism, which he had begun studying well before he met Fidel Castro and other leaders of the July 26 Movement in Mexico.

As Che traveled throughout the Americas in the years before and after graduation from medical school, he absorbed the reality of imperialist domination of these countries, the human consequences of the superexploitation and wretched poverty forced upon millions of his Latin American compatriots. He met revolutionary-minded workers and others with whom he argued and exchanged ideas.

In the works of Karl Marx (whom Guevara affectionately referred to in his youthful letters to family and friends as "St. Karl") and Frederick Engels, the founders of the modern communist workers movement, and of Russian communist leader V.I. Lenin, Guevara increasingly found observations about and explanations for the workings of capitalism that confirmed his experiences. The scientific world view he discovered widened his horizons and helped him understand the exploitative class relations throughout Latin America that he was becoming less and less willing to accept, and more and more deeply committed to changing by whatever means necessary.

In the years preceding the launching of the revolutionary war in Cuba, Guevara concentrated on political economy through an intensive study of Marx's *Capital.* Later, as part of his responsibilities in Cuba, he sought to deepen his knowledge of Lenin's writings and speeches from the opening years of the workers and peasants republic in Soviet Russia and from congresses of the Communist International. Together with several colleagues in the ministry of industry and others, he devoted each Thursday night—often between midnight and dawn—to the study of *Capital.* In his writings and speeches, Che frequently went back to this book, to *The Critique of the Gotha Programme,* and to other works by Marx and Engels, including their rich, pre-1847 writings, prior to when they became consistently scientific in their new world outlook.

Following the revolutionary victory over the Batista dictatorship on January 1, 1959, Guevara—thirty years old at the time of the triumph—worked not only to set a practical example but to help lay a theoretical foundation for the transition to socialism in Cuba. As he did so, Guevara was in the thick of daily central leadership responsibilities in the revolutionary government and party. Photographs reproduced in this book record his activity as he carried out this work: his frequent meetings with assemblies of workers in various factories and enterprises, his participation in Sunday voluntary work mobilizations on priority social projects, his international responsibilities. Guevara immersed himself in the literature discussing the most modern industrial processes in use in other countries. He learned the principles of accounting and took classes in mathematics so he could help advance the application of computerization to economic planning and financial controls in Cuba, a task he considered vital.

It was common, Castro noted in his October 1967 tribute, to see the lights on in Guevara's office until all hours of the night, as he worked and studied. "For he was a student of all problems; he was a tireless reader. His thirst for learning was practically insatiable, and the hours he stole from sleep he devoted to study."[13]

The political and social course Guevara worked to implement as he carried out his leadership responsibilities was far from unanimously or enthusiastically supported by all in Cuba. In 1963–64 a public debate touching on many of the political and economic questions at stake took place in several Cuban journals and received considerable international attention. The debate reflected a growing conflict between two politically irreconcilable approaches to economic planning and management and the social organization of labor. Both approaches were being used in Cuba during those years.[14]

Guevara championed what was called the budgetary finance system, which was being applied under his direction in state enterprises responsible to the Ministry of Industry. The other was known as the economic accounting system (or sometimes the financial self-management system). Drawing heavily on contemporary experience in the USSR and Eastern Europe, this system had been chosen for use in enterprises organized by the National Institute of Agrarian Reform, then headed by Carlos Rafael Rodríguez, as well as those accountable to the Ministry of Foreign Trade, directed by Alberto Mora. Together these latter two comprised some 30 percent of industry in Cuba.

The articles written by Guevara in the course of this rich debate are generously cited by Tablada. For Che the budgetary finance system was not a "thing," not a set of administrative rules to be counterposed to a different set called the economic accounting system. Instead, the course he advocated and sought to apply was "part of a general conception of the development of the construction of socialism," and, what was essential, this course had to be evaluated as such in class terms.[15]

Guevara's aim was not to come up with ways to administer economic production and distribution, approaching the working class from the outside, as one "input" or "factor of production" (albeit the most important one, the "human factor," as post-Lenin, Soviet-trained economists often put it). The goal was, from within the vanguard of the working class, to organize and raise the political consciousness of workers, making possible their growing control over the economic and social decisions that simultaneously shape production and their daily lives. The aim was to increase workers' powers to determine society's collective needs, as well as their conscious command over the allocation of labor and resources to meet those needs. Through this effort, working people would transform their own values and attitudes; their creativity and imagination would begin to be freed from the stunting and alienating conditions of life and work under capitalist social relations.

The "muck of the ages" would begin to be washed away.

*   *   *

In the 1987 speech that serves as a prologue to this book, Castro remarks that "at a given moment some of Che's ideas were incorrectly interpreted and, what's more, incorrectly applied. Certainly no serious attempt was ever made to put them into practice, and there came a time when ideas diametrically opposed to Che's economic thought began to take over."

As a result, Castro said, while "much has been done to recall his other qualities," Guevara's contribution on these questions of economic and political policy "is largely unknown in our country."[16] Publication of this book in a print run of a quarter million in 1987 helped advance a timely recovery and discussion of Guevara's political-economic ideas in the context of what was known in Cuba as the "rectification process."

Following a series of costly mistakes in the closing years of the 1960s, the government and party leadership in Cuba decided to adopt the system of economic planning and management used in one or another variant throughout the Soviet Union and Eastern Europe. From the early 1970s to the mid-1980s it was this political course, not Guevara's budgetary finance system, that predominated on questions of economic policy. Guevara's rich legacy of practical activity and theoretical contributions was largely obscured behind the public image of Che the Heroic Guerrilla and man of spotless moral purity ("St. Che," as this icon has been dubbed in Cuba by partisans of Guevara's communist course).

By the early 1980s, however, the devastating political consequences of the course that had been copied and imported were becoming increasingly clear as communist political consciousness among Cuba's working people faltered, demoralization spread, and corruption grew. A relatively privileged layer of administrative personnel in the state and party apparatus, industrial enterprises, economic planning agencies, and mass organizations such as the trade unions began more and more to promote and implement policies that expressed their interests and improved their own living standards and working conditions, while disregarding many of the most pressing needs of the large majority of Cuban toilers.

During this "disgraceful period of building socialism," as Castro calls it in the speech reprinted here,[17] revolutionary victories elsewhere in the Americas simultaneously released new energies among Cuba's working people. Tens of thousands of teachers, doctors, engineers, construction workers, and others volunteered to risk their lives taking part in internationalist missions to aid the people of Nicaragua and Grenada. At the same time, hundreds of thousands of Cubans were responding to the request of the Angolan government for help to defeat the invading forces of the South African apartheid government intent on preventing the newly independent government of the former Portuguese colony from being consolidated.

By 1986 Cuba's communist leadership, with Fidel Castro in the lead, had launched the revolutionary political counteroffensive on questions of economic policy that became known as the rectification process. Corruption and privilege were systematically addressed and substantially reduced. Living and working conditions of agricultural workers and others in the lowest-paid categories were improved. Child care and other needs of women workers were given new priority.

From the outset of the rectification process, volunteer labor—"one of the best things [Che] left us during his stay in our country and his part in the revolution," said Castro—was revived in Cuba. It was promoted by the leadership as a lever of revolutionary action to take steps forward, through collective efforts, to address the most pressing social needs such as housing, nurseries, clinics, and schools. For some fifteen years, Castro said, such efforts had been steadily on the decline because of "the bureaucrat's view, the technocrat's view that voluntary work was neither basic nor essential," but rather "kind of silly, a waste of time." Beginning in 1986, however, voluntary labor was reborn. The construction "minibrigades," as they were called, assumed an even greater centrality to the revolution and working class than similar efforts during the early years of the Cuban or Russian revolutions.

Rectification took on the character of a growing social movement led by Cuba's most conscious and disciplined working people who were convinced that the brigades opened the road toward a return to proletarian methods that could advance the revolution and strengthen social consciousness.

Just as the bureaucratic parties and regimes of Eastern Europe and the USSR were finally beginning to shatter in face of irresolvable economic, social, and political crises building up for decades, the Cuban revolution was gaining strength along the lines of the communist political course of rectification. This renewal, Fidel explained in his October 1987 tribute, would have given Guevara much joy and confidence, just as he would have been "appalled" by what had preceded it. Because, Castro said, Che "knew that communism could never be attained by wandering down those worn capitalist paths and that to follow along those paths would mean eventually to forget all ideas of solidarity and even internationalism."[18]

As the rectification process was gaining new momentum in 1989, the Cuban revolution was suddenly confronted with the most severe economic crisis in its history. The crisis was precipitated by the abrupt decline in aid and trade on favorable terms with the disintegrating regimes in the Soviet bloc. The "special period," as it is known in Cuba, registered a decline in economic production estimated at some 35 percent—equal to or greater than the fall in U.S. output during the opening years of the Great Depression of the 1930s. Stepped-up efforts by Cuba's revolutionary government to find new trading partners and sources of development capital were met by intensified economic warfare instigated and organized by Washington.

Enemies of the working class the world over gleefully predicted that the revolutionary government of Cuba would soon suffer a fate similar to the regimes of Eastern Europe and the USSR. Once again they were wrong. They failed to understand—as they had many times before—that the proletarian internationalist course Che's name was associated with in Cuba and around the world was not his alone, but was indeed the trajectory of Cuba's communist leadership, deeply rooted among the big majority of Cuba's working people. This was not a variant of the course in the Soviet Union and Eastern Europe, but its antipode.

No other government in the world could have survived the test of popular support that Cuba's revolutionary leadership has faced in the 1990s. In meeting the challenge of the special period, moreover, the Cuban working class has emerged stronger, not weaker. Today it is more conscious of its historic responsibilities, and more confident of its collective capacity to resist, to fight, and to win. The rectification process of the previous decade was decisive in this outcome.

The slow and difficult economic recovery that has taken place since the bottom of the crisis in 1994 has been achieved only by taking countless measures that involve painful, temporary retreats from positions conquered earlier by Cuban working people—such as allowing use of the U.S. dollar as one of the legal currencies within Cuba. This and other steps taken to marshal the resources and capital investments required to reverse the accelerating decline in production have increased social inequalities, eroded social solidarity, and destabilized social relations that arose on the basis of previous revolutionary conquests.

What Cuba faces today is not a crisis of socialism, however. Above all, the Cuban toilers are confronting the brutal realities of an economically underdeveloped country in a world still dominated by capitalism, and the terms of struggle imposed by the exploiting classes on those who are determined to chart a way forward for humanity.

"We do not fight principally for ourselves," Fidel Castro told a convention of the Central Organization of Cuban Workers in April 1996. Cuba, he said, has become a standard bearer for the exploited and oppressed of the world. "That is why we are pleased to call ourselves internationalists, to call ourselves socialists, to call ourselves communists." These are three things that fortify us, Castro added, "the expression of what we have wanted to be, of what we are, and of what we will always be."

It is the capitalist world that will face the gravest crisis in the years ahead. "The exploiters are starting to get afraid again," Castro noted. "They're afraid of social upheaval, afraid of social explosions, afraid of chaos . . . because they don't really know what's going to happen."[19]

That is why Che's course, Fidel Castro's course, is not a question of past history, or only of interest to some future communist society. It remains at the heart of the ability of Cuba's working people to resist, to limit the temporary retreat that has been forced upon them, to hold the line at not one step further than necessary to assure the survival of their political power, of their revolutionary government.

The new edition of this book, both timely and necessary, is a weapon that will help increase the battle-readiness and political effectiveness of a new generation of revolutionary-minded fighters.

Che Guevara's legacy—an irreplaceable part of the web of lessons learned by the modern working class through enormous effort and sacrifice—is a piece of our collective patrimony that Pathfinder Press is honored to publish.

Mary-Alice Waters
September 1997

CHE'S IDEAS ARE

ABSOLUTELY RELEVANT

TODAY

Speech by Fidel Castro on October 8, 1987, at the main

ceremony marking the twentieth anniversary of the death

of Ernesto Che Guevara

Nearly twenty years ago, on October 18, 1967, we met in the Plaza of the Revolution with a huge crowd to honor Compañero Ernesto Che Guevara. Those were very bitter, very difficult days when we received news of the developments in Vado del Yeso, in the Yuro Ravine, when news agencies reported Che had fallen in battle.

It didn't take long to realize that those reports were absolutely correct, for they consisted of news items and photos that proved it beyond doubt. For several days the news was coming in, until with all that information in hand—although many of the details we know today were not known at the time—we held the large mass rally, the solemn ceremony in which we paid our last respects to the fallen compañero.

Nearly twenty years have passed since then, and now, on October 8, we are marking the date he fell in battle. According

The ceremony marking Guevara's death was held at a newly completed electronic components factory in the city of Pinar del Río. The text of this speech was originaly published in the October 12, 1987, issue of Granma, *newspaper of the Communist Party of Cuba.*

to reliable reports we have now, he was actually murdered the following day, after having been captured unarmed and wounded; his weapon had been rendered useless in battle. That's why it has become a tradition to commemorate that dramatic event on October 8.

The first year passed and then five, ten, fifteen, and now twenty years, and it was necessary to recall the historic dimensions of that development, and particularly the man. Thus in a natural way, rather than a very deliberate or pondered way, the entire people have been recalling the date in recent months. It was possible to commemorate the twentieth anniversary on a solemn note as we have seen here today: the playing of taps, the anthem, the magnificent poem by Nicolás Guillén, which rang out with the same voice we heard twenty years ago.

I could try to give a very solemn, grandiloquent speech, perhaps a written speech, but in these times the pressure of work barely leaves a minute free for thinking more carefully about all those events and the things I could say here, let alone for writing a speech.

That's why I'd prefer to recall Che, share my thoughts with you, because I've thought a lot about Che.

I did an interview, part of which was made public yesterday in our country, in answer to the questions of an Italian journalist who had me in front of the television cameras nearly sixteen hours straight—actually, they were movie, not TV cameras, because in order to get a better image in everything he did, he didn't use videocassettes, some of which last two hours, but rather movie cameras. He'd change reels every twenty or twenty-five minutes, and so it was quite an exhausting interview. We should have taken three days to do it, but we had to do it in one because there was no more time. We started before noon on a Sunday and finished at 5:00 a.m. the following day. There were more than 100 questions. Among the variety of subjects and themes, the journalist was very interested in talking about Che, and between 3:00 and 4:00 a.m. we got to the subject. I made an effort to answer each of his questions, and I made a special effort to summarize my memories of Che.

I told him how I felt, and I think many compañeros feel the

same way, regarding Che's permanent presence. We must keep in mind the special relationship with Che, the affection, the fraternal bonds of comradeship, the united struggle over nearly twelve years, from the moment we met in Mexico until the end, a period rich in historic events, some of which have been made public only in the last couple of days.

It was a period filled with heroic and glorious deeds, from the time Che joined us to go on the *Granma* expedition, the landing, the setbacks, the most difficult days, the resumption of the struggle in the mountains, rebuilding an army virtually from scratch, the first clashes, and the last battles.

Then the intense period that followed the victory of the revolution: the first revolutionary laws, in which we were absolutely loyal to the commitments we'd made to the people, carrying out a really radical transformation in the life of the country. There were the things that followed, one after another, such as the start of imperialist hostility; the blockade; the slander campaigns against the revolution as soon as we started to do justice to the criminals and thugs who had murdered thousands of our fellow citizens; the economic blockade; the Girón invasion; the proclamation of the socialist nature of the revolution; the struggle against the mercenaries; the October crisis; the first steps in the construction of socialism when there was nothing—neither experience nor cadres nor engineers nor economists and hardly any technicians, when we were left almost without doctors because 3,000 of the 6,000 doctors in the country left.

Then came the First and Second Declarations of Havana, the start of the isolation imposed on our country, the collective rupture of diplomatic relations by all Latin American governments except Mexico. It was a period in which, along with all these developments, we had to organize the economy of the country. It was a relatively brief but fruitful period replete with unforgettable events.[1]

It must be kept in mind that Che persisted in an old desire, an old idea: to return to South America, to his country, to make the revolution based on the experience he'd gained in our country. We should recall the clandestine way in which his departure had to be organized, the barrage of slanders against the revolution, when there was talk of conflicts, of differences with Che, that Che had disappeared. It was even said that he had been murdered because of splits in the ranks of the revolution.

Meanwhile, the revolution calmly and firmly endured the ferocious attack, because over and above the irritation and bitterness caused by those campaigns, the important thing was for Che to be able to fulfill his goals; the important thing was to ensure his safety and that of the compatriots with him on his historic missions.

In the interview I explained the origin of that idea, how when he joined us he had set only one condition: that once the revolution was made, when he wanted to return to South America he would not be prevented from doing so for reasons of state or for the state's convenience, that he would not be held back. We told him he could go ahead and that we would support him. He would remind us of this pledge every so often until the time came when he decided it was time to leave.

Not only did we keep the promise of agreeing to his departure, but we gave him all the help we could. We tried to delay the departure a little. We gave him other tasks to enrich his guerrilla experience, and we tried to create a minimum of conditions so that he would not have to go through the most difficult stage of the first days of organizing a guerrilla force, something we knew full well from our own experience.

We were well aware of Che's talent, his experience, and his role. He was a cadre suited to major strategic tasks and we felt it might be better if other compañeros undertook the initial organizational work and that he join at a more advanced stage in the process. This also fit in with our policy during the war of saving cadres, as they distinguished themselves, for increasingly important and strategic assignments. We did not have many experienced cadres, and as they distinguished themselves we would not send them out every day with a squad to ambush; rather, we gave them more important tasks in keeping with their ability and experience.

Thus, I remember that during the days of Batista's final offensive in the Sierra Maestra mountains against our militant but small forces, the most experienced cadres were not in the front lines; they were assigned strategic leadership assignments and saved for our devastating counterattack. It would have been pointless to put Che, Camilo [Cienfuegos],[2] and other compañeros who had participated in many battles at the head of a squad. We held them back so that they could subsequently lead columns that would undertake risky missions of great importance, and it was then that we did send them into enemy territory with full responsibility and awareness of the risks, as in the case of the invasion of Las Villas led by Camilo and Che, an extraordinarily difficult assignment that required men of great experience and authority as column commanders, men capable of reaching the goal.

In line with this reasoning, and considering the objectives, perhaps it would have been better if this principle had been observed and Che had joined at a later stage. It really was not so critical for him to handle everything right from the start. But he was impatient, very impatient really. Some Argentine comrades had been killed in the initial efforts he had made years before, including Ricardo Massetti, the founder of Prensa Latina.[3] He remembered that often and was really impatient to start to participate personally in the work.

As always, we respected our commitments and his views, for our relationship was always based on absolute trust, absolute brotherhood, regardless of our ideas about what would be the right time for him to join in. And so we gave him all the help and all the facilities possible to start the struggle.

Then news came of the first clashes and contact was completely lost. The enemy detected the initial stage of organization of the guerrilla movement, and this marked the start of a period lasting many months in which almost the only news we received was what came via international news dispatches, and we had to know how to interpret them. But that's something our revolution has become very experienced at: determining when a report is reliable or when it is made up, false.

I remember, for example, when a dispatch came with the news of the death of Joaquín's group (his real name was Vilo

Acuña).[4] When we analyzed it, I immediately concluded that it was true; this was because of the way they described how the group had been eliminated while crossing a river. Because of our own guerrilla experience, because of what we had lived through, we knew how a small guerrilla group can be done away with. We knew the few, exceptional ways such a group can be destroyed.

When it was reported that a peasant had made contact with the army and provided detailed information on the location and plans of the group, which was looking for a way to cross the river; how the army set up an ambush on the other bank at a spot on the route the same peasant had told the guerrilla fighters to use; the way the army opened fire in midstream, there was no doubt as to the truth of the explanation. If the writers of false reports, which came in often, tried to do it again, it was impossible to admit that they, who were always so clumsy in their lies, would have had enough intelligence and experience to make up the exact and only circumstances in which the group could be eliminated. That's why we concluded the report was true.

Long years of revolutionary experience had taught us to decipher dispatches and tell the difference between the truth and falsehood of each development, although, of course, there are other things to keep in mind when making a judgment. But that was the type of information we had about the situation until the news of Che's death arrived.

As we have explained, we had hopes that even with only twenty men left, even in a very difficult situation, the guerrillas still had a chance. They were headed toward an area where sectors of the peasants were organized, where some good Bolivian cadres had influence, and until that moment, until almost the very end, there was a chance that the movement could be consolidated and could develop.

But the circumstances in which my relationship with Che developed were so unique—the almost unreal history of the brief but intense saga of the first years of the revolution when we were used to making the impossible possible—that, as I explained to that journalist, one had the permanent impression that Che had not died, that he was still alive. Since his was such an exemplary personality, so unforgettable, so familiar, it was difficult to resign oneself to the idea of his death.

Sometimes I would dream—all of us dream of things related to our lives and struggles—that I saw Che, that he returned, that he was alive. How often this happened! I told the journalist that these are feelings you seldom talk about, but they give an idea of the impact of Che's personality and also of the extraordinary degree to which he really lives on, almost as if his was a physical presence, with his ideas and deeds, with his example and all the things he created, with his continued relevance and the respect for him not only in Latin America but in Europe and all over the world.

As we predicted on October 18, twenty years ago, he became a symbol for all the oppressed, for all the exploited, for all patriotic and democratic forces, for all revolutionaries. He became a permanent and invincible symbol.

We feel Che's presence for all these reasons, because of this real force that he still has today which, even though twenty years have gone by, exists in the spirit of all of us, when we hear the poem, when we hear the anthem, or the bugle is sounded before a moment's silence, when we open our newspapers and see photographs of Che during different stages of his life, his image, so well known throughout the world—because it has to be said that Che not only had all the virtues and all the human and moral qualities to be a symbol, he also had the appearance of a symbol, the image of a symbol: his look, the frankness and strength of his look; his face, which reflects character, irrepressibly determined for action, at the same time showing great intelligence and great purity—when we look at the poems that have been written, the episodes that are recounted, and the stories that are repeated, we feel the reality of Che's relevance, of his presence.

It's not strange if one feels Che's presence not only in everyday life, but even in dreams if one imagines that he is alive, that Che is in action and that he never died. In the end we must reach the conclusion that to all intents and purposes in the life of our revolution Che never died, and in the light of what has been done, he is more alive than ever, has more influence than ever, and is a more powerful opponent of imperialism than ever.

Those who disposed of his body so that he would not become a symbol; those who, under the guidance of the methods of their imperial masters, did not want any trace to remain, have discovered that although his tomb is unmarked, there are no remains, and there is no body, nevertheless a frightening opponent of imperialism, a symbol, a force, a presence that can never be destroyed, does exist.

When they hid Che's body they showed their weakness and their cowardice, because they also showed their fear of the example and the symbol. They did not want the exploited peasants, the workers, the students, the intellectuals, the democrats, the progressives, or the patriots of this hemisphere to have a place to go to pay tribute to Che. And in the world today, in which there is no specific place to go to pay tribute to Che's remains, tribute is paid to him everywhere. [*Applause*]

Today tribute is not paid to Che once a year, nor once every five, ten, fifteen, or twenty years; today homage is paid to Che every year, every month, every day, everywhere, in a factory, in a school, in a military barracks, in a home, among children, among Pioneers. Who can count how many millions of times in these twenty years the Pioneers have said: "Pioneers for communism, we will be like Che!" [*Applause*]

This one fact I've just mentioned, this one idea, this one custom in itself constitutes a great and permanent presence of Che. And I think not only our Pioneers, not only our children, but children all over the hemisphere, all over the world could repeat this same slogan: "Pioneers for communism, we will be like Che!" [*Applause*]

Really, there can be no superior symbol, there can be no better image, there cannot be a more exact idea, when searching for the model revolutionary man, when searching for the model communist. I say this because I have the deepest conviction—I always have had and I still have today, just the same or more so than when I spoke that October 18 and I asked how we wanted our fighters, our revolutionaries, our party members, our children to be, and I said that we wanted them to be like Che. Because Che is the personification, Che is the image of that new man, the image of that human being if we want to talk about a communist society; [*Applause*] if our real objective is to build, not just socialism but the higher stages of socialism, if humanity is not going to renounce the lofty and extraordinary idea of living in a communist society one day.

If we need a paradigm, a model, an example to follow to attain these elevated ideas, then men like Che are essential, as are men and women who imitate him, who are like him, who think like him, who act like him; men and women whose conduct resembles his when it comes to doing their duty, in every little thing, every detail, every activity; in his attitude toward work, his habit of teaching and educating by setting an example; his attitude of wanting to be first at everything, the first to volunteer for the most difficult tasks, the hardest ones, the most self-sacrificing ones; the individual who gives his body and soul to a cause, the individual who gives his body and soul to others, the person who displays true solidarity, the individual who never lets down a compañero; the simple man; the man without a flaw, who doesn't live any contradiction between what he says and what he does, between what he practices and what he preaches; a man of thought and a man of action—all of which Che symbolizes. [*Applause*]

For our country it is a great honor and privilege to have had Che as a son of our people even though he wasn't born in this land. He was a son because he earned the right to consider himself and to be considered a son of our country, and it is an honor and a privilege for our people, for our country, for our country's history, for our revolution to have had among its ranks a truly exceptional man such as Che.

That's not to say that I think exceptional people are rare; that's not to say that amid the masses there are not hundreds, thousands, even millions of exceptional men and women. I said it once during the bitter days after Camilo disappeared. When I recounted the history of how Camilo became the man he was, I said: "Among our people there are many Camilos." I could also say: "Among our peoples, among the peoples of

Latin America and the peoples of the world there are many Ches."

But, why do we call them exceptional? Because, in actual fact, in the world in which they lived, in the circumstances in which they lived, they had the chance and the opportunity to demonstrate all that man, with his generosity and solidarity, is capable of being. And, indeed, seldom do ideal circumstances exist in which man has the opportunity to express himself and to show everything he has inside as was the case with Che.

Of course, it's clear that there are countless men and women among the masses who, partly as a result of other people's examples and certain new values, are capable of heroism, including a kind of heroism I greatly admire: silent heroism, anonymous heroism, silent virtue, anonymous virtue. But given that it's so unusual, so rare for all the necessary circumstances to exist to produce a figure like Che—who today has become a symbol for the world, a symbol that will grow—it is a great honor and privilege that this figure was born during our revolution.

And as proof of what I said earlier about Che's presence and force today, I could ask: Is there a better date, a better anniversary than this one to remember Che with all our conviction and deep feelings of appreciation and gratitude? Is there a better moment than this particular anniversary, when we are in the middle of the rectification process?

What are we rectifying? We're rectifying all those things— and there are many—that strayed from the revolutionary spirit, from revolutionary work, revolutionary virtue, revolutionary effort, revolutionary responsibility; all those things that strayed from the spirit of solidarity among people. We're rectifying all the shoddiness and mediocrity that is precisely the negation of Che's ideas, his revolutionary thought, his style, his spirit, and his example.

I really believe, and I say it with great satisfaction, that if Che were sitting in this chair, he would feel jubilant. He would be happy about what we are doing these days, just like he would have felt very unhappy during that unstable period, that disgraceful period of building socialism in which there began to prevail a series of ideas, of mechanisms, of bad habits, which would have caused Che to feel profound and terrible bitterness. [*Applause*]

For example, voluntary work, the brainchild of Che and one of the best things he left us during his stay in our country and his part in the revolution, was steadily on the decline. It became a formality almost. It would be done on the occasion of a special date, a Sunday. People would sometimes run around and do things in a disorganized way.

The bureaucrat's view, the technocrat's view that voluntary work was neither basic nor essential gained more and more ground. The idea was that voluntary work was kind of silly, a waste of time, that problems had to be solved with overtime, with more and more overtime, and this while the regular workday was not even being used efficiently. We had fallen into the bog of bureaucracy, of overstaffing, of work norms that were out of date, the bog of deceit, of untruth. We'd fallen into a whole host of bad habits that Che would have been really appalled at.

If Che had ever been told that one day, under the Cuban revolution there would be enterprises prepared to steal to pretend they were profitable, Che would have been appalled. Or if he'd been told of enterprises that wanted to be profitable and give out prizes and I don't know what else, bonuses, and they'd sell the materials allotted to them to build and charge as though they had built whatever it was, Che would have been appalled.

And I'll tell you that this happened in the fifteen municipalities in the capital of the republic, in the fifteen enterprises responsible for house repairs; and that's only one example. They'd appear as though what they'd produced was worth 8,000 pesos a year, and when the chaos was done away with, it turned out they were producing 4,000 pesos worth or less. So they were not profitable. They were only profitable when they stole.

Che would have been appalled if he'd been told that enterprises existed that would cheat to fulfill and even surpass their production plan by pretending to have done January's work in December.

Che would have been appalled if he'd been told that there were enterprises that fulfilled their production plan and then distributed prizes for having fulfilled it in monetary value but not in goods produced, and that engaged in producing items that meant more monetary value and refrained from producing others that yielded less profit, despite the fact that one item without the other was not worth anything.

Che would have been appalled if he'd been told that production norms were so slack, so weak, so immoral that on certain occasions almost all the workers fulfilled them two or three times over.

Che would have been appalled if he'd been told that money was becoming man's concern, man's fundamental motivation. He who warned us so much against that would have been appalled. Work shifts were being shortened and millions of hours of overtime reported; the mentality of our workers was being corrupted and men were increasingly being motivated by the pesos on their minds.

Che would have been appalled for he knew that communism could never be attained by wandering down those worn capitalist paths and that to follow along those paths would mean eventually to forget all ideas of solidarity and even internationalism. To follow those paths would imply never developing a new man and a new society.

Che would have been appalled if he'd been told that a day would come when bonuses and more bonuses of all kinds would be paid, without these having anything to do with production.

Were he to have seen a group of enterprises teeming with two-bit capitalists—as we call them—playing at capitalism, beginning to think and act like capitalists, forgetting about the country, the people, and high standards (because high standards just didn't matter; all they cared about was the money being earned thanks to the low norms), he would have been appalled.

And were he to have seen that one day they would not just make manual work subject to [quantitative] production norms—which has a certain logic to it, like cutting cane and doing many other manual and physical activities—but even intellectual work, even radio and television work, and that here even a surgeon's work was likely to be subject to norms—putting just anybody under the knife in order to double or triple his income—I can truthfully say that Che would have been appalled, because none of those paths will ever lead us to communism. On the contrary, those paths lead to all the bad habits and the alienation of capitalism.

Those paths I repeat—and Che knew it very well—would never lead us to building real socialism, as a first and transitional stage to communism.

But don't think that Che was naive, an idealist, or someone out of touch with reality. Che understood and took reality into consideration. But Che believed in man. And if we don't believe in man, if we think that man is an incorrigible little animal, capable of advancing only if you feed him grass or tempt him with a carrot or whip him with a stick—anybody who believes this, anybody convinced of this will never be a revolutionary; anybody who believes this, anybody convinced of this will never be a socialist; anybody who believes this, anybody convinced of this will never be a communist. [*Applause*]

Our revolution is an example of what faith in man means because our revolution started from scratch, from nothing. We did not have a single weapon, we did not have a penny, even the men who started the struggle were unknown, and yet we confronted all that might, we confronted their hundreds of millions of pesos, we confronted the thousands of soldiers, and the revolution triumphed because we believed in man. Not only was victory made possible, but so was confronting the empire and getting this far, only a short way off from celebrating the twenty-ninth anniversary of the triumph of the revolution. How could we have done all this if we had not had faith in man?

Che had great faith in man. Che was a realist and did not reject material incentives. He deemed them necessary during the transitional stage, while building socialism. But Che attached more importance—more and more importance—to the conscious factor, to the moral factor.

At the same time, it would be a caricature to believe that Che was unrealistic and unfamiliar with the reality of a society and a people who had just emerged from capitalism.

But Che was mostly known as a man of action, a soldier, a leader, a military man, a guerrilla, an exemplary person who always was the first in everything; a man who never asked others to do something that he himself would not do first; a model of a righteous, honest, pure, courageous man, full of human solidarity. These are the virtues he possessed and the ones we remember him by.

Che was a man of very profound thought, and he had the exceptional opportunity during the first years of the revolution to delve deeply into very important aspects of the building of socialism because, given his qualities, whenever a man was needed to do an important job, Che was always there. He really was a many-sided man and whatever his assignment, he fulfilled it in a completely serious and responsible manner.

He was in INRA [National Institute of Agrarian Reform] and managed a few industries under its jurisdiction at a time when the main industries had not yet been nationalized and only a few factories had been taken over. He headed the National Bank, another of the responsibilities entrusted to him, and he also headed the Ministry of Industry when this agency was set up. Nearly all the factories had been nationalized by then and everything had to be organized, production had to be maintained, and Che took on the job, as he had taken on many others. He did so with total devotion, working day and night, Saturdays and Sundays, at all hours, and he really set out to solve far-reaching problems. It was then that he tackled the task of applying Marxist-Leninist principles to the organization of production, the way he understood it, the way he saw it.

He spent years doing that; he spoke a lot, wrote a lot on all those subjects, and he really managed to develop a rather elaborate and very profound theory on the manner in which, in his opinion, socialism should be built leading to a communist society.

Recently, all these ideas were compiled, and an economist wrote a book that was awarded a Casa de las Américas prize.

The author compiled, studied, and presented in a book the essence of Che's economic ideas, retrieved from many of his speeches and writings—articles and speeches dealing with a subject so decisive in the building of socialism. The name of the book is *The Economic Thought of Ernesto Che Guevara.* So much has been done to recall his other qualities that this aspect, I think, is largely unknown in our country. Che held truly profound, courageous, bold ideas, which were different from many paths already taken.

In essence—in essence!—Che was radically opposed to using and developing capitalist economic laws and categories in building socialism. He advocated something that I have often insisted on: Building socialism and communism is not just a matter of producing and distributing wealth but is also a matter of education and consciousness. He was firmly opposed to using these categories, which have been transferred from capitalism to socialism, as instruments to build the new society.

At a given moment some of Che's ideas were incorrectly interpreted and, what's more, incorrectly applied. Certainly no serious attempt was ever made to put them into practice, and there came a time when ideas diametrically opposed to Che's economic thought began to take over.

This is not the occasion for going deeper into the subject. I'm essentially interested in expressing one idea: Today, on the twentieth anniversary of Che's death; today, in the midst of the profound rectification process we are all involved in, we fully understand that rectification does not mean extremism, that rectification cannot mean idealism, that rectification cannot imply for any reason whatsoever lack of realism, that rectification cannot even imply abrupt changes.

Starting out from the idea that rectification means, as I've said before, looking for new solutions to old problems, rectifying many negative tendencies that had been developing; that rectification implies making more accurate use of the system and the mechanisms we have now, an Economic Management and Planning System which, as we said at the enterprises meeting,[5] was a horse, a lame nag with many sores that we were treating with Mercurochrome and prescribing medicines for, putting splints on one leg, in short, fixing up the nag, the horse. I said that the thing to do now was to go on using that horse, knowing its bad habits, the perils of that horse, how it kicked and bucked, and try to lead it on our path and not go wherever it wishes to take us. I've said, let us take up the reins! [*Applause*]

These are very serious, very complicated matters and here we can't afford to take shots in the dark, and there's no place for adventures of any kind. The experience of so many years that quite a few of us have had the privilege of accumulating through a revolutionary process is worth something. And that's why we say now, we cannot continue fulfilling the plan simply in terms of monetary value; we must also fulfill it in terms of goods produced. We demand this categorically, and anyone who does otherwise must be quickly replaced, because there's no other choice! [*Applause*]

We maintain that all projects must be started and finished quickly so that there is never a repeat of what happened to us on account of the nag's bad habits: that business of doing the earthmoving and putting up a few foundations because that was worth a lot and then not finishing the building because that was worth little; that tendency to say, "I fulfilled my plan as to value but I didn't finish a single building," which made us waste hundreds of millions, billions, and we never finished anything.

It took fourteen years to build a hotel! Fourteen years wasting iron bars, sand, stone, cement, rubber, fuel, manpower before the country made a single penny from the hotel being used. Eleven years to finish our hospital here in Pinar del Río! It's true that in the end it was finished and it was finished well, but things of this sort should never happen again.

The minibrigades,[6] which were destroyed for the sake of such mechanisms, are now rising again from their ashes like a phoenix and demonstrating the significance of that mass movement, the significance of that revolutionary path of solving the problems that the theoreticians, technocrats, those who do not believe in man, and those who believe in two-bit capitalism had stopped and dismantled. This was how they were leading us into critical situations.

In the capital, where the minibrigades emerged, it pains us to think that over fifteen years ago we had found an excellent solution to such a vital problem, and yet they were destroyed in their peak moment. And so we didn't even have the manpower to build housing in the capital; and the problems kept piling up, tens of thousands of homes were propped up and were in danger of collapsing and killing people.

Now the minibrigades have been reborn and there are more than 20,000 minibrigade members in the capital. They're not in contradiction with the nag, with the Economic Management and Planning System, simply because the factory or workplace that sends them to the construction site pays them, but the state reimburses the factory or workplace for the salary of the minibrigade member. The difference is that whereas the worker would normally work five or six hours, on the minibrigade he works ten, eleven, or twelve hours doing the job of two or three men, and the enterprise saves money.

Our two-bit capitalist can't say his enterprise is being ruined. On the contrary, he can say, "They're helping the enterprise. I'm doing the job with thirty, forty, or fifty less men and spending less on wages." He can say, "I'm going to be profitable or at least lose less money; I'll distribute more prizes and bonuses since wage expenditures will be cut down." He organizes production better, he gets housing for his workers, who in turn are happier because they have new housing. He builds community projects such as special schools, polyclinics, daycare centers for the children of working women, for the family; in short, so many extremely useful things we are doing now and the state is building them without spending an additional cent in wages. That really is miraculous!

We could ask the two-bit capitalists and profiteers who have blind faith in the mechanisms and categories of capitalism: Could you achieve such a miracle? Could you manage to build 20,000 housing units in the capital without spending a cent more on wages? Could you build fifty day-care centers in a year without spending a cent more on wages, when only five had been included in the five-year plan and they weren't even built, and 19,500 mothers were waiting to get their children a place, which never materialized.

At that rate it would take 100 years! By then they would be dead, and fortunately so would all the technocrats, two-bit capitalists, and bureaucrats who obstruct the building of socialism. [*Applause*] They would have died without ever seeing day-care center number 100. Workers in the capital will have their 100 day-care centers in two years, and workers all over the country will have the 300 or so they need in three years. That will bring enrollment to 70,000 or 80,000 easily, without paying out an additional cent in wages or adding workers, because at that rate, with overstaffing everywhere, we would have ended up bringing workers in from Jamaica, Haiti, some Caribbean island, or some other place in the world. That was where we were heading.

It can be seen in the capital today that one in eight workers can be mobilized, I'm sure. This is not necessary because there would not be enough materials to give tasks to 100,000 people working in Havana, each one doing the work of three. We're seeing impressive examples of feats of work, and this is achieved by mass methods, by revolutionary methods, by communist methods, combining the interests of people in need with the interests of factories and those of society as a whole.

I don't want to become the judge of different theories, although I have my own theories and know what things I believe in and what things I don't and can't believe in. These questions are discussed frequently in the world today. And I only ask modestly, during this process of rectification, during this process and this struggle—in which we're going to continue as we already explained: with the old nag, while it can still walk, if it walks, and until we can cast it aside and replace it with a better horse, as I think that nothing is good if it's done in a hurry, without analysis and deep thought—What I ask for modestly at this twentieth anniversary is that Che's economic thought be made known; [*Applause*] that it be known here, in Latin America, in the world: in the developed capitalist world, in the Third World, and in the socialist world. Let it be known there too!

In the same way that we read many texts, of all varieties,

and many manuals, Che's economic thought should be known in the socialist camp. Let it be known! [*Applause*] I don't say they have to adopt it, we don't have to get involved in that. Everyone must adopt the thought, the theory, the thesis they consider most appropriate, that which best suits them, as judged by each country. I absolutely respect the right of every country to apply the method or systems it considers appropriate; I respect it completely!

I simply ask that in a cultured country, in a cultured world, in a world where ideas are discussed, Che's economic theories should be made known. [*Applause*] I especially ask that our students of economics, of whom we have many and who read all kinds of pamphlets, manuals, theories about capitalist categories and capitalist laws, also begin to study Che's economic thought, so as to enrich their knowledge.

It would be a sign of ignorance to believe there is only one way of doing things, arising from the concrete experience of a specific time and specific historical circumstances. What I ask for, what I limit myself to asking for, is a little more knowledge, consisting of knowing about other points of view, points of view as respected, as deserving, and as coherent as Che's points of view. [*Applause*]

I can't conceive that our future economists, that our future generations will act, live, and develop like another species of little animal, in this case like the mule, who has those blinders only so that he can't see to either side; mules, furthermore, with grass and the carrot dangling in front as their only motivation. No, I would like them to read, not only to intoxicate themselves with certain ideas, but also to look at other ones, analyze them, and think about them.

Because if we were talking with Che and we said to him, "Look, all this has happened to us," all those things I was talking about before, what happened to us in construction, in agriculture, in industry, what happened in terms of the goods actually produced, work quality, and all that, Che would have said, "It's as I said, it's as I said." He'd have said, "It's as I warned, what's happening is exactly what I thought would happen," because that's simply the way it is. [*Applause*]

I want our people to be a people of ideas, of concepts. I

want them to analyze those ideas, think about them, and, if they want, discuss them. I consider these things to be essential.

It might be that some of Che's ideas are closely linked to the initial stages of the revolution, for example his belief that when a quota was surpassed, the wages received should not go above that received by those on the scale immediately above. What Che wanted was for the worker to study, and he associated his concept with the idea that our people, who in those days had a very poor education and little technical expertise, should study. Today our people are much better educated, more cultured. We could discuss whether now they should earn as much as the next level or more. We could discuss questions associated with our reality of a far more educated people, a people far better prepared technically, although we must never give up the idea of constantly improving ourselves technically and educationally.

But many of Che's ideas are absolutely relevant today, ideas without which I am convinced communism cannot be built, like the idea that man should not be corrupted; that man should never be alienated; the idea that without consciousness, simply producing wealth, socialism as a superior society could not be built, and communism could never be built. [*Applause*]

I think many of Che's ideas—many of his ideas!—have great relevance today. Had we known, had we learned about Che's economic thought we'd be a hundred times more alert, including in riding the horse, and whenever the horse wanted to turn right or left, wherever it wanted to turn—although, mind you, here this was without a doubt a right-wing horse—we should have pulled it up hard and got it back on the track, and whenever it refused to move, use the spurs hard. [*Applause*]

I think a rider, that is to say, an economist, that is to say, a party cadre, an administrative cadre, armed with Che's ideas would be better equipped to lead the horse along the right track.

Just being familiar with Che's thought, just knowing his ideas would enable him to say, "I'm doing badly here, I'm doing badly there, that's a consequence of this, that, or the other," provided that the system and mechanisms for building socialism and communism are really being developed and improved on.

I say this because it is my deepest conviction that if his thought remains unknown it will be difficult to get very far, to achieve real socialism, really revolutionary socialism, socialism with socialists, socialism and communism with communists. I'm absolutely convinced that ignoring those ideas would be a crime. That's what I'm putting to you.

We have enough experience to know how to do things; and there are extremely valuable principles of immense worth in Che's ideas and thought that simply go beyond the image that many people have of Che as a brave, heroic, pure man, of Che as a saint because of his virtues, as a martyr because of his selflessness and heroism. Che was also a revolutionary, a thinker, a man of doctrine, a man of great ideas, who was capable with great consistency of working out instruments and principles that unquestionably are essential to the revolutionary path.

Capitalists are very happy when they hear people talk about rent, profit, interest, bonuses, superbonuses; when they hear about markets, supply and demand as elements that regulate production and promote quality, efficiency, and all those things. For they say, "That's my kind of talk, that's my philosophy, that's my doctrine," and the emphasis that socialism may place on them makes them happy, for they know these are essential aspects of capitalist theory, laws, and categories.

We ourselves are being criticized by quite a few capitalists; they try to make people think that the Cuban revolutionaries are unrealistic, that the thing to do is go for all the lures of capitalism; that's where they aim their fire. But we'll see how far we get, even riding on the old nag full of sores, but correctly led, for as long as we don't have anything better than the old nag. We'll see how far we get in the rectification process with the steps we're taking now.

That's why on this, the twentieth anniversary, I'm making an appeal for our party members, our youth, our students, our economists to study and familiarize themselves with Che's political and economic thought.

Che is a figure with enormous prestige. Che is a figure whose influence will grow. Needless to say, those who feel frustrated or who dare to fight Che's ideas or use certain terms to describe Che or depict him as a dreamer, as someone who is out of touch with reality, do not deserve any revolutionary's respect. That's why we want our youth to have that instrument, to wield that weapon, even if for the time being it only serves to say, don't follow that mistaken path foreseen by Che; even if it only serves to increase our knowledge; even if it only serves to force us to meditate or to delve deeper into our revolutionary thought.

I sincerely believe that more than this ceremony, more than formal activities, more than all the honors, what we accomplish in action is really the best homage we can pay Che. The work spirit that is starting to appear in so many places and that is evident in so many examples in this province: those workers in Viñales who are working twelve and fourteen hours building minidams, starting them and finishing them one right after the other, and building them at half what they otherwise would have cost, with the result that in comparison with other projects—were we to use a capitalist term, although Che was opposed even to using capitalist terms when analyzing questions of socialism—were we to use the term profitability, we could say that those men on the minidam construction brigade working in Viñales are more than 100 percent profitable—more than 100 percent profitable! [*Applause*]

Che devoted absolute, total, priority attention to accounting, to analyzing expenditures and costs, cent by cent. Che could not conceive of building socialism and running the economy without proper organization, without efficient controls and strict accounting of every cent. Che could not conceive of development without an increase in labor productivity. He even studied mathematics to use mathematical formulas to implement controls and measure the efficiency of the economy. What's more, Che even dreamed of computers being used in running the economy as an essential, fundamental, and decisive way of measuring efficiency under socialism.

And those men I mentioned have made a contribution: for every peso spent they produce two; for every million pesos spent they produce two million. They and those working on the Guamá Dam, those working on the canal, those working on the thruway to Pinar del Río, those who are going to work on the Patate Dam, those who have started to work on roads and the waterworks in the city—there are a number of groups of workers who are carrying out real feats with pride, honor, discipline, loyalty to work. They are working with great productivity.

A few days ago we met with a group of construction workers building an avenue in the capital. They're all members of the party or the Union of Young Communists, or they're outstanding workers, about 200 men in all. Rather than linking their wages to production norms—I don't mean to say that this is negative, there are a number of fields where it is perfectly correct—since they move about in powerful trucks and machines, we don't have to tell them to work more but rather to work less. People like that are doing a lot, sometimes too much with too much effort. At times we'd have to tell them to take less trips because at the proper speed they can't make twenty-five trips with materials in a truck but twenty, because we don't want them to get killed. What we're interested in is not only what they do but the quality with which it is done. We told them we were much more interested in the quality than the quantity. [*Applause*] Quantity without quality is a waste of resources; it's throwing away work and materials.

Awareness of the need for water conservation, which had virtually died out in the shameful period when nothing was finished, is being regained, and the province of Pinar del Río is playing a leading role in this regard. [*Applause*]

The road brigades in the mountains of Pinar del Río are working with the same spirit, and the awareness of the need for water conservation is spreading all over the country along with the desire to build roads and highways and improve the efficiency of our economy, factories, agriculture, hospitals, and schools, to go full speed ahead with the economic and social development of the country.

Fortunately, during these years we have trained a large number of people with a high degree of technical knowledge and experience—university graduates and intermediate-level technicians. How does this compare to what we had in the early years of the revolution? When Che headed the Ministry of Industry, how many engineers did the country have, how many technicians, designers, researchers, scientists? Now we must have about twenty times the number we had then, perhaps more. If he had been able to draw on the collective experience of all the cadres that we have now, who knows what he could have accomplished.

Let's look at the medical sector alone. Back then we had 3,000 doctors and now we have 28,000. Each year our twenty-one medical schools graduate as many doctors as the total number in the country at that time. What a privilege! What a power! What force! As of next year we'll be graduating more doctors than those who stayed in the country in the early years. Can we or can we not do what we set our minds to in the field of public health? And what doctors they are! They work in the countryside, in the mountains, or in Nicaragua, Angola, Mozambique, Ethiopia, Vietnam, Kampuchea, or at the end of the world! Those are the doctors trained by the revolution! [*Applause*]

I'm sure Che would be proud, not of the shoddy things that have been done with such a two-bit profiteering mentality; he'd be proud of the knowledge and technology our people have, of our teachers who went to Nicaragua and the 100,000 who offered to go. He'd be proud of our doctors willing to go anywhere in the world, of our technicians, of our hundreds of thousands of compatriots who have been on internationalist missions! [*Applause*]

I'm sure Che would be proud of that spirit just like we all are, but we cannot permit what we have built with our heads and hearts to be trampled on with our feet. [*Applause*] That's the point, that and the fact that with all the resources that we have built up, with all that force, we should be able to advance and take advantage of all the potential opened up by socialism and the revolution to get people to move ahead. I would like to know if the capitalists have people like those I mentioned.

They are extraordinary internationalists and workers; you have to talk to them to see how they think and feel, to see how deeply they love their work, and this is not because they're workaholics but because they feel the need to make up for lost time, time lost during the revolution, time lost during almost 60 years of neocolonial republic, time lost during centuries of colonialism.

We must regain this time! And hard work is the only way, not waiting 100 years to build 100 day-care centers in the capital when we can really do it in two; not waiting 100 years to build 350 all over the country when we can do it in three with our work; not waiting 100 years to solve the housing problem when we can do it in a few years with our work, our stones, our sand, our materials, our cement, even with our oil and steel produced by our workers.

As I said this afternoon at the hospital ceremony, the year 2000 is just around the corner. We must set ourselves ambitious goals for the year 2000, not for the year 3000 or 2100 or 2050, and if someone suggests that we should, we must reply: "That may suit you but not us! We have the historic mission of building a new country, a new society, the historic mission of making a revolution and developing a country; those of us who have had the honor and privilege of not just promoting development but a socialist development and working for a more humane and advanced society."

To those who encourage laziness and frivolity we will say, "We will live longer than you, not just better than you, or like we would live if everyone were like you. We will live longer than you and be healthier than you because with your laziness you will be sedentary and obese, you will have heart problems, circulatory ailments, and all sorts of other things, because work doesn't harm your health, work promotes health, work safeguards health, and work created man."

These men and women doing great things must become models. We could say that they're being true to the motto, "We will be like Che!" They are working like Che worked or as

Che would have worked. [*Applause*]

When we were discussing where this ceremony should be held, there were many possible places. It could have been in the Plaza of the Revolution in the capital, it could have been in a province, it could have been in one of the many workplaces or factories that the workers wanted to name after Che.

We gave the matter some thought and recalled this new and important factory, the pride of Pinar del Río, the pride of the country and example of what can be done with progress, study, education in this province, which in the past was so neglected and backward and now has young workers capable of running such a complex and sophisticated factory. We need only say that the rooms where the circuits are printed must be ten times cleaner than an operating room to meet the required standard. It was necessary to do such complex work, with such quality and good equipment, and Pinar del Río residents are doing it marvelously. [*Applause*]

When we toured it we were deeply impressed and we talked with many compañeros, the members of the Central Committee, about what you were doing in the factory; in the machine industry, which is advancing at a rapid pace; what was being done in construction. We realized the great future of this factory as a manufacturer of components, of vanguard technology, which will have a major impact on development and productivity, on the automation of production processes.

When we toured your first-rate factory and saw the ideas you had which are being put into practice, we realized it will become a huge complex of many thousands of workers, the pride of the province and the pride of the country. In the next five years more than 100 million pesos will be invested in it to make it a real giant. When we learned that the workers wanted to name it after Che because he was so concerned with electronics, computers, and mathematics, the leadership of our party decided that this was where the ceremony marking the twentieth anniversary of Che's death should be held, [*Applause*] and that the factory should be given the glorious and beloved name of Ernesto Che Guevara. [*Applause*]

I know that its workers, its young workers, its dozens and dozens of engineers, its hundreds of technicians will do honor to that name and work as they should. This doesn't only mean being here fourteen, twelve, or ten hours, for often on certain jobs eight hours of work well done is a real feat. We've seen compañeros, especially many women workers doing microsoldering, which is really difficult work that requires rigor and tremendous concentration. We've seen them, and it's hard to imagine how these compañeras can spend eight hours doing that work and turn out up to 5,000 units daily.

Compañeros, don't think that we feel that the only way to solve problems is to work twelve or fourteen hours a day. There are jobs where you can't work twelve or fourteen hours. In some even eight hours can be a lot. One day we hope that not all workdays will be the same. We hope that in certain fields—if we have enough personnel, and we will if we employ them efficiently—we can have six-hour workdays.

What I mean to say is that being true to Che's example and name also means using the workday with the right pace, being concerned about high standards, having people do various tasks, avoiding overstaffing, working in an organized manner, and developing consciousness.

I'm sure that the workers of this factory will be worthy of Che's name, [*Applause*] just as I'm sure that this province was deserving of hosting the anniversary and will continue to be deserving.

If there is something left to say tonight it's that despite our problems; despite the fact that we have less hard currency than ever before, for reasons we have explained in the past; despite the drought; despite the intensification of the imperialist blockade—as I see our people respond, as I see more and more possibilities open up, I feel confident, I feel optimistic, and I am absolutely convinced that we will do everything we set our minds to! [*Applause*]

We'll do it with the people, with the masses; we'll do it with the principles, pride, and honor of each and every one of our party members, workers, youth, peasants, and intellectuals!

I can proudly say that we are giving Che well-deserved tribute and honor, and if he lives more than ever, so will the homeland! If he is an opponent of imperialism more powerful than ever, the homeland will also be more powerful than ever against imperialism and its rotten ideology! [*Applause*] And if one day we chose the path of revolution, of socialist revolution and of communism, the path of building communism, today we are prouder to have chosen that path because it is the only one that can give rise to men like Che and a people composed of millions of men and women capable of being like Che! [*Applause*]

As [José] Martí said, whereas there are men without dignity, there are also men who carry inside them the dignity of many men![7] We might add that there are men who carry inside them the dignity of the world, and one of those men is Che!

Patria o muerte! [Homeland or death]
Venceremos! [We will win] [*Ovation*]

PART ONE

The economic management

system under socialism:

Theoretical and

methodological questions

discussed by Che

CHAPTER 1

The economic management system and its categories

ONE OF THE GREAT theoretical contributions in Che's writings on the period of the transition to socialism and communism is his synthesis of two elements that are *indissolubly linked*, forming a single whole, in the very structure of the theoretical works of Marx and Engels. The first of these two elements is economic production. The second is the production and reproduction of the *social relations* through which economic production takes place—that is, the economic relations and other social relations that men establish both inside and outside the production process. In the theory of Marx and Engels, these elements take on life once they are seen as elements of a totality (of a particular social formation). These two elements were separated by bourgeois theoreticians and by the Social Democrats of the Second International; reunited by Lenin in the course of building the first proletarian state power; and have been separated again today by some contemporary theoreticians.

The divorce of these two elements since the time of the Second International has produced the most colossal distortion that the theory of Marx and Engels has ever been subjected to. It constitutes a return to pre-Marxist philosophical positions. This regression drives a wedge between revolutionary theory and practice—neither of which, without the other, can retain its revolutionary power and potential.

Che's originality lies, among other things, in the fact that he defended this and other important principles of Marxist-Leninist economic theory on the period of transition to communism, starting from the new factors arising from the socioeconomic and political system in which he lived.

Che laid the groundwork for a theory of the period of transition to communism. The system of economic management associated with this theory affirms the possibility of building a new society, in an underdeveloped country, by genuinely revolutionary means. This system regards moral incentives as the fundamental lever for building socialism in human society, "without neglecting, however, a correct use of material incentives—especially of a social character."[1] It is a model, moreover, that allows for the constant development of theory itself, which is the only way to create a Marxist-Leninist science of the transition period that is useful to concrete revolutionary activity.

Che's revolutionary duties in the many-sided tasks he carried out, together with his critical spirit and profound and original thinking, led him to see the revolution not just as something in which he had played an outstanding role as part of the vanguard, but also as something in which he could make a contribution in theory toward building a communist society. This meant cultivating a highly critical outlook, in order to avoid errors that could block rapid progress toward creating and developing new human relations. An apologetic attitude, to take just one example, could become a brake on the revolutionary process:

> Unfortunately, in the eyes of most of our people, and in mine as well, apologetics for a system can have more impact than scientific analysis of it. This does not help us in the task of clarification, and our whole effort is aimed at inviting people to think, to treat Marxism with the seriousness this towering doctrine deserves.[2]

Somewhat later, in 1965, Che wrote:

> If we add to this the scholasticism that has held back the development of Marxist philosophy and impeded a systematic treatment of the transition period, whose political economy has not been developed, we must agree that we are still in diapers and that it is necessary to devote ourselves to investigating all the principal

characteristics of this period before elaborating an economic and political theory of greater scope.[3]

From early in his political life, Che had been conscious of one of the most distressing facts about theory in his times: the stagnation of Marxist thought.

The Cuban revolution marks a crucial moment in the history of Marxist-Leninist thought—the point at which it definitively took root in *Our America*,[4] linking up with the best revolutionary traditions. What the imperialists pejoratively call "Castroism" is in fact a stage—a vital one, to be sure—in the development of Marxist-Leninist theory and practice.

Just as Lenin rescued revolutionary ideas from the reformist swamp of Social Democracy, Fidel Castro revitalized Marxism-Leninism, developing it in accordance with the specific characteristics and requirements of the Latin American revolution. He was able to do this because the Cuban revolution, the opening shot in the continental revolution, had been ever since Moncada[5] a "rebellion against oligarchies and against revolutionary dogmas,"[6] as Che characterized that epic deed.

Che was the most brilliant and creative student of that school of revolutionary thought and action. He not only played a part in the formulation of many of its ideas and writings, but later added to it the stamp of his own blood. That's why Che, like Fidel, and like Lenin, was a profound critic of dogmas and erroneous conceptions that opened cracks that the class enemy could slip through.

Che's understanding of the need for critical analysis in building socialism and communism led him to deepen his study of revolutionary theory—both as an irreplaceable necessity to avoid theoretical, ideological, and political errors, and as a weapon for the practical work of building the new society.

The spirit permeating Marx's tireless criticism of apologetic tendencies in bourgeois social science guided the Cuban revolutionaries' road to Marxism-Leninism. As Che put it, "One should be a 'Marxist' with the same naturalness with which one is a 'Newtonian' in physics or a 'Pasteurian' in biology. . . ."[7]

What exactly is political economy in the transition period? Is there really a need to formulate such a political economy with its own special characteristics? If the answer is yes, will it survive beyond the transition period? Or will it disappear in communist society and be replaced by a sort of "social technology"? What *economic policies* should be adopted? What relation do these policies have to the political economy of the transition period? How is the new society to be organized?

These and other questions swirled in the heads of the young revolutionaries. Searching in vain for some book that would provide the answers, they went back to the classics. In Cuba this study of Marx had different motivations than those in Europe. What was involved in Europe was a *turn* to the young Marx. Some believed they had found anthropological theories in Marx's early writings that justified a return to prior humanist positions, and that this offered an alternative to the reductionist theoretical simplifications of some of the standard manuals and treatises on Marxism.

Nonetheless, what is found in Marx, as we shall see, is not a "Political Economy of the Transition Period," but instead some observations by this leader of the world proletariat on the historically conditioned character of all human thought. The object of Marx's studies, he always stressed, was "the capitalist mode of production, and the relations of production and forms of exchange that correspond to it,"[8] with the aim of carrying out the communist revolution. The present explains the past, Marx pointed out, but the past is not always needed to understand the present.

> Bourgeois society is the most developed and multifaceted historical organisation of production. The categories which express its relations, an understanding of its structure, therefore, provide, at the same time, insights into the structure and the relations of production of all previous forms of society the ruins and elements of which were used in the creation of bourgeois society.
>
> Some of these remnants are still dragged along unassimilated within bourgeois society, while elements

which previously were barely indicated have developed and attained their full significance. The anatomy of man is a key to the anatomy of the ape. On the other hand, indications of higher forms in the lower species of animals can only be understood when the higher forms themselves are already known.

Bourgeois economy thus provides a key to that of antiquity, and so on. But by no means in the manner of those economists who obliterate all historical differences and see in all forms of society the bourgeois forms. One can understand tribute, the tithe, etc., if one understands rent. But they must not be treated as identical.

Since bourgeois society is, moreover, only a contradictory form of development, it contains relations of earlier forms of society often only in very stunted shape or as mere travesties, e.g., communal property. Thus if it is true that the categories of bourgeois economy are valid for all other forms of society, this has to be taken *cum grano salis* [with a grain of salt], for they may contain them in a developed, stunted, caricatured, etc., form always with substantial differences.[9]

Thus the idea of the specific nature of the new social system took on ever greater clarity. The establishment of the dictatorship of the proletariat expressed a turning point not only in history itself, but also in the *way* history is made. For the first time man *consciously* takes up the task of organizing society. The possibility of making political and economic decisions transforms man into the architect of his own destiny. Previously society was atomized and dispersed in various directions. Society was unaware of the forces that came into play in the unfolding of history and was, in fact, largely a toy of those forces.

In the *Manifesto of the Communist Party*, Marx and Engels give a precise image of the "blind" way history is made:

Modern bourgeois society with its relations of production, of exchange, and of property, a society that has conjured up such gigantic means of production and of exchange, is like the sorcerer who is no longer able

> to control the powers of the nether world whom he has
> called up by his spells.[10]

Society produced a history as seemingly incoherent and contradictory as society itself. Economic forces were totally outside any field of knowledge—imposing themselves like superhuman laws—but were at the same time the only possible clue for social science to begin untangling the mess and drawing initial conclusions. Only when political economy emerged as a social science did the tendencies and regularities that characterize various aspects of the capitalist system begin to be grasped and given a rational explanation. Even then, the apologetic character of bourgeois economic science prevented many of capitalism's significant features from being detected. Marxism, by making a conscious critique of capitalist reality, succeeded to a large degree in finally understanding it.

It is obvious however that knowledge about social phenomena, while important, is not sufficient to subject them to human will. Understanding the meaning of surplus value does not, in and of itself, eliminate it; the structures that give rise to surplus value must be eliminated.

To take control of their destiny, revolutionary forces have found two instruments: revolution and the dictatorship of the proletariat. With the first they overthrew the bourgeois government. With the second they destroyed the bourgeois state, replaced it, and brought social forces under their control, thereby opening a new *way* of making history. Revolutionary aims were now expressed through the *economic plan*. In addition to understanding reality, there was now also the power to make decisions that affected reality.

Given these considerations, what can theory accomplish? Everything indicates that centralized decision making can contribute increasing organization to the various elements of society, eventually bringing to them some of the regularities and tendencies of scientific thought. But these *tendencies* do not "impose themselves as iron necessities," because they are in fact the product of man's conscious action, on which they continue to depend.

With the revolution of October 1917, the revolution of Lenin, man acquired a new consciousness. The men of the French revolution, who told humanity so many beautiful things, who set so many examples, and whose tradition is still preserved, were nevertheless simple instruments of history. Economic forces were in motion, and the French revolutionaries sought to interpret popular sentiments, the sentiments of the men of that era. Some of them saw farther than others, but none were capable of taking history into their own hands, of consciously making their own history.

This became possible after the October revolution. And after the Second World War, the bloc of countries that made up the camp of peace and socialism was very strong. Now there were a billion men taking history in their own hands, who knew what they were doing. And among this billion, like a drop, but a drop that could be discerned, with its own features, and with our deepest pride—were the seven million people of Cuba.[11]

From these initial conclusions a corollary can be derived: despite similar premises (dictatorship of the proletariat, social ownership of the means of production, and so forth) and similar objectives (creation of a communist society), each process of transition to communism indisputably has its individual identity stemming from particular decisions made by various political leaderships in response to problems that emerge under different conditions.

This discovery had immense methodological implications. On the one hand, it laid bare the danger of importing by extrapolation solutions to real problems that required concrete answers. On the other hand, it helped clarify that the problems each revolutionary process had to face were closely related to the historical framework in which the process occurred and had to be grasped as *experiences* in *that* context.

What was needed, therefore, was to construct a model for building communism that corresponded both to the general laws governing the transition period—that is, to the common characteristics of revolution and the construction of socialism formulated in the declaration of the Conference of Communist and Workers' Parties of the socialist countries in 1957—as well as to the socioeconomic, historical, ideological, and cultural characteristics of the Cuban revolution that began in 1868.[12]

In other words, what was needed was a general conception of *how* the transition to communism would be carried out. It would have to be an *integrated* model; it would have to encompass all levels of society (economic, political, juridical, ideological, and so forth) in a coherent fashion. Such a model should also make us conscious of its provisional nature—that it is an instrument requiring constant renewal in order to revolutionize reality.

In drawing up such a model, politics establishes the goals, while science lays out the possibilities for attaining them and determines the roads to be taken. No one can develop a science of something that does not yet exist. That's why ideology and consciousness about *what we want to overcome* play such an important role.

For Che, "the budgetary finance system is *part of a general conception* of the development of the construction of socialism and should therefore be studied in its totality."[13]

The rationality of an economic model must therefore be measured by its *social rationality*, and not the reverse. Said another way, the rational functioning of society requires rational economic functioning as its premise, but economic rationality does not imply *social rationality* in and of itself. At issue here is not the quantity and quality of material goods produced, but rather *how* they are produced, and the social relations that flow from that way of producing them.

The general conception on the basis of which such a model would be drawn up was summarized by Che in this incisive response to a question from a journalist:

> A socialist economy without communist moral values does not interest me. We fight poverty but we also fight alienation. One of the fundamental aims of Marxism is to eliminate material interest, the factor of "individual self-interest" and profit from man's psychological motivations.

Marx was concerned with both economic facts and their reflection in the mind, which he called a "fact of consciousness." If communism neglects facts of consciousness, it can serve as a method of distribution but it will no longer express revolutionary moral values.[14]

Che hit the nail on the head with this conceptual negation. It captures both the strategic objective and the general conception of our transition.

Che described the ultimate objective of the entire effort in the following way: creating a social structure that will provide optimum conditions for the *type* of "human nature" aspired to. The *new* man will emerge both as a result of revolutionary effort and as the product of conditions inherent to the structures created by the revolution. He will take hold of his own existence in order to dominate the forces that previously imposed their destiny upon him, but that can now be dominated and directed. Social processes will be led consciously and with the active involvement of the masses. The masses will raise themselves to the level of the present vanguard and to even higher levels.[15] Political power will not just be *popular,* it will be a political power *of the people.* Che had confidence in the capacity of human beings to transform themselves.

In *The German Ideology,* Marx and Engels made the following point:

> Both for the production on a mass scale of this communist consciousness, and for the success of the cause itself, *the alteration of men on a mass scale is necessary, an alteration which can only take place in a practical movement, a revolution;* the revolution is necessary, therefore, not only because the *ruling* class cannot be overthrown in any other way, but also because the class *overthrowing* it *can only in a revolution succeed in ridding itself of all the muck of ages* and become fitted to found society anew.[16]

Che believed that the new social consciousness would not be attained simply as the end product of the first stage of development of society's material and technical base and the advance of economic efficiency. Instead, the transformation of human consciousness had to start in the first phase of the transition from capitalism to communism.

Che understood that the creation of a new social consciousness would require the same effort as that devoted to the development of a material base for socialism. He saw consciousness as an active element, a material force, an engine to develop the material and technical base. He did not believe consciousness could be relegated to a secondary position. He took care to ensure that the methods and means used to attain the goal would not distort the goal itself or push it into the background.

Che idealized neither human beings, classes, nor the masses. He knew very well, both in theory and in practice, their aspirations, desires, psychology, ideology, and the "inheritance" they carried over from capitalist society. He was fully aware of the historical context of human thought and conduct, and he adhered to Marxist-Leninist principles in interpreting them.[17]

Socialist society has to be built by human beings who are fighting to climb out of the bourgeois muck, but not surrendering to their past motivations. The new and the old must be combined in a dialectical way.

For Che the following concepts are not identical: *material* base and *economic* wealth, development of the *productive forces* and development of *production*,[18] *social* relations of production and *economic* relations, the production and reproduction of *material life* and the production and reproduction of *consumer goods*. Marxist categories burst beyond economic factors to offer a complex and comprehensible picture of reality. In their richness they cannot be reduced to economic concepts whose equivalents can easily be found in the history of bourgeois economic thought. It is the social relations of production, not purely *economic* relations, that condition the social consciousness of an era.

Che believed that mixing up a number of these different concepts could lead to models for building socialism that leave out the element of politics and ideology. In referring exclusively to the economic level, such models could overlook the importance of superstructural factors.

Che understood that according to this line of thinking, the first phase of communism could be viewed as a stage of *economic* transformations—or, to be more precise, of *economic* development—from which new forms of social consciousness would flow *automatically* during the second phase. This way of approaching the transition period could suggest that the *base* and *superstructure* are independent phenomena that can be dealt with in different stages, or at least that the superstructure is a passive element.[19] Che agreed with Marx that "circumstances make men just as much as men make circumstances."[20] And Che agreed with the order of importance of the factors Marx laid down in his *Critique of the Gotha Programme* to characterize communism:

> In a higher phase of communist society, when the enslaving subordination of the individual to the division of labour, and therewith also the antithesis between mental and physical labour, has vanished; *when labour has become not only a means of keeping alive but has itself become a vital need; when the productive forces have also increased with the all-round development of the individual,* and all the springs of co-operative wealth flow more abundantly. . . .[21]

As can be seen, the factor "co-operative wealth" is preceded by a whole series of elements that condition it. Among these, and directly preceding it, is "the all-round development of the individual."

Che gave some thought to what is often understood as economic rationality, observing that this always revolves around concepts such as efficiency, productivity, maximum utility, optimal decision making, profit, and so forth. And he posed a question that was seldom asked: What objective is being pursued through the application of these economic methods? If the aim is simply economic *development*, then the *methods* used don't matter, since that goal itself defines what is socially rational. But if society is pursuing higher and more complex objectives than economic development, then a different conclusion is indicated: that an organic link exists between longer range goals and economic management. This link, in turn, is related to the question: How should economic factors be handled to attain the objectives that society as a whole is pursuing?

The role of economic rationality was thus limited to simply one element—and a subordinate element—in establishing social rationality.

> If material incentives are counterposed to the development of consciousness, but are a great lever for increasing production, does this mean that giving priority to the development of consciousness retards production? In comparative terms, in a given period, that may be, although no one has made the relevant calculations. We maintain that in a relatively short time, however, the development of consciousness does more for the development of production than material incentives do. We state this based on the overall development of society toward communism, which presupposes that work will cease to be a tedious necessity and become a pleasant duty.[22]

At issue, then, is not an innocent choice between one or another theoretical position that may be to our liking. The real stakes can only be grasped once we realize that the choice made immediately involves the creation of the material and ideological relations that will mark the production of daily life and consciousness for years to come. In other words, the simple fact of state ownership of the means of production is not sufficient to stamp the mode of production with a socialist character.

What needs to be examined are how the management apparatus of the state is structured; the nature of the incentives used; the forms of property that may or may not coexist, and their extent (social or cooperative, for example); the existence and functioning of the market and/or the plan, according to the case; the existence or not of generalized commodity production; and so forth. These are the elements that give shape to a specific mode of production, a specific mode of activity, a specific mode of living for individuals. And the formation of the ideas and attitudes of those individuals will flow continually from that social and political structure.

Che thought it was simplistic to explain advances, stagnation, or retreats on the ideological plane on the basis of how well or how poorly political work and ideological education had been carried out. Such work, Che believed, is conditioned by the totality of material relations noted above.

The education of generations that will overcome the selfishness and personal ambition that motivate man in class society is not consistent with the principle of material interest as the *main* lever to build the new society. Che stressed the need to keep in mind some essential tenets of Marxism—the interrelation between consciousness and the production of material life, the relationship between the base and superstructure, the interrelation between changing circumstances and human activity.

Che warned against the dangerous path of pragmatism in face of these realities. That is why the search for the parameters of our transition process remained of vital importance to him.

One of Che's main theoretical merits is undoubtedly his understanding of the complex relationship between the base and the superstructure during the transition (the period of socialism).

In *The German Ideology,* their first outstanding joint work, Marx and Engels uncovered the way in which material relations (the economic structure), particularly economic relations, determined and conditioned the resulting ideological relations (superstructure). This discovery of cardinal importance made possible the emergence of a genuine social science: historical materialism.

Nevertheless it is interesting to note that among the existing literature that Che found concerning the transition period—works published in the most diverse places and from various ideological standpoints—none tackled in a clear way the question of how the new economic organization of society, and the overall remodeling of social relations, would condition the forms of social consciousness.

In the literature referred to, the question of the transition is approached in two main ways:

• the establishment of the dictatorship of the proletariat per se is taken as a guarantee of the increasing emergence of communist consciousness;

• the economy is treated as something independent of the superstructural forms that accompany it.

Both approaches display a lack of understanding of the Marxist-Leninist approach to the social base and superstructure, and both can be the source of serious errors not only on the theoretical plane but also—and primarily—of a practical nature.

In regard to the first approach, it should first be pointed out that the "dictatorship of the proletariat" is an abstraction—in fact a synthesis of many abstractions—that expresses an objective phenomenon made up of a multitude of elements. That's why an equal sign should not be placed between the revolutionary triumph and the establishment of the revolutionary dictatorship in its most complete and finished form. The triumph makes it possible to begin the process of progressively establishing such a dictatorship. But this process has its own stages and, in the first phase, must undoubtedly concentrate its main efforts on the struggle against counterrevolutionary elements and on the consolidation of revolutionary power.

As explained in the Marxist classics, the dictatorship of the proletariat is the period during which—once power has been taken—the social relations of production that characterize capitalism are eliminated and replaced by others of a new, communist type.

In this sense it can be said that the dictatorship of the proletariat *implies* the formation of communist consciousness. But this is a *programmatic* implication of a goal still to be attained. So the question of whether or not such consciousness is attained, and whether it will take a longer or shorter period of time, depends on the actions of the revolutionary dictatorship, on the political vision of its leaders, on the real internal and external possibilities to carry it out, and many other factors.

A lesson emerges here: the initial revolutionary triumph

opens the *possibility* for social change but cannot *by itself* guarantee it. The vanguard must act in an organized and conscious way to promote the creation of structures that help develop a communist attitude in the new generations. This delicate process cannot be left to spontaneity.

With regard to the second approach—the tendency to treat the economy of the transition period as something independent, with no connection to superstructural factors—Che believed that such a conception tended to give rise to dangerous errors in both theory and practice.

There is a tendency among some economists to treat their field of study in a technical, academic way, in an effort to leave to one side political, ideological, or philosophical considerations. Dealing with such factors, they believe, would reduce, or perhaps even nullify, the scientific validity of their theoretical findings. This position—false and mistaken under any circumstances—is the source of innumerable errors with incalculable consequences when the subject to be analyzed is the socialist economy (in the transition period).

Such an attitude accounts for the existence of a body of literature on the economy of the transition period that gives no consideration whatsoever to political and ideological questions during this stage or to the complex interplay of base and superstructure.

As Che pointed out, it is precisely this attitude that makes possible "the danger that the forest will not be seen for the trees" and that in pursuing economic development indiscriminate use will be made of the "dull instruments left to us by capitalism,"[23] only later to discover the damage done by these newly established economic forms and *structures* in undermining consciousness. In a nutshell, this is a technocratic and administrative attitude. Its complete failure to examine the problem of base-superstructure relations in the transition period opens a deep channel for revisionism in theory and counterrevolution in practice, consciously or unconsciously, whether or not that is the author's intent.

The way that each of the new economic structures and institutions affects, expresses, and conditions the motivations of ordinary people is a vital consideration that should be taken up in any study of the transition period. Che's understanding of the base-superstructure phenomenon in this stage enabled him to take a revolutionary position on the socialist economy, a position in which economic rationality in itself was not assumed to be the absolutely surefire barometer of revolutionary transformation.

On occasion, in analyzing the causes of certain tensions or anomalies that crop up—particularly those that could be linked to enemy activity or used to the enemy's advantage—a narrow superstructural standpoint is adopted. Blame is placed on erroneous political methods, on a lack of organic connection between the government and the masses, on bad political work by the party, and other factors of this sort.

Never included, however, is an analysis of the *economic structure* of the society, which is "above all suspicion" because of its declared socialist character. But it is clear that this structure is the product of human actions, actions that have been taken just as consciously as setting in motion a program of political education. It is therefore possible that the economic structure possesses defects, shortcomings, and distortions resulting from errors or incorrect interpretations by the human beings who created it. These defects and shortcomings are to some degree inherent in the socialist character of the economy and must be detected and corrected to improve the health of the economy and of society in general. Moreover, the existence of such shortcomings or defects in the economic structure affects the entire superstructure, including political work itself, which is the basic factor in developing social consciousness during this stage.

Che thought that perpetuating and developing the economic laws and categories of capitalism would prolong bourgeois social relations of production, and with them, the habits of thought and motivations of capitalist society. This was true even though the underlying phenomenon had now gone through a metamorphosis under socialist forms.

This is not a case of vulgar economism leading us to blame the economic structure for every anomaly in the superstructure. At issue is understanding that the *base* must not be viewed as "above all suspicion" when something happens; instead, it must be "the first suspect" to be "interrogated."

Often, however, the debate has not consistently followed this path of rounded and rigorous analysis. In general, a problem is raised or reraised when a crisis is detected in the way the economy is functioning. Discussion therefore inevitably tends to revolve around economic efficiency. The focus is placed on the need for a new model of economic management capable of attaining such efficiency and surpassing previous methods.

But what is being discussed here is not a capitalist monopoly or a capitalist state, but a revolution that pursues as its most important strategic objective the establishment of a new order of human relations—communist relations. That is why the discussion takes on profound and complex implications that transcend economic matters and require a precise, detailed, and comprehensive examination.

Nevertheless, the existing body of literature on past debates on the transition period tends to concentrate almost exclusively on technical and administrative aspects of the question and to omit the social and political dimension of the options under discussion. This in turn serves as a source of new errors, since the legitimacy, validity, and effectiveness of management systems are measured strictly in terms of economic efficiency. All research into whether or not a correct choice of management systems has been made is centered on analyzing indicators of economic efficiency.

There is a danger in this flawed methodological approach. If the superstructure is affected negatively by existing economic relations, and if there is no further analysis of this fact in any subsequent discussion on possible changes in those relations—then the possibility of a gradual regression in social consciousness increases dramatically.

This is the dialectical relationship Che was referring to when he stressed that market-economy mechanisms and the indiscriminate, unthinking use of direct material incentives to encourage production would tend to take on an existence of their own and impose their independent dynamic on social relations as a whole. Lenin also noted such a possibility when, after putting forward the need for the New Economic Policy, he called for a halt to the retreat and for a return to the offensive against capitalism. Unfortunately Lenin did not live long enough to work out the strategy and tactics of the retreat and the offensive.[24]

What was needed therefore was a model for the transition—a model with which to transform capitalist structures and advance toward communist consciousness and forms of production.

The first difficulty emerged immediately. How does one work out a theory for a transition that has not yet occurred? How does one conduct a scientific analysis of something that does not yet exist? The solution could arise only out of the concrete transformation of conditions, *in the framework of a general conception* of the goals being pursued. In this way, the concrete steps taken would be consistent with the overall conception they aimed to advance. That would give them the status of a system, whose model would be established by the general conception.[25] This conception in turn would function as a theoretical premise, readjusted as necessary on the basis of information fed back by the model.

At the same time, the general conception establishes the model's strategic objective: the shaping of a new mode of production, of a new set of social relations intrinsically antagonistic to those of capitalism—in short, a change in the material conditions simultaneous with the transformation of men into communists, the antithesis of the *homo economicus* [economic man] of class society, particularly of the capitalist mode of production. And the aim was to carry this out in an underdeveloped country such as Cuba.

This is not revolutionary romanticism, not a dream of a utopian paradise. It should be self-evident that the development of consciousness must be the strategic objective of the first social system ever to be constructed in a conscious way. ·

While it is true that the *new man* cannot be precisely defined, it is nonetheless perfectly clear what we *do not want him to be*. The new man is the antithesis of the *homo economicus* of the prehistory of humanity, as Marx called the long road of suffering and struggle to give the world a new face. The point therefore is to discover and sweep away the structures that generate selfishness and personal ambition, replacing them with new social institutions and mechanisms capable of molding future generations in a different way.

To repeat, this is not romanticism. It is a Marxist-Leninist understanding of how social being determines social consciousness, and how both elements can only be transformed jointly, through social practice.

Once a goal has been set, it is necessary to gauge the possibilities of attaining it. In other words, it is necessary to evaluate all the elements that affect the will to carry through revolutionary change and therefore establish the framework of what is possible *at a given moment*. These objective factors set the *initial* limits and possibilities of revolutionary measures. While recognizing this objective reality from the outset, communists set out to transform that reality—basing themselves on the elements in the situation that are most favorable to carrying out these revolutionary measures. This in turn broadens the framework of what is possible.

The dichotomy between "determinism" and "voluntarism" is a false one. Instead, revolutionaries must adopt a genuine Marxist-Leninist position. Man always finds himself in a given *historical* situation; that is, a situation that he himself did not directly participate in creating but rather "inherited" from preceding generations. These are the *objective* conditions he *confronts*, regardless of his will, and that affect his actions *at every moment*. Within that framework of what is possible, however, it is precisely *man's own actions that transform his conditions and create a new objective situation that opens up new options and possibilities.*

Che's model for the transition period steers clear of the two poles of this dichotomy. It is not voluntarist, since—as a prerequisite to applying the laws that govern the communist socioeconomic formation—this model demands exact knowledge of the objective reality to be confronted, as well as knowledge of the experiences of sister socialist countries. It is not determinist, since it calls for transforming this reality, not *adapting* to it.

So what was Cuban reality like at the beginning of the 1960s?

Cuba was a country with a backward and single-crop agri-

culture, little industry, tremendous technological backwardness, and low levels of productivity. It was unable to feed itself. It was absolutely dependent on foreign trade but had no
merchant fleet. It had a poorly skilled labor force and few technicians and engineers. It was without sources of energy or an
organized irrigation system that would enable agriculture—
the basic pillar of the economy—to cope with seasonal and
climatic problems. Social needs of all types had accumulated
for decades. There was a serious unemployment problem. In
addition the country was a neocolony.

Cuba was a small country with a transportation system that
was adequate in comparison with other Latin America countries of the time. It had a considerable communications network, ranging from telex to telephone, radio, microwave re-
lay, cable, telegraph, and television. During the 1950s U.S.
companies used Cuba as a testing ground for their latest innovations in communications. Cuban communications therefore became disproportionately developed in relation to other
Latin American countries. This was even true—all proportions
guarded—in relation to the United States itself, which in some
cases never put into operation certain communications systems installed in Cuba.

In addition some foreign corporations had introduced into
Cuba the latest technical innovations in accounting, the organization and management of production, and overall economic
controls.

In his article "On the Budgetary Finance System," Che cites
a long quotation from the Polish economist Oskar Lange in
which Lange lists the latest technical-economic advances of
state capitalism. Che adds immediately: "It should be noted
that Cuba had not made its transition nor even begun its revolution at the time this was written. Many of the advanced techniques described by Lange existed in Cuba. . . . "[26]

The Cuban revolution was inaugurated at a singular moment in history, as well. Its emergence coincided with the existence of an already powerful socialist camp whose economic,
military, and political consolidation was well known and beyond question. It also came at a time of unusual strides in
science and technology—in particular in cybernetics, electron-

ics, and data processing, all of which had very important effects on economic organization. The most vital fact in our objective reality was that Cuba, unlike Bolshevik Russia some forty years earlier, was not alone.

These factors indicated the possibility and necessity of constructing a model of economic management in Cuba based on the experience of the socialist countries, our existing system of communications, our country's geographic size, and the latest economic techniques of analysis, control, and organization of production. Such a model, combined with centralized administrative management and adequate facts and figures, would permit a step toward consolidating economic planning.

Che's views on the transition period were not the result of a dogmatic extremism, nor of fear of a capitalist "contagion." While vehemently denouncing the dangers implicit in the attempt of some economists to understand the socialist economy by using the categories of capitalist political economy, Che pointed out at the same time the possibilities to take advantage of capitalism's latest technical and economic advances in matters of accounting, organization, and implementation of controls in enterprises and production. Referring to these systems of controls, he stated:

> We said we were not going to invent anything new, that this was the accounting system of the monopolies. And it's true, it has a lot in common with the accounting system of the monopolies. But no one can deny that the monopolies have a very efficient system of controls. They really look after their pennies; it doesn't matter to them that they have millions, they always take care of the pennies. And they have very rigorous techniques for determining costs.[27]

But Che opposed utilizing categories from capitalist political economy, such as the market, interest, direct material incentives, and profit. He thought that socialism could not be built using the elements of capitalism without changing the real meaning of socialism. Taking such a road would produce a hybrid system that would require new concessions to capitalist economic levers and would therefore lead to a retreat.

In this regard, Che's insistence that communists not use terms taken from capitalist political economy to describe phenomena of the transition period should also be noted. He argued this not only because of the confusion this would create in economic analysis, but also because using such categories would set in motion a logic in which Marxist thought would become completely distorted.

The problem then was not a simple one. Not at all. It amounted to structuring specific forms for our transition at a time when no developed theory on such a period existed. All that was available was the arsenal of previous experiences of other countries in the socialist camp.

CHAPTER 2

The Marxist conception of politics as concentrated

economics and its importance in economic management

under socialism

T HE CONSTRUCTION of the model of building socialism we have referred to must be organically linked to the revolutionary leadership's general conception of the specific features of our transition.[28] The model should closely adhere to that conception and function as one of the mechanisms to carry it out. That is, any system of economic management under consideration should above all contribute to the revolution's strategic objective: the creation of a new social order and a new man, communist man.

To ensure that the battle against poverty goes hand in hand with a simultaneous effort to create a new communist consciousness, an ongoing relationship must exist between the operation of the economy and the organization of socialist leadership. The capacity of the economic model proposed by Che (the budgetary finance system) to harmonize economic and social rationality would be measured by the degree to which it helped attain the strategic goals embodied in the general conception of our transition.

Looked at from the angle of a model for the socialist economy, the budgetary finance system would have to demonstrate its success on two levels. From a technical point of view, it would have to demonstrate its capacity for efficient administration and management. From a structural point of view, it would have to mesh with the political and ideological needs of the transition, promoting first and foremost the communist transformation of social relations as a whole.

The system's successes in the economic sphere would assure the possibility of constructing a new order. But the *way* these successes were attained would be of the greatest importance, because this would set the framework for the new model of society that was being built. In other words, economic successes, both in terms of final results and the way they were attained, will be genuine to the degree they give a decisive impetus to the formation of communist social relations and, therefore, of new forms of social consciousness.

Here an important fact should be taken into account: the efficiency of the budgetary finance system can neither be evaluated solely by how well it makes use of the resources at its command, nor by the quantity of revenues and earnings generated by its enterprises. It also has to be gauged by its capacity to improve economic management *through* the development of communist education; by its capacity to harmonize strategic and tactical objectives, social and economic goals. In short it must be judged by its capacity to harmonize social and economic rationality.

As a revolutionary economist, Che never lost sight of the fact that, under socialism, what is economically rational could not in itself serve as the barometer of what is socially rational. The formation of a new type of human relations would have to be the central objective of every effort; other factors would be positive or negative to the degree they helped accelerate or retard that process. Otherwise, a grave risk would be run that the need to overcome the poverty accumulated over centuries would lead the revolutionary vanguard to view success in production as the sole central goal, losing sight of the reason for making the revolution in the first place. Seeking purely economic gains could lead to the application of methods that, while producing economic successes in the short run, could mortgage the revolutionary future through gradual erosion of the process of raising consciousness. No one described this phenomenon better than Che:

> A complete education for social labor has not yet

taken place in these countries, and wealth is far from being within the reach of the masses through the simple process of appropriation. Underdevelopment, on the one hand, and the usual flight of capital to the "civilized countries, on the other, make a rapid transition without sacrifices impossible. There remains a long way to go in constructing the economic base, and the temptation is very great to follow the beaten track of material interest as the lever with which to accelerate development.

There is the danger that the forest will not be seen for the trees. The pipe dream that socialism can be achieved with the help of the dull instruments left to us by capitalism (the commodity as the economic cell, profitability, individual material interest as a lever, etc.) can lead into a blind alley. And you wind up there after having traveled a long distance with many crossroads, and it is hard to figure out just where you took the wrong turn. Meanwhile, the economic foundation that has been laid has done its work of undermining the development of consciousness. To build communism it is necessary, simultaneous with the new material foundations, to build the new man.[29]

And once again, he made the same point:

It is not a matter of how many kilograms of meat one has to eat, nor of how many times a year someone can go to the beach, nor how many pretty things from abroad you might be able to buy with present-day wages. It is a matter of making the individual feel more complete, with much more internal richness and much more responsibility.[30]

Thus for Che economic rationality meant the best possible use of resources so as to enhance the multifaceted development of both society and communist education.

That does not mean that building communism can be compatible with economic bankruptcy. The point is that the efficiency of administrative management under socialism cannot be measured *exclusively* by the total amount of values created.

It must also be gauged by the degree to which the economic structures help bring closer the new society, through the transformation of men. It must be gauged by how well man is developed socially in a communist direction, precisely on the basis of the new economic structures.

In building communism the relative weight of economic achievements, on the one hand, and achievements in raising consciousness, on the other, was clearly established by Che:

> Socialism is not a welfare society, nor is it a utopian society based on the goodness of man as man.
> Socialism is a system *that arises historically,* and that has as its pillar the socialization of the basic means of production along with equitable distribution of all of society's wealth, in a framework of social production.[31]
>
> In our view *communism is a phenomenon of consciousness and not solely a phenomenon of production.* We cannot arrive at communism through the simple mechanical accumulation of quantities of goods made available to the people. By doing that we would get somewhere, to be sure, to some peculiar form of socialism.
>
> But what Marx defined as communism, what is aspired to in general as communism, cannot be attained if man is not conscious. That is, if he does not have a new consciousness toward society.[32]

This conception was summed up in a few words by Che to a ceremony on August 21, 1962, honoring outstanding Cuban workers, as well as some visiting workers from the German Democratic Republic:

> Productivity, more production, consciousness—these are the foundations upon which the new society can be built.[33]

It is extremely important to clarify this question, since revisionist theories of the transition period are sometimes cloaked under technocratic formula used by bourgeois social theorists to argue that Marxism-Leninism is outmoded. These revisionist theories separate economic from political-ideological considerations. They assign primacy to economic models whose central aim is to maximize profits, frankly pushing off to the side the revolution's reason for being. Their watchword is: "Let's concern ourselves with maximizing economic growth, the rest will follow." And that is how they seek to smuggle in the rotten fruit of capitalism. To understand that there is no automatic relationship between abundance and communist consciousness, it should be sufficient to analyze the motivations of the typical citizen of U.S. 'consumer society.'

On April 4, 1982, speaking at the closing session of the Fourth Congress of the Union of Young Communists, Fidel stated:

> Marxism-Leninism must continue evolving every day in actual practice in a revolutionary sense. We have yet to see a revolution that regresses while correctly applying the principles of Marxism-Leninism, creatively applying them and, above all, if the principle of applying the principles themselves is applied. Because little problems start cropping up when principles are not correctly applied, a fact so widely exploited by the enemies of socialism, by the capitalists, in their bid to resuscitate their decrepit, inhuman, and prehistoric system.
>
> This is a task that we revolutionaries have to tackle. For it is easy to make a mistake and mistakes are often made. Often they are the result of a lack of serious, in-depth analysis, the result of a lack of collective analysis, which is also one of the fundamental principles of Marxism-Leninism. . . .
>
> Nevertheless, we've had to adopt a number of specific measures imposed by necessity, by reality. These measures help in many ways, they develop the economy. And the development of the economy makes for greater resources which, in turn, makes for greater possibilities for the development of society and of society's wealth. If there's no wealth there will be very few things to distribute. That is a reality, and in correcting its idealistic mistakes the revolution had the courage to adopt the pertinent measures.
>
> But contradictions do arise. And we must guard

against allowing socialist formulas to compromise communist consciousness. We must prevent socialist formulas from compromising our loftiest objectives, our aspirations, our communist dreams. We must not allow ourselves to be diverted from our goal of developing communist man because of neglect of ideology or a lack of understanding of these truths. . . .

No, no one can expect communist consciousness to be based solely on an abundance of wealth.

The way I see it, in the development of communist society, wealth and the material base must grow hand in hand with consciousness, because it can even happen that as wealth increases consciousness diminishes. . . . I'm convinced that it's not only wealth or the development of the material base that will develop consciousness—far from it. There are some countries much richer than ours—there are some. I don't want to make comparisons of any kind; that would not be correct. But we do know of revolutionary countries where wealth has advanced more than consciousness, leading even to counterrevolutionary problems and things of that sort. But you can have a great deal of consciousness without much wealth. . . .

We must search for socialist formulas rather than capitalist formulas to solve problems, because before we realize it capitalist formulas can begin to corrupt us and contaminate us. . . .[34]

With these problems clearly in mind, Che carefully selected the elements that were to make up the budgetary finance system of economic management, its institutional forms, its incentive mechanisms, and its methods of implementing controls. Ninety miles from the shores of imperialism, Cuban socialism could not allow itself the luxury of not seeing the forest and wandering down the wrong path.

CHAPTER 3

The relationship between the budgetary finance system

and the economic accounting system

in the management of the socialist economy

ONE OF THE most hotly debated points in the literature of the period of transition to communism is undoubtedly the series of measures taken in Russia in the early 1920s under the name New Economic Policy (NEP).[35]

In his essay "On the Budgetary Finance System," Che wrote:

> Lenin's theory[36] was proven in practice by the victory in Russia that gave birth to the USSR.
>
> We are faced by a new phenomenon: the advent of the socialist revolution in a single country, economically backward, with 22 million square kilometers, a low population density, further impoverished as a result of the war, and, as if all this were not enough, under attack by the imperialist powers.
>
> After a period of war communism, Lenin laid the bases of the NEP and, with it, the basis for the development of Soviet society up to today.
>
> It is important to describe here the conjuncture the Soviet Union was living through, and no one can do this better than Lenin:
>
> "Thus, in 1918, I was of the opinion that with regard to the economic situation then obtaining in the Soviet Republic, state capitalism would be a step forward. This

sounds very strange, and perhaps even absurd, for already at that time our Republic was a socialist republic and we were every day hastily—perhaps too hastily—adopting various new economic measures which could not be described as anything but socialist measures.

"Nevertheless, I held the view that in relation to the economic situation then obtaining in the Soviet Republic state capitalism would be a step forward, and I explained my idea simply by enumerating the elements of the economic system of Russia. In my opinion these elements were the following: '(1) patriarchal, i.e., the most primitive form of agriculture; (2) small commodity production (this includes the majority of peasants who trade in grain); (3) private capitalism; (4) state capitalism; and (5) socialism.'

"All these economic elements were present in Russia at that time. I set myself the task of explaining the relationship of these elements to each other, and whether one of the non-socialist elements, namely, state capitalism, should not be rated higher than socialism. I repeat: it seems very strange to everyone that a non-socialist element should be rated higher than, regarded as superior to, socialism in a republic which declares itself a socialist republic.

"But the fact will become intelligible if you recall that we definitely did not regard the economic system of Russia as something homogeneous and highly developed; we were fully aware that in Russia we had patriarchal agriculture, i.e., the most primitive form of agriculture, alongside the socialist form. What role could state capitalism play in these circumstances? . . .

"Now that I have emphasized the fact that as early as 1918 we regarded state capitalism as a possible line of retreat, I shall deal with the results of our New Economic Policy. I repeat: at that time it was still a very vague idea, but in 1921, after we had passed through the most important stage of the Civil War—and passed through it victoriously—we felt the impact of a grave—I think it was the gravest—internal political crisis in

Soviet Russia. This internal crisis brought to light discontent not only among a considerable section of the peasantry but also among the workers. This was the first and, I hope, the last time in the history of Soviet Russia that feeling ran against us among large masses of peasants, not consciously but instinctively.

"What gave rise to this peculiar, and for us, of course, very unpleasant situation? The reason for it was that in our economic offensive we had run too far ahead, that we had not provided ourselves with adequate resources, that the masses sensed what we ourselves were not then able to formulate consciously but what we admitted soon after, a few weeks later, namely, that the direct transition to purely socialist forms, to purely socialist distribution, was beyond our available strength, and that if we were unable to effect a retreat so as to confine ourselves to easier tasks, we would face disaster."[37]

As can be seen, the economic and political situation in the Soviet Union made necessary the retreat Lenin spoke of. *The entire policy, therefore, can be characterized as a tactic closely linked to the country's historical situation. Therefore, not all of Lenin's statements should be accorded universal validity. It seems to us that two extremely important factors should be considered regarding their introduction into other countries.*

1. The characteristics of tsarist Russia at the time of the revolution, including the development of technology on every level; the special character of its people; and the country's general condition—adding to this the destruction caused by a world war, the devastation wrought by the White hordes and the imperialist invaders.[38]

2. The general characteristics of the period with respect to techniques of economic administration and controls.[39]

Che clearly believed the New Economic Policy constituted an *emergency* policy of a *transitory* character, and that Lenin *never* viewed it as a phase in the period of transition to communism, obligatory for every country that begins to construct communist society. It was a tactical retreat, a response to the *specific* political, economic, social, and historical situation of Russia in those years.

Wlodzimiers Brus,[40] one of the best known representatives of one of the schools of thought Che differed with, wrote the following:

> The adoption of the New Economic Policy partially changed the situation among theoreticians. It became necessary to work out theoretically the function of the forms of market relations between city and countryside, along with the consequences stemming from the resurgence of the commodity-monetary economy in the socialist sector itself (economic accounting). Analysis of the market and of the conclusions for planning was to occupy an important place in both economic policy and theoretical discussions. The question of money in particular was taken up.
>
> The first signs began to appear at this time of a change in opinion among Marxist economists on the relationship between the plan and the market. For some, the idea that the market and commodity-monetary forms were the opposite of planning began to be transformed into the conception of the market as a mechanism under the plan.[41]

But there is an enormous difference between Lenin's views and those of the economists who hold an assessment of the New Economic Policy and the transition period different from Che's.

Since the April Theses[42] the Bolshevik leader had stated the impossibility, without the help of the international revolution and under the prevailing conditions in Russia, of undertaking the construction of socialism—that is, the first phase of the communist revolution—immediately after the overthrow of bourgeois rule. When the Menshevik pseudorevolutionaries,[43] *who had never been able to make a revolution,* began to mock the revolution in Russia, pointing to its temporary inability to take up transitional tasks, Lenin's reply went to the heart of the matter:

> "The development of the productive forces of Russia
> has not attained the level that makes socialism possible."
> All the heroes of the Second International, including, of
> course, Sukhanov, beat the drums about this
> proposition. They keep harping on this incontrovertible
> proposition in a thousand different keys, and think that
> it is the decisive criterion of our revolution.
>
> But what if the situation, which drew Russia into the
> imperialist world war that involved every more or less
> influential West-European country and made her a
> witness of the eve of the revolutions maturing or partly
> already begun in the East, gave rise to circumstances
> that put Russia and her development in a position
> which enabled us to achieve precisely that combination
> of a "peasant war" with the working-class movement
> suggested in 1856 by no less a Marxist than Marx
> himself as a possible prospect for Prussia?[44]
>
> What if the complete hopelessness of the situation, by
> stimulating the efforts of the workers and peasants
> tenfold, offered us the opportunity to create the
> fundamental requisites of civilisation in a different way
> from that of the West-European countries? Has that
> altered the general line of development of world
> history? Has that altered the basic relations between the
> basic classes of all the countries that are being, or have
> been, drawn into the general course of world history?
>
> If a definite level of culture is required for the building
> of socialism (although nobody can say just what that
> definite "level of culture" is, for it differs in every West-
> European country), why cannot we begin by first
> achieving the prerequisites for that definite level of
> culture in a revolutionary way, and *then,* with the aid of
> the workers' and peasants' government and the Soviet
> system, proceed to overtake the other nations?[45]

Lenin never forgot this reality, despite the ups and downs
the revolution experienced (including civil war, foreign invasion, economic chaos, and sabotage). These conditions forced

the revolution to adopt a course that was necessary for its survival (punitive nationalizations, forced agricultural requisitions), but for which it was not prepared.

By the fall of 1921, however, conditions were so bad that even the most romantic revolutionary had to take note of the situation. There had been a series of peasant uprisings, the proletariat had virtually disappeared, the Kronstadt sailors were rebelling against the revolutionary power, the country had been drained by war (the First World War, then the civil war), millions of Russians were literally dying of hunger,[46] the economy was suffering a collapse that tended to feed on itself, and the world revolution had not occurred. "[We are fighting] 'single-handed'—we told ourselves."[47]

Amid these indescribable and distressing conditions Soviet Russia faced a choice, in Lenin's words, "between economic relations of this [NEP] type and nothing at all."[48]

It is important therefore to stress two things:

• the New Economic Policy was the result of a particular conjuncture in the history of the revolutionary movement;

• Lenin viewed it as a tactical retreat offering "the opportunity to create the fundamental requisites of civilisation,"[49] in order to later take up the socialist tasks.

The situation was reflected in the rupture of the worker-peasant alliance at a time, moreover, when the alliance barely existed. Topping things off was the absence by then of the international revolution, which was an essential condition for bringing the Russian revolution to its ultimate outcome. Lenin's remark on this is worth recalling:

> . . . in adopting a policy to be pursued over a number of years we do not for a moment forget that everything may be altered by the international revolution, its rate of development and the circumstances accompanying it.[50]

The aim then was to try, in a country of small peasants, to begin building sturdy bridges that would "lead from a small-peasant economy via state capitalism to socialism."[51]

This was not a period of transition to communism. Two factors not foreseen in theory had come together to produce this phase. First, the revolution had occurred in an imperialist country marked by very uneven development. Second, the victory of the revolution had not extended beyond the country's borders. The New Economic Policy in no way represented a transition to communism. It was instead a desperate and bold attempt to attain "the fundamental requisites of civilisation" in order to then take up the questions of the transition—a point not always obvious to those who lost sight of the connection between the retreat and the aspirations to return to the offensive:

> We must reveal this link so that we may see it clearly, so that all the people may see it, and so that the whole mass of the peasantry may see that there is a connection between their present severe, incredibly ruined, incredibly impoverished and painful existence and the work which is being done *for the sake of remote socialist ideals*.[52]

The fact that the measures adopted by the Bolshevik-led government involved "turning back towards capitalism"[53] was sufficiently obvious to evoke support for these steps from the counterrevolution. Lenin stated:

> It is in this sense that we must speak of halting the retreat; and the proper thing to do is, in one way or another, to make this slogan a Congress decision.
>
> In this connection, I should like to deal with the question: what is the Bolsheviks' New Economic Policy—evolution or tactics? This question has been raised by the *Smena Vekh* people, who, as you know, are a trend which has arisen among Russian émigrés; it is a socio-political trend led by some of the most prominent Constitutional-Democrats, several Ministers of the former Kolchak government, people who have come to the conclusion that the Soviet government is building up the Russian state and therefore should be supported.[54] They argue as follows: "What sort of state is the Soviet government building? The Communists say they are building a communist state and assure us that the new policy is a matter of tactics: the Bolsheviks are making use of the private capitalists in a difficult situation, but

later they will get the upper hand. The Bolsheviks can say what they like; *as a matter of fact it is not tactics but evolution, internal regeneration; they will arrive at the ordinary bourgeois state, and we must support them.* History proceeds in devious ways."

Some of them pretend to be Communists, but there are others who are more straightforward, one of these is Ustryalov. I think he was a Minister in Kolchak's government. He does not agree with his colleagues and says: "You can think what you like about communism, but I maintain that it is not a matter of tactics, but of evolution." *I think that by being straightforward like this, Ustryalov is rendering us a great service. We, and I particularly, because of my position, hear a lot of sentimental communist lies, "communist fibbing," every day, and sometimes we get sick to death of them.*

But now instead of these "communist fibs" I get a copy of *Smena Vekh,* which says quite plainly: "Things are by no means what you imagine them to be. As a matter of fact, you are slipping into the ordinary bourgeois morass with communist flags inscribed with catchwords stuck all over the place."

This is very useful. It is not a repetition of what we are constantly hearing around us, but the plain class truth uttered by the class enemy. It is very useful to read this sort of thing; and it was written not because the communist state allows you to write some things and not others, but because it really is the class truth, bluntly and frankly uttered by the class enemy. "I am in favour of supporting the Soviet government," says Ustryalov, although he was a Constitutional-Democrat, a bourgeois, and supported intervention. "I am in favour of supporting Soviet power because it has taken the road that will lead it to the ordinary bourgeois state."

This is very useful, and I think we must keep it in mind. It is much better for us if the *Smena Vekh* people write in that strain than if some of them pretend to be almost Communists, so that from a distance one cannot tell whether they believe in God or in the communist revolution. We must say frankly that such candid enemies are useful. We must say frankly that the things Ustryalov speaks about are possible. History knows all sorts of metamorphoses. Relying on firmness of convictions, loyalty, and other splendid moral qualities is anything but a serious attitude in politics. A few people may be endowed with splendid moral qualities, but historical issues are decided by vast masses, which, if the few do not suit them, may at times treat them none too politely.

There have been many cases of this kind; that is why we must welcome this frank utterance of the *Smena Vekh* people. The enemy is speaking the class truth and is pointing to the danger that confronts us, and which the enemy is striving to make inevitable. *Smena Vekh* adherents express the sentiments of thousands and tens of thousands of bourgeois, or of Soviet employees whose function it is to operate our New Economic Policy.

This is the real and main danger. And that is why attention must be concentrated mainly on the question: "Who will win?" I have spoken about competition. No direct onslaught is being made on us now; nobody is clutching us by the throat. *True, we have yet to see what will happen tomorrow; but today we are not being subjected to armed attack. Nevertheless, the fight against capitalist society has become a hundred times more fierce and perilous, because we are not always able to tell enemies from friends.*

When I spoke about communist competition, what I had in mind were not communist sympathies but the development of economic forms and social systems. This is not competition but, if not the last, then nearly the last, desperate, furious, life-and-death struggle between capitalism and communism.[55]

Lenin, who never tired of comparing the New Economic Policy with the Brest-Litovsk peace accord,[56] did not try to sugarcoat the harsh reality. He preferred to call things by their right names so as to avoid dangerous confusion:

What is free exchange? *It is unrestricted trade, and that*

means turning back towards capitalism. Free exchange and freedom of trade mean circulation of commodities between petty proprietors. All of us who have studied at least the elements of Marxism know that this exchange and freedom of trade *inevitably* lead to a division of commodity producers into owners of capital and owners of labour-power, a division into capitalists and wage-workers, i.e., a revival of capitalist wage-slavery, which does not fall from the sky but springs the world over precisely from the agricultural commodity economy. This we know perfectly well in theory, and anyone in Russia who has observed the small farmer's life and the conditions under which he farms must have seen this.[57]

Changes in the forms of socialist development are necessary because the Communist Party and the Soviet government are now adopting special methods to implement the general policy of transition from capitalism to *socialism* and in many respects are operating differently from the way they operated before: they are capturing a number of positions by a "new flanking movement", so to speak; they are *retreating* in order to make better preparations for a new offensive *against capitalism*. In particular, a free market and capitalism, both subject to state control, are now being permitted and are developing; on the other hand, the socialised state enterprises are being put on what is called a *profit basis,* i.e., they are being reorganised *on commercial lines,* which, in view of the general cultural backwardness and exhaustion of the country, will, to a greater or lesser degree, *inevitably give rise to the impression among the masses that there is an antagonism of interest between the management of the different enterprises and the workers employed in them. . . .*

The transfer of state enterprises to the *so-called profit basis is inevitably and inseparably connected* with the New Economic Policy. . . .[58]

The New Economic Policy nevertheless left a legacy in the field of economic theory: the conception that identified economic rationality with social rationality and dissolved the latter into the former. This identification emerged at a moment when the survival of workers' power depended on the efficiency of economic management. And it stuck in the minds of some economists who—despite all Lenin's warnings—began to see the New Economic Policy as a necessary and unique form of socialism. So, in 1921 are found the roots of using and developing the law of value under socialism, of financial self-management, of agricultural cooperatives as a form of socialist property, and so forth. The categories of the New Economic Policy thus tend to reappear in utilitarian garb: "They help increase productivity."

Overlooked in all this, however, is the warning that qualitative increases and decreases in forms of social consciousness are not easy to measure, although in the final analysis these changes will determine the future.

For Karl Marx, the period of transition to communism was a single process with two phases: the dictatorship of the proletariat (socialism) and communism. Based on the specific situation of Russia in 1921, some writings generalize the tragic situation of the USSR in those years and give the phase of the New Economic Policy the character of an "objective law." They claim there are three *obligatory* phases for any socialist process, in place of the two put forward by Marx.

Che believed, along with Lenin, that the New Economic Policy was a step backward. It should not be forgotten that Lenin compared it to the Brest-Litovsk treaty. The circumstances under which the glorious Soviet revolution developed were very complex. Decisions were extremely difficult. Reading the last writings and speeches of the leader of the revolution enables us to consider carefully his doubts about the effects of the NEP. It is safe to assume that had Lenin lived a few years longer, he would have corrected its most backward effects, including that giant Trojan horse in the new society—direct material self-interest as the main economic lever.

In Che's view, the New Economic Policy was not created to combat small commodity production but, more correctly, was a policy made necessary by small commodity production.

As we shall see in the next chapter, the budgetary finance system was the way in which industry was brought under social ownership and operated in Cuba. It was the form through which Cuba established socialist relations of production in virtually its entire industrial sector.

PART TWO

The economic management system in the first stage of building socialism in Cuba

CHAPTER 4

Emergence of the budgetary finance system

T HE MAIN POINTS of the budgetary finance system first
emerged as a series of practical steps (such as centralizing the
bank accounts of various enterprises) to deal with concrete
problems in industry. Some enterprises, for example, had surplus financial resources, others none, at a time when the revolution still faced social problems such as unemployment. These
initial steps gradually evolved into a coherent body of political and economic considerations that began to take shape as a
theory sometime around 1962–63. In practice its application
was limited to the industrial sector.

On October 7, 1959, Fidel announced that Che had been
named to head the Department of Industrialization of the
National Institute of Agrarian Reform (INRA).[59]

Since the days of the Sierra Maestra,[60] Che had shown his
mettle as a builder. To tackle the Rebel Army's problems in
obtaining supplies, he helped organize a number of small
workshops that turned out weapons, clothing, bread, shoes,
dried meat, tobacco, and cigarettes. After the victory of the
revolution, Che was named head of Havana's La Cabaña fortress, where he showed similar capacities.

The Department of Industrialization was created in response to the industrial development generated by the
agrarian reform.[61] In practice, it also began to administer a
series of industries and small workshops that had been "intervened" by the revolutionary government.[62] Some of these
came under its control because the owners were linked to
the old regime and had enriched themselves from public
funds; others because their owners had abandoned them to

go abroad, or because of labor conflicts.

In the early months of the revolution, the number of factories under the department's administration grew rapidly. As the revolution advanced, a wave of interventions and nationalizations occurred. By the second half of 1960, the department was administering more than 60 percent of Cuba's industry. By 1961, it accounted for more than 70 percent.

In the early phase of the socialist revolution state-owned industry was organized and run under the budgetary finance system. The roots of that system can be traced back to INRA's Department of Industrialization. Many of the factories and small workshops it administered lacked funds to purchase raw materials, pay for other supplies, and meet their payrolls. Some enterprises, because of what they produced, were essential; others, less so.

A decision was made to combine the funds of all factories and workshops into a single centralized account. State-managed enterprises deposited their income into the account and, according to a preestablished budget, withdrew the amounts set aside for their operations. This centralization of funding helped prevent a rise in unemployment, which at the time was still a problem. It assured that society would continue receiving the goods these plants produced, even though not all of them made a profit.

Che implemented a policy of merging the small workshops. This created larger enterprises in which technology could be introduced, which in turn increased productivity and lowered costs. Workers not needed in one workplace were relocated to branches of production with employment openings. Those not rapidly rehired were paid while they went back to school and added to their technical and cultural qualifications. Above all, Che held, no make-work, artificially created jobs should be permitted. In a meeting on March 16, 1962, he stated the following:

> What is better for the state: To maintain today's absurd inefficiency throughout our industry, so that everybody works and receives a disguised subsidy? Or to increase productivity to the maximum, take all the

workers who aren't needed, and pay them to study and improve their skill level, to make this their major job? Our answer is that it's much more useful for the country to increase the productivity of labor—not simply by intensifying the labor of each worker, but fundamentally through rationalizing work and, in some cases, mechanizing it.[63]

A subsequent chapter on the wage structure explains the social and economic situation facing Cuba at the beginning of the 1960s and how these conditions justified Che's recommendations on raising workers' educational levels.

A section of the Department of Industrialization responsible for finances, accounting, and budgets administered the centralized funds. As part of its work, this section established budgets and a program for applying them in accordance with an annual plan. So the Department of Industrialization also took Cuba's first steps in economic planning.

The centralized funds were deposited in the National Bank. The Department of Industrialization sent the bank copies of the various units' budgets, and the banking agencies authorized only those payments stipulated in the budgets.[64]

On June 13, 1959, four months before being named head of the Department of Industrialization, Che went abroad as head of a governmental delegation that visited Egypt, India, Japan, Indonesia, and Yugoslavia. Based on his six-day visit to Yugoslavia he wrote a report, which said in part:

All collective bodies in Yugoslavia, whether made up of peasants or industrial workers, are guided by the principle of what they call self-management. In the framework of a plan, well defined in terms of its parameters but not in specific details, the enterprises compete among themselves in the national market as if they were private capitalist entities.

In broad strokes, with an element of caricature, you could describe Yugoslav society as managerial capitalism with socialist distribution of the profits. Each enterprise is viewed not as a group of workers but as a unit functioning more or less in a capitalist manner, obeying laws of supply and demand, and engaged in violent struggle with its competitors over prices and quality—engaged in what is called, in economics, free competition. But we should never lose sight of the fact that the total profits of this enterprise are going to be distributed not in the disproportionate manner of a capitalist enterprise, but among the workers and salaried employees of the factory.

It would be very risky on my part to give a definitive diagnosis, an opinion on this social system, especially since I have no personal knowledge of orthodox communism as practiced in the countries of the Warsaw Pact, of which Yugoslavia is not a member. . . . This freedom of discussion was made clear when, during an amiable after-dinner meeting in one of the republics that make up the federation, I was asked my opinion on the Yugoslav system.

It's an opinion that's difficult to express. Even today, understanding a little more about its mechanisms, I simply can't express an opinion in general terms. In any event, it was very interesting, all the new things shown to us, representatives of a capitalist country in the process of developing its economy and fighting for its national liberation.

We saw a communist country and, at the same time, a communism that is moving away from the orthodoxy expressed in the standard manuals, taking on its own characteristics. *But it also seemed dangerous, because competition among enterprises dedicated to producing the same article may introduce factors that distort what the socialist spirit should presumably be.*

These were the points I made, including the practical example of the evils such a system could, in my opinion, bring with it.[65]

These notes are extremely valuable for us today. Because as early as August 1959—in his first contact with an economy governed by the so-called financial self-management system, without direct knowledge of the other socialist countries or of specialized economic literature, and without yet having a post in government that compelled him to look into these questions—Che was already concerned about the self-management system because it "may introduce factors that distort what the socialist spirit should presumably be." Months later, when he held direct responsibility for administering, organizing, and developing Cuban industry, that experience influenced the decisions that went into creating the budgetary finance system.

In February 1961 the revolutionary government passed a number of laws regarding the country's political and economic structure. This included creation of the Ministry of Industry, to which Che was named director by the Council of Ministers.[66]

In the previous chapter, in the section on the system of economic management and its categories, another factor was noted that Cuban revolutionaries could not ignore in formulating an economic model. The budgetary finance system was developed with the aim of strengthening the revolutionary state and eliminating the anarchy inherited from Cuba's neocolonial and underdeveloped socioeconomic structure. At the same time, Cuba already had an adequate network of roads and a good communications system, including telex, telephone, radio, microwave, cable, telegraph, and television. Some foreign corporations had installed the most advanced techniques that state monopoly capitalism had to offer in organizing, managing, checking, and planning production, along with the latest developments in accounting. A number of foreign companies had established centralized accounting systems based in Havana or in the United States. Cuba had public accountants who had mastered these new techniques. To a certain extent, use of these methods had spread to managerial personnel in Cuban companies, as well.

In formulating the budgetary finance system, Che drew on the following:

• advanced accounting techniques that permitted a better system of controls and an efficient, centralized management; as well as studies and practical application of methods of central-

ization and decentralization by the monopoly corporations;[67]
• computer technology applied to the economy and management, and the application of mathematical methods to the economy;[68]
• techniques of programming production and production controls;
• use of budgetary techniques as an instrument of financial planning and controls;
• techniques of economic controls through administrative means;
• the experience of the socialist countries.
Che summed up the spirit of the system as follows:

> We propose a centralized system of economic management based on rigorous supervision within the enterprises and, at the same time, conscious supervision by their directors. We view the entire economy as one big enterprise. In the framework of building socialism, our aim is to establish collaboration between all the participants as members of one big enterprise, instead of treating each other like little wolves.[69]

The name budgetary finance system comes from the fact that the enterprise turns all its revenues over to the national budget; that is, it does not accumulate its revenues or retain them in the form of cash in an account of its own. Moreover, the enterprise makes expenditures in accordance with a financial plan. Through its budget it has access to funds kept in a banking agency that keeps track of the enterprise's operations through three accounts: wages, investments, and other costs.[70]

In this way, the enterprise receives all the funds it needs to carry out its activities. There is no need to resort to banking credit and all the accounting fictions that accompany it. Che applied the same modern techniques used by multinational corporations in establishing relations between the parent company and its subsidiaries. The sole source of an enterprise's financing is the national budget. In the chapter "The Role of Money, the Banking System, and Prices," Che's views on this will be explained in more detail.

In a bimonthly meeting of the Ministry of Industry's Management Council, Che said:

> I believe the budgetary finance system and its conceptions mark a step forward. It at least puts us in a position to deepen the analysis, to take the measures necessary, and to carry them out without a great deal of commotion. Because it is clear this system offers a road forward in terms of management, a progressive path, which is the path of the monopoly corporations. This may seem contradictory, but it is true.
>
> Marxist analysis is based upon the development of capitalism to its utmost limits, and upon the contradictions that finally give rise to the transitional society. Things turned out differently, due to the emergence of monopoly capitalism. Lenin developed his theory of the weakest link, which he applied to the Soviet Union.[71] The Soviet Union is not therefore a typical example of a fully developed capitalist country that passes over to socialism.
>
> The economic system taken over by the Soviets was not a developed one. Consequently, they began with a series of approaches borrowed from sources including from before the rise of monopoly capitalism. That's why, from the point of view of developing an industrial society, the system of financial self-management is more backward than the system that several big monopoly corporations put into effect in Cuba. In other words, the accounting methods of the budgetary finance system, which are those of the monopolies, are more progressive than the self-management system.[72]

In his essay "On the Budgetary Finance System," Che pointed out the following with regard to the use of such techniques:

> With this series of quotations, we have tried to lay out the themes that we consider basic to explaining the budgetary finance system.
>
> 1. Communism is a goal of humanity that is achieved

consciously. Therefore, education, the elimination of the vestiges of the old society in people's consciousness, is an extremely important factor. It should be kept in mind, however, that without parallel advances in production, such a society will never be achieved.

2. The forms of economic administration, from the technological standpoint, must be borrowed from wherever they are most developed and can be adapted to the new society. The socialist camp can use the petrochemical technology of the imperialist camp without fear of being "infected" by bourgeois ideology. This also applies to the economic field, in all that refers to the norms of administration and production controls.

At the risk of being considered pretentious, we could paraphrase Marx's reference to the use of Hegel's dialectics and say that such techniques have been turned right side up.

An analysis of the accounting techniques commonly used today in the socialist countries shows us that there is a conceptual difference between theirs and ours, perhaps comparable to the one that exists in the capitalist camp between competition and monopoly. Finally, the past techniques were the basis for the development of both systems; from the moment they are "turned right side up," the roads diverge, since socialism has its own relations of production and therefore its own requirements.

We could say, then, that as a technique the forerunner of the budgetary finance system was the imperialist monopoly implanted in Cuba. It had already gone through the variations inherent in the long process of the development of the techniques of administration and review—a process extending from the beginning of the monopoly system until today, when it reaches its higher levels.[73]

On the same point, on another occasion, Che pointed out the following:

The important thing is not who invented the system.

The system of accounting used in the Soviet Union was also undoubtedly invented by capitalism; and in applying it today in the Soviet Union no one cares who invented it. . . . The same is true here. We have nothing to be afraid of in using the capitalists' techniques of auditing and financial controls . . . and their general techniques of budgetary accounting. At present, naturally, the capitalists implement budgetary accounting on the basis of a certain autonomy for the factories or enterprises, and on the basis of the direct material self-interest of each participant. Under capitalism, autonomy tied to material self-interest is an absolutely essential condition; the two cannot be separated.[74]

It was necessary, therefore, to make a distinction between the different methods of managing the economy.

In considering these methods from the technical point of view, Che was of the opinion that techniques should be taken from wherever they were the most developed. These could be adapted to the new society without fear of being *infected* by bourgeois ideology, he believed, *so long as* what was being adopted were *simply technical norms* for managing and checking on production.

From the political point of view, however, Che thought it would be wrong to administer the economy for very long or to any great degree on the basis of capitalist incentive mechanisms and criteria of economic management. In short, Che favored a critically minded assimilation of advanced techniques in economic management and controls, but he rejected the use and development of what he called "the dull instruments left to us by capitalism."

Che was never of the opinion that the budgetary finance system was a finished product. When he left for internationalist duties in 1965, the system still needed development in some aspects and correction in others. There was no better critic of the system than Che himself. In meeting after meeting in the Ministry of Industry, in speeches to workers, and in television appearances, Che continually pointed to the weaknesses still to be eliminated from the budgetary finance system.

What are the system's basic weaknesses? We believe that first of all there is its lack of maturity. Second, at all levels there is a scarcity of really qualified cadres. Third, there is a lack of widely disseminated information on the system and its operation so that the people understand it better. We could also cite the lack of a central planning apparatus that would operate in a uniform way and with an absolute hierarchical order, which would make the job easier. We can list shortcomings in the supply of materials, in the transportation system, that sometimes force us to stockpile items and at other times impede production. There are shortcomings in our entire quality-control apparatus and in relations (which should be very close, very harmonious, and very well defined) with distribution agencies, particularly the Ministry of Domestic Trade, and with some supply organizations, especially the Ministry of Foreign Trade and INRA. It is still difficult to specify exactly which shortcomings result from inherent weaknesses in the system and which are due largely to our present level of organization.

Neither the factory nor the enterprise use collective material incentives at the moment. This is not due to any overriding idea, but because we haven't yet attained sufficient organizational depth to establish incentives based on anything other than the simple fulfillment or overfulfillment of the enterprise's main plans. The reasons for this have already been noted above.

The system is said to have a tendency toward bureaucratism. One point that must therefore be constantly stressed is the rational organization of the entire administrative apparatus so that there is as little bureaucratism as possible. Now, from the standpoint of objective analysis, it is evident that the more we centralize all the recording and accounting operations of the enterprise or unit, the less bureaucracy there will be. If all the enterprises could centralize all their administrative activities, their apparatus would be reduced to a small nucleus of unit directors plus whatever might be necessary to collect information to pass on to the central administration.

That, for the moment, is impossible. We must, however, proceed with setting up production units of optimum size. This is something that is very much facilitated by the budgetary finance system. The establishment of work norms with a single wage scale breaks down narrow ideas about the enterprise as the center of an individual's activity, and he will more and more turn to society as a whole.[75]

And Che added in this regard:

Our task is to continue perfecting the system of management, which is nothing more than a system, the budgetary finance system; we must seek the causes, the real internal motors, the unique interrelations that exist under socialism between man, the individual, and society, to be able to use the new tools that are available and develop them to the maximum, something we have yet to do.[76]

CHAPTER 5

Economic planning: its function as principal generator

of the socialist economy

Throughout their writings Marx and Engels clearly pointed to economic planning as one of the key concepts of the transition period. From the *Theses on Feuerbach* and *The German Ideology* (both written in 1845–46) to the *Manifesto of the Communist Party* (1848) and *A Contribution to the Critique of Political Economy* (1859), and concluding with *Capital* and *Critique of the Gotha Programme,* Marx and Engels implicitly or explicitly put forward the elements that constitute the concept of the *planned economy* and its role in both the transition period and communist society.

The emergence of the idea of economic planning is tied to the concepts of anticapitalist revolution and dictatorship of the proletariat. In other words, anticapitalist revolution, establishment of the dictatorship of the proletariat, and the planned economy are inseparably linked in Marxist theory. They signify the synthesis of a new way of making history. They express the fact that for the first time in history men have taken on the task of consciously transforming society. The planned economy becomes the instrument by which men can know reality and make decisions about it, thereby creating and shaping both their present and their future. "[With Marxism] man ceases to be the slave and instrument of his environment and becomes an architect of his own destiny."[77]

Through economic planning men can, within the bounds of what is objectively possible, bring economic forces under their control. Until the communist revolution these forces had operated beyond man's consciousness, beyond the organized and conscious will of man, who was unable to affect them. Che once wrote that economic planning should be seen as humanity's first chance to reign over economic forces.

In carrying out the anticapitalist revolution, establishing the dictatorship of the proletariat, and instituting planning in social production, humanity closed what Marx termed our prehistory and opened a new stage characterized by man becoming the architect of his own destiny. For this reason economic planning, unlike other commonly accepted concepts in the theory and practice of the transition period, constitutes a key, decisive, and fundamental concept in the building of communism. It is, as Che put it, an *element that characterizes and defines* the transition period and communist society as a whole:

> We can therefore state that centralized planning is the mode of existence of socialist society, its defining characteristic, and the point at which man's consciousness finally succeeds in synthesizing and directing the economy toward its goal: the full liberation of the human being within the framework of communist society.[78]

In the period of the transition to communism, the plan establishes and maintains the current and future proportions in which various goods are produced for society. In this sense the plan has features similar to the law of value. What distinguishes it from the law of value is its character as an instrument that men consciously *create, shape, dominate, and use*. The plan is the *only* instrument that makes it possible to develop the productive forces, form new human relations, create the new man, and reach the stage of communist society.

Thus, to reduce the concept of planning to an economic notion, Che thought, would be to deform it from the outset and limit its possibilities. In Che's opinion, the plan embraced *material* relations as a whole (in the sense Marx gave to the term). For that reason the plan should incorporate and unite two elements:

• creating the basis for economic development of the new

society, as well as for economic regulation and controls;
 • creating a new type of human relations, a new man.

This raises a principle of planning, and thus a principle of the period of transition to communism, that cannot be overlooked without distorting the plan and endangering the transition to communism itself. The effectiveness of the plan cannot be evaluated *solely* by whether or not it improves economic management and, therefore, augments the goods available to society. Nor can it be evaluated by the earnings obtained in the production process.

The real measure of the plan's effectiveness lies in its potential to improve economic management in terms of advancing toward the central objective: communist society. In other words, the true gauge lies in the plan's ability to combine what is rational socially with what is rational economically. Its effectiveness can be measured by the degree to which the economic apparatus succeeds in creating the technical and material base for the new society, spurring a transformation in the habits and values of those who participate in the productive process, and helping to create and instill the new communist values.

Nearly all the literature on the political economy of the transition period lacks original conceptual tools suited to the topic. From the theoretical point of view, this literature tends to distort the very object of study by applying Marxist categories that pertain to capitalism, thus losing the possibility of critically examining the new reality. In other words, the use of such categories—and of their structure and relations in Marxist terms as elements of the capitalist social formation—makes it difficult to grasp a reality whose unique characteristics have not been recognized on the theoretical plane. The law of value is one such element of Marxist economic theory that more than once has been extrapolated beyond its context and converted into a fundamental theoretical pillar of the political economy of the transition period.

Before proceeding with our investigation of Che's economic thought, we must go back to Marx, especially to the chapter in *Capital* on the theory of value. We don't intend to take up the concept of value in any great depth here. We will limit ourselves to pointing out some of Marx's own views.

Marx's theory of value differed from that of both his predecessors and his contemporaries. His theory indissolubly fused two elements that until then had been analyzed separately: the quantitative relations between products and the historically conditioned relations between producers.

In chapter one of *Capital*, Marx begins by analyzing the commodity. He points out that a commodity is both a use-value—that is, a useful object—and an exchange-value. For Marx value is a social category that expresses a set of social relations prevailing at a given historical moment. The production and reproduction of the social relations embodied in commodity production does not constitute the universal form of economic existence in human history. For him, the categories used to describe the capitalist mode of production "are forms of thought which are socially valid, and therefore objective, for the relations of production belonging to this historically determined mode of social production, i.e., commodity production."[79]

More so than anywhere else in Marx's theory, the social character of the categories is central to his analysis of value; that is, these categories express historically determined relations between human beings. Under the capitalist mode of production social relations take on the appearance of relations between things. Marx demonstrated this in the opening chapter of *Capital* in the section entitled "The Fetishism of the Commodity and Its Secret." This constitutes the heart of Marx's theory of value. The quantitative relation between things, between commodities, is no more than the external manifestation of social relations between men. Marx put it this way:

> The mysterious character of the commodity-form
> consists therefore simply in the fact that the commodity
> reflects the social characteristics of men's own labour
> as objective characteristics of the products of labour
> themselves, as the socio-natural properties of these
> things. Hence it also reflects the social relation of the

producers to the sum total of labour as a social relation between objects, a relation which exists apart from and outside the producers. Through this substitution, the products of labour become commodities, sensuous things which are at the same time suprasensible or social. . . . It is nothing but the definite social relation between men themselves which assumes here, for them, the fantastic form of a relation between things. . . . I call this the fetishism which attaches itself to the products of labour as soon as they are produced as commodities, and *is therefore inseparable from the production of commodities.*

As the foregoing analysis has already demonstrated, this fetishism of the world of commodities arises from the peculiar social character of the labour which produces them.[80]

For Marx the law of value explains how the general equilibrium of capitalism comes about. What Marx called the law of value is simply the theoretical explanation of how an equilibrium is established in capitalist society among various economic forces: the amount of commodities produced, the extent to which they are exchanged, how labor power is apportioned among different sectors of the economy, and the allotment of resources among these sectors. Understood in this way, the aim of Marx's theory of value becomes clear. This concept enables us to grasp the structure of the capitalist system, as well as its internal workings, which—as demonstrated throughout the first chapter of *Capital*—are otherwise concealed from our eyes.

To sum up the idea that pulls together the questions that have been discussed and that is present throughout Marx's theory, we quote the following passage from *Capital:*

Political economy has indeed analysed value and its magnitude, however incompletely, and has uncovered the content concealed within these forms. But it has never once asked the question why this content has assumed that particular form, that is to say, why labour is expressed *in value*, and why the measurement of labour by its duration is expressed in the *magnitude of the value* of the product. These formulas . . . bear the unmistakable stamp *of belonging to a social formation in which the process of production has mastery over man, instead of the opposite. . . .*[81]

Che's position on the law of value and the use of this law and other capitalist categories—both in economic management during the transition period and in the creation of a theory of the construction of communist society—can be summed up as follows:

• rejection of the law of value as the *guiding principle* in the period of transition to communism;

• the distinction between *acknowledging* the existence of a series of capitalist relations that necessarily persist during the transition period (including the law of value, given its character as an economic law—that is, as an expression of certain economic tendencies); and *affirming* the possibility of managing the economy by the conscious use of the law of value and the other categories that go along with it;

• rejection of the view that the period of transition to communism, even in its first phases, has to unfold in accordance with the law of value and the other categories of commodity production implied by its use;

• rejection of the view that not only recommends use of the law of value and monetary-commodity relations in the transition period, but also asserts the need to *develop* these capitalist relations as a vehicle for reaching communist society;

• rejection of the inevitable use of "the *commodity* category in relations among state enterprises," and instead considering "all such establishments to be part of the single large enterprise that is the state";[82]

• the need for economic policies that tend toward the gradual withering away of the old categories, including the market, money (so long as its functions are distorted), and thus the lever of direct material self-interest; or, more accurately, policies that tend toward the elimination of the conditions that give rise to these categories;

• rejection of the practice of using capitalist categories. If capitalist categories such as "the commodity as the economic cell, profitability, individual material interest as a lever, etc.,"[83] are used in building the new society, they will rapidly take on an existence of their own, in the end imposing their own influence on relations among men;

• acknowledgement that the free play of the law of value in the period of transition to communism implies the impossibility of fundamentally restructuring social relations, since it means perpetuating the "umbilical cord"[84] that ties alienated man to society; and that it leads instead in the direction of a hybrid system in which a fundamental transformation of the social nature of man and society will not occur;

• the construction of socialism and communism is a question, simultaneously, of both production and consciousness. As Che put it:

> In our view, communism is a phenomenon of consciousness *and not solely* a phenomenon of production. We cannot arrive at communism through the simple mechanical accumulation of quantities of goods made available to the people. By doing that we would get somewhere, to be sure, to some peculiar form of socialism.
>
> But what Marx defined as communism, what is aspired to in general as communism, cannot be attained if man is not conscious. That is, if he does not have a new consciousness toward society.[85]

The very definitions of economic planning and the law of value demonstrate the impossibility of their coexistence throughout the period of the transition to communism. Such coexistence can occur only in the first phase of the transition, in which the law of value persists as a form inherited from the previous system. The law of value continues to exist in the period that spans the destruction of the bourgeois political machinery through the establishment of the dictatorship of the proletariat and the transfer of the means of production from the capitalists to the revolutionary state. Nonetheless, the goal during this period should not be to develop monetary-commodity relations, but rather to begin developing the new socialist relations. The law of value must be eliminated, not by decree, but through a process of gradual withering away as we develop the new forms inherent in the system we are building.

As the means of production are transferred to the revolutionary state, new relations of production emerge and become established. This stage requires a new conception of production—a new conception of its inner workings and of its goals. It also requires new *ways* of operating the mechanisms of supervision, organization, management, and incentives.[86] During this stage, some means of production remain in the hands of capitalists and small producers, both private and cooperative.

Even in the period when commodity production still exists as a sector of production, however, *the law of value no longer governs in a "pure" form*. Measures taken by the revolutionary state, on social questions as well as on strictly economic matters, tend to distort the way the law of value functions. These measures include lowering the rent on housing; providing medical care and social assistance either free of charge or at prices below those set by the market; setting and controlling prices in order to combat counterrevolutionary speculation; establishing control over foreign currency, foreign trade, and domestic wholesale trade; bringing previously marginalized sectors of the population into the economic life of the country; and taking steps to reduce and eventually eliminate unemployment. *In practice, such measures make it impossible for the law of value to reign.*

Value no longer establishes the quantities in which commodities are produced or exchanged. It no longer determines how labor power is allotted among different sectors of the economy, or how resources are allocated. It ceases being a regulatory mechanism with the character of a law. Of key importance in this regard is the fact that prices are no longer set spontaneously, through market fluctuations in supply and demand. These market operations are responsible for the automatic, anarchic, and brutal way in which proportions and equilibrium are established in capitalist society.

In this stage the leadership of the revolution establishes distribution not on the basis of value, but in accordance with its political program; the concrete conditions of the country and the rest of the world; and the revolution's political, ideological, and military strength. Centralized planning is an objective, an ideal to be attained.

What is important in the management of society's productive forces is the *overall* data of profitability. What does this mean? That on the basis of an exact, rigorous analysis of the costs of production and the value of the goods produced, socialism can permit itself the luxury—impossible for a capitalist society—of setting prices above or below the value of a particular item. In other words, prices of particular items become interchangeable, so long as required levels of profitability and efficiency are maintained overall.

This might be taken as proof that in the final analysis the law of value does govern under socialism, that it regulates the overall social equilibrium. That would be a complete illusion, however. Economic equilibrium (here understood as overall "profitability" in the management of society's productive forces) is a feature inherent in any society if it is to continue to exist. No tribe could have survived, much less developed, if it consumed more than it was capable of producing. But this elementary principle, this measure of economic rationality, *is not* the law of value. If it were, then we would have to say this law is *universal*, that it always has and always will govern, in an inexorable fashion. But the law of value is simply the theory that explains *the manner* in which this equilibrium is established—in a spontaneous way—in bourgeois society. The plan, for its part, is *the manner* in which this equilibrium is attained—in a conscious and rational way—in socialist and communist societies.

On the other hand, the function and advantages of the plan in comparison with capitalism hardly rest in establishing the costs of manufacturing a given product in order to set its price. That would make planning an absurdity, with no real advantages, since the plan would in fact remain subject to the law of value. Such a course would lead to renouncing socialism, as in the case of Czech economist Ota Sik and Polish political economist Wlodzimiers Brus. They argued in the 1960s that complete freedom of operation for market mechanisms would save the national planning commissions from having to make millions of mathematical calculations. The law of value in and of itself, they said, would spontaneously set prices without the necessity of all that "tiresome" work.

The plan has a different task—to serve as a tool in rationally and consciously building the new society. Its main advantage is precisely that the plan, unlike the capitalist business executive, is not bound by the level of profitability of a particular production unit, or even an entire sector of production. Everything it manages can be financed centrally and regulated on the basis of overall calculations. The key to its success is the rigor, detail, exactitude, and accuracy of both the data at its disposal and the analysis of that data.

Looked at from another angle, once the prices of products are no longer regulated by their values through the mechanism of supply and demand, that fact alone is sufficient to establish that the law of value no longer dominates. From then on, overall equilibrium is regulated not through the mechanisms of the law of value, but through conscious decisions.

Even if we accept the existence of commodity production—given the survival of small private producers and cooperatives—it is still not completely true that exchanges between the state sector and private sector are carried out in accordance with the laws governing commodity transactions in societies where the law of value reigns. In fact, the money that changes hands in such transactions *does not constitute a measure of value* during the transition period. The exchange with the private sector does not involve equal amounts of socially necessary labor, because the prices of the commodities are not set in accord with their value and the mechanism of supply and demand. As for the means of production used by the private sector, it is the state—on the basis of specific economic policies implemented through the plan—that determines both the quantities in which such production inputs are available and the prices at which these commodities are sold.

No less important than the matters we have taken up so far

is the relationship that must exist between planning and the categories and mechanisms through which the plan is expressed. Che's position was the following: the fact that commodity production continues for a certain time in the transition period *does not mean* the plan should operate on the basis of capitalist mechanisms or that its functioning should be explained through the use of capitalist categories.

In its general conception of how to build a communist society, the budgetary finance system is an original contribution to the theory of the transition period. But it is also more than that. It is a model of economic management and controls in the period of transition to communism. It is a model that serves as a weapon for destroying capitalist economic relations, economic categories derived from commodity production, as well as capitalist ideology. It is, in a nutshell, the driving force behind new forms of human relations and communist consciousness.

We reprint below some of what Che wrote on the foundations of the budgetary finance system and its position on the law of value, in contrast to the standpoint of what is called the economic accounting system. We turn first to what Che said in the essay "On the Budgetary Finance System," under the heading "On the law of value":

> There is a profound difference (at least in the rigor of the terms employed) between our position and that of the proponents of economic accounting regarding the concept of the law of value and the possibility of using it consciously.
> The *Manual of Political Economy*[87] says:
> "Unlike capitalism, where the law of value operates as a blind, spontaneous force imposed on man, the socialist economy is conscious of it. The state takes it into account and uses it in the planned administration of the economy.
> "A knowledge of the operation of the law of value and its *intelligent use* must necessarily help the economy's directors to channel production rationally, to systematically improve work methods, and to make

use of untapped reserves in order to increase and improve production."

The words we have italicized indicate the spirit of the paragraphs.

The law of value would act as a blind force, but once it is understood it can be handled, or used, by man.

But this law has certain characteristics: First, it assumes the existence of a commodity society. Second, its results cannot be measured a priori; they have to reveal themselves in the market, where exchange takes place between producers and consumers. Third, it is a coherent whole, including the world market; changes and distortions in certain branches of production are reflected in the total result. Fourth, given its nature as an economic law, it operates fundamentally as a tendency, and, in the transition periods, its tendency must logically be to disappear.

Some paragraphs further on, the *Manual* states:

"The socialist state uses the law of value, exercising—through the financial and credit system—control over production and distribution of the social product.

"Control over the law of value, and its use in conformity with a plan, represents an enormous advantage of socialism over capitalism. Thanks to control over the law of value, its operation in the socialist economy does not imply the waste of social labor, characteristic of capitalism's anarchy of production. The law of value and its related categories—money, prices, commerce, credit, finance— are used successfully in the USSR and the people's democracies in the interests of building socialism and communism, in the planned administration of the national economy."

This may be considered accurate only as regards the total amount of value produced for direct use by the population and the respective funds available to purchase them—which any capitalist treasury minister could do with relatively balanced finances. Within this framework all of the law's partial distortions apply.

Further on the *Manual* states:

"Commodity production, the law of value, and money will disappear only when the higher stage of communism is reached. But in order to make the disappearance of commodity production and circulation possible in the higher stage of communism, it is necessary *to develop* and use the law of value as well as monetary and commodity relations during the period when the communist society is being built."

Why *develop?* We understand that capitalist categories are retained for a time and that the length of this time cannot be determined beforehand. But the characteristics of the transition period are those of a society throwing off its old bonds in order to arrive quickly at the new stage.

The *tendency* must be, in our opinion, to eliminate as vigorously as possible the old categories, including the market, money, and, therefore, the lever of material interest—or, to put it better, to eliminate the conditions for their existence. Otherwise, one would have to assume that the task of building socialism in a backward society is something in the nature of a historical accident and that its leaders, in order to *make up* for the "mistake," should set about consolidating all the categories inherent in the intermediate society. All that would remain as foundations of the new society would be the distribution of income according to work and the tendency toward elimination of man's exploitation of man. These things by themselves seem inadequate to bring about the gigantic change in consciousness necessary to tackle the transition. That change must take place through the multifaceted action of all the new relations, through education and socialist morality—with the individualistic way of thinking that direct material incentives instill in consciousness acting as a brake on the development of man as a social being.

To summarize our differences: We consider the law of value to be partially operative because remnants of the commodity society still exist. This is also reflected in the type of exchange that takes place between the state as supplier and the consumer. We believe that particularly in a society such as ours, with a highly developed foreign trade, the law of value on an international scale must be recognized as a fact governing commercial transactions, even within the socialist camp. We recognize the need for this trade to assume a higher form in countries of the new society, to prevent a widening of the differences between the developed and the more backward countries as a result of the exchange. In other words, it is necessary to develop terms of trade that permit the financing of industrial investments in the developing countries even if it contravenes the price systems prevailing in the capitalist world market. This would allow the entire socialist camp to progress more evenly, which would naturally have the effect of smoothing off the rough edges and of unifying the spirit of proletarian internationalism. (The recent agreement between Cuba and the USSR is an example of the steps that can be taken in this direction.)

We reject the possibility of consciously using the law of value in the absence of a free market that automatically expresses the contradiction between producers and consumers. We reject the existence of the commodity category in relations among state enterprises. We consider all such establishments to be part of the single large enterprise that is the state (although in practice this has not yet happened in our country). The law of value and the plan are two terms linked by a contradiction and its resolution. We can therefore state that centralized planning is the mode of existence of socialist society, its defining characteristic, and the point at which man's consciousness is finally able to synthesize and direct the economy toward its goal—the full liberation of the human being in the framework of communist society.[88]

In his essay "Considerations on the Costs of Production," Che writes:

The capitalist market functions on the basis of the law of value, which in turn is directly expressed in the market. It is impossible to analyze the law of value separate from its natural medium, the market. In fact, the capitalist market is itself the expression of the law of value. During the process of building socialist society, many of the relations of production change as changes occur in ownership of the means of production. They change as the market is no longer characterized by free competition (leaving aside previous limits already imposed by monopolistic practices), and acquire other, new characteristics as market operations are restricted by the influence of the socialist sector, which consciously regulates the commodity sector.[89]

In his polemical essay "On the Law of Value," Che noted:

Turning to the first paragraph of the article in question,[90] we would say this assessment is not correct. We look at the question of value in a different light. I refer back to our article published in *Nuestra Industria: Revista Económica*, no. 1,[91] which states:

"When all products respond to prices that have an internal relationship among themselves distinct from the relationship among these products on the capitalist market, then we will have created a new price structure that has no parallel on the world market. How do we then ensure that these prices coincide with value? How can we consciously use our knowledge of the law of value to attain equilibrium in the market sector, on the one hand, and a faithful price reflection of real costs on the other? This is one of the most serious problems faced by the socialist economy."

In other words, no one questions that the law of value remains in effect. What we are saying is that this law operates in its most developed form through the capitalist market, and that modifications introduced into the market by social ownership of the means of production and the distribution apparatus obscure how the law operates.

We view the law of value as the regulator of commodity relations under capitalism. Therefore, to the extent the market is distorted for whatever reason, certain distortions will also occur in the operation of the law of value itself.

The form and degree to which this happens have not been given the same in-depth study that Marx conducted of capitalism. Marx and Engels did not foresee that the transition period might begin in economically backward countries and thus did not devote much study or consideration to the economic characteristics of such a situation.

Lenin, for all his genius, did not have enough time—an entire lifetime in Marx's case—to make a lengthy study of the economic problems of the transitional stage. This period combines two elements: on the one hand, the historical fact of a society that is emerging from capitalism without completing the stage of capitalist development (and in which remnants of feudalism still survive); on the other, ownership of the means of production concentrated in the hands of the people.

This possibility was foreseen by Lenin in his study of the uneven development of capitalism, the emergence of imperialism, and his theory of the imperialist system breaking at its weakest link at times of social upheavals such as wars. With the Russian revolution and the creation of the first socialist state, Lenin proved the feasibility of such an occurrence. He did not have time to pursue his investigation, however, since he devoted himself in full to consolidating power and participating in the revolution, as announced in the abrupt ending to his book *State and Revolution*. (The whole of Lenin's writings on the economy of the transition period serve as an extremely valuable introduction to the topic. But they lack the development and depth that time and experience would have given them.)"[92]

In "Socialism and Man in Cuba," Che pointed out:

Marx outlined the transition period as resulting from

the explosive transformation of the capitalist system destroyed by its own contradictions. In historical reality, however, we have seen that some countries that were weak limbs on the tree of imperialism were torn off first—a phenomenon foreseen by Lenin.

In these countries capitalism had developed sufficiently to make its effects felt by the people in one way or another. But it was not capitalism's internal contradictions that, having exhausted all possibilities, caused the system to explode. The struggle for liberation from a foreign oppressor; the misery caused by external events such as war, whose consequences privileged classes place on the backs of the exploited; liberation movements aimed at overthrowing neocolonial regimes—these are the usual factors in unleashing this kind of explosion. Conscious action does the rest.

A complete education for social labor has not yet taken place in these countries, and wealth is far from being within the reach of the masses through the simple process of appropriation. Underdevelopment, on the one hand, and the usual flight of capital, on the other, make a rapid transition without sacrifices impossible. There remains a long way to go in constructing the economic base, and the temptation is very great to follow the beaten track of material interest as the lever with which to accelerate development.

There is the danger that the forest will not be seen for the trees. The pipe dream that socialism can be achieved with the help of the dull instruments left to us by capitalism (the commodity as the economic cell, profitability, individual material interest as a lever, etc.) can lead into a blind alley. And you wind up there after having traveled a long distance with many crossroads, and it is hard to figure out just where you took the wrong turn. Meanwhile, the economic foundation that has been laid has done its work of undermining the development of consciousness. To build communism it is necessary, simultaneous with the new material foundations, to build the new man.[93]

CHAPTER 6

The role of money, the banking system, and prices

F̶OR METHODOLOGICAL reasons, this is the appropriate point to examine Che's concepts of money. The reader nonetheless may have already found some basic elements of Che's views implicit in the preceding pages, especially those discussing the law of value.

Che held that the characteristics of the transition period, and the correct theoretical approach to it, were fundamentally distinct from those under capitalism. Flowing from this conviction, Che assigned money a different role from that conferred on it by partisans of the economic accounting system. Che's ideas on money should therefore be analyzed and explained in the framework of his conception of the transition period. It is in this context that Che's views take on their full relevance.

Che's ideas on the role of money in the transition period are mostly found in his writings between 1963 and 1965, especially in the article "On the Budgetary Finance System," and in the article "Banking, Credit, and Socialism." While both articles are polemical in nature, the former offers more of a positive explanation of the budgetary finance system advocated by Che.

With the aim of retaining Che's method in tackling the problem of money and banking in the transition period, his views on these matters will be discussed in the context of the budgetary finance system. We will follow as closely as possible the order in which Che himself presented his views in the article "Banking, Credit, and Socialism." We will forgo, for obvious reasons, a discussion of the origin of banking, its characteristics, and its functions in the capitalist mode of production.[94]

Money is a product of commodity relations and therefore expresses certain relations of production. For that reason, money is a social category historically conditioned by those relations. It is not possible to destroy commodity relations in a day; they survive into the transition period. Their presence may be of greater or lesser duration, depending on the pace of development of the new relations of production and the policy adopted toward these new relations. Whatever the case, commodity relations must be combated; the tendency should be for them to gradually wither away until they have totally disappeared. To develop commodity relations further is to endanger the realization of the communist program.

These same considerations apply to the role of banking in the transition period. As Che noted:

> It is important to point out, for reasons we will come to later, that money reflects the relations of production; it cannot exist without a commodity society. We can also say that a bank cannot exist without money and, for that reason, that the existence of banking is dependent on commodity relations of production, however developed they may be.[95]

Of the five functions that the money form possesses in all commodity production, according to Marx, only two should exist in the transition period. These are:

• *money of account*, that is, money as a measure of value; and

• *money as a medium of circulation* and / or *distribution*—beween the state and the remaining small private proprietors, and between the state and individual consumers.[96]

Contrasting the budgetary finance and economic accounting systems, Che explained:

> Another difference is the way money is used. Under our system, it functions only as money of account, as a reflection, in prices, of an enterprise's performance that can be analyzed by the central bodies in order to review its functioning. Under the system of economic accounting, money serves not only this purpose but is

also a means of payment that acts as an indirect instrument of auditing and review, since it is these funds that permit the production unit to operate. The production unit's relations with the bank are similar to those a private producer maintains with capitalist banks, to whom it must thoroughly explain plans and prove its solvency. Naturally, in such cases decisions are not arbitrary but are subject to a plan, and these relations take place between state bodies.

Consistent with the way in which money is used under the budgetary finance system, our enterprises have no funds of their own. At the bank there are separate accounts for withdrawals and for deposits. The enterprise may withdraw funds in accordance with the plan from the general expense account and the special wage account. But its deposits automatically pass into the hands of the state.

In the majority of the fraternal countries, enterprises have their own funds in the banks, which they can add to with bank loans for which they pay interest. But it must not be forgotten that the enterprise's "own" funds, as well as the loans, belong to society, and their movement reflects the enterprise's financial situation.[97]

In *Capital*, we read:

There is a contradiction immanent in the function of money as the means of payment. When the payments balance each other, money functions only nominally, as money of account, as a measure of value. But when actual payments have to be made, money does not come onto the scene as a circulating medium, in its merely transient form of an intermediary in the social metabolism, but as the individual incarnation of social labour, the independent presence of exchange-value, the universal commodity.[98]

Che's conviction that money could function as money of account was reinforced, among other things, by the development by the imperialists of the most modern techniques of economic organization, accounting, administration, and analysis. To avoid unnecessary expenditures, the Yankee monopolies had even begun using money of account in operations among their subsidiaries. They deemed it absurd to send bills and issue payments to their own subsidiaries. Development of these techniques relegated money to the role of simply recording the value of what had been produced.

The use of money as a measure of value means it can be used, in the form of prices, to measure how well an enterprise is being managed. In this way, money of account serves as an instrument of analysis, *as an economic indicator,* enabling the central state economic bodies to evaluate the functioning of an enterprise.

The budgetary finance system gives finance a content and role different from that conferred on it by the economic accounting system. Finance is no longer the mechanism through which one supervises, directs, analyzes, and organizes the economy. Financial compulsion is replaced by technical-administrative compulsion. As Che explained:

> In this way, and with steps toward improving our apparatus, we can avoid the problems of the financial self-management system. We can convert financial compulsion (because financial self-management is really nothing more than financial compulsion) into administrative compulsion. That is, we can carefully monitor our apparatus—as well as the concrete results of efforts in factories and workplaces—and immediately sound the alarm when one or another aspect of the plan is not being fulfilled, thereby making it possible to remedy the problem.[99]
>
> Administrative measures exist. We should keep one thing in mind. Do you think the workers in a U.S. factory are fond of the owner? Absolutely not. But do the police have to stand watch over production? No. Because there is a series of administrative mechanisms so that whenever production falls short, steps are taken to assure that the careless worker makes less money; that he himself suffers, quietly, in proportion to the

degree of his mistake. In this way, whoever makes mistakes is singled out for attention. So it is no secret how the employers keep watch over the smooth functioning of a workplace.[100]

The budgetary finance system views each enterprise as part of a whole, of one big enterprise, the state. No enterprise has, or needs, its own funds. Under this system the enterprise has separate bank accounts for deposit and withdrawal.

> Once the means of production are socially owned, through the state, and once this financial system is applied to transactions between the socialist enterprises, it becomes possible within the state sector to convert the buying and selling of commodities on the market into simply the mutual delivery of products. It also becomes possible to limit the function of money as a means of payment, reducing it to a measure of value; and to eliminate the function of accounts payable and accounts receivable as credit instruments, transforming them conceptually into simple administrative or accounting acts. These acts take the concrete form of payment orders, whose sole purpose is to maintain accurate banking records.[101]

The survival of money as an expression of the value of products and as a means of distribution stems from the maintenance of a private sector and of a commodity sector for consumer goods. These functions of money will disappear with the development of the new society; they do not endanger the creation of communist consciousness and human relations of a new type.

The banking system will disappear over the long run in the period of transition to communism. It will survive during the period in which commodity relations persist, because the existence of banking is "dependent on commodity relations of production, however developed they may be."[102] In this same article, Che also pointed out:

> In periods of building socialist society, all previous concepts of the political role of the banking system

change, and other ways must be sought to put its experience to use.[103]

As a result of transformations in society's socioeconomic relations, the banking system ceases to play a dominant role in the economy. Its economic functions are not the same as those under capitalism. It does not possess capital of its own, nor can it act as though it does. This presents us with a good number of limitations. Since it does not possess its own capital, the banking system can continue to exist only as property of the state, which uses it for specific economic functions. It is the state that encompasses the entire economy; the bank is an instrument to carry out these specific functions. It is not possible to claim "that the banks continue maintaining a dominant position in the economy, independently of socioeconomic changes."[104]

The budgetary finance system is a partisan of centralization. But as Che pointed out, this does not mean it must be the banks that assume major responsibility for the state's accounting and supervision of economic performance; nor does it mean the banks will dictate the nation's economic policy.

There is a widely held belief that direct relations with the banking system assure an accurate analysis of all factors of production and make it impossible for an enterprise to escape the scrutiny of the bank. This is simply an illusion under prevailing conditions in Cuba today. The banking system itself offers proof positive of this fact in its relations with the enterprises that operate under the financial self-management (or economic accounting) system.

In 1931, Stalin made the following point:

"But that is not all. To it must be added the fact that owing to inefficient management the principles of business accounting are grossly violated in a large number of our factories and business organisations. It is a fact that a number of enterprises and business organisations have long ceased to keep proper accounts, to calculate, to draw up sound balance-sheets of income and expenditure. It is a fact that in a number of enterprises and business organisations such concepts as 'regime of economy,' 'cutting down on unproductive expenditure,' 'rationalisation of production' have long gone out of fashion. Evidently they assume that the State Bank 'will advance the necessary money anyway.' It is a fact that production costs in a number of enterprises have recently begun to increase. They were given the assignment of reducing costs by 10 per cent and more, but instead they are increasing them."[105]

We cite this simply *to demonstrate that we face a stubborn task of administrative organization before any system at all can be put into effect. This should be the thrust of our efforts at the present time.*[106]

The fact that money serves as a means of payment does not presuppose the need for banking credit. It can function as money of account in all transactions between state and cooperative enterprises. Historically, the need for credit in the state sector stemmed from the form the young Soviet government adopted to oversee and direct its economy.

Under the budgetary finance system the bank has no power to grant loans to state enterprises, much less to collect interest from them. Che supported this policy by citing some passages from *Capital*. Among them was the following:

It must never be forgotten, however, firstly that money in the form of precious metal remains the foundation from which the credit system can *never* break free, by the very nature of the case. Secondly, that the credit system presupposes the monopoly possession of the social means of production (in the form of capital and landed property) on the part of private individuals, that it is itself on the one hand *an immanent form of the capitalist mode of production* and on the other hand a driving force of its development into its highest and last possible form.

As was already asserted in 1697, in *Some Thoughts of the Interests of England*, the banking system, by its organization and centralization, *is the most artificial and elaborate product brought into existence by the capitalist mode of production. . . .*

Finally, there can be no doubt that the credit system will serve as a powerful lever in the course of transition from the capitalist mode of production to the mode of production of associated labour; however, only as one element in connection with other large-scale organic revolutions in the mode of production itself. On the other hand, illusions about the miraculous power of the credit and banking system, in the socialist sense, arise from complete ignorance about the capitalist mode of production and about the credit system as one of its forms. *As soon as the means of production cease to be transformed into capital (which also means the abolition of private property in land), credit as such no longer has any meaning,* something incidentally that even the Saint-Simonians have realized. As long as the capitalist mode of production persists, however, interest-bearing capital persists as one of its forms, and in fact forms the basis of its credit system. Only that same sensationalist writer who wanted commodity production to continue while money was abolished (Proudhon) could dream up the enormity of a *crédit gratuit* [interest-free credit], the ostensible realization of the pious wish arising from the petty-bourgeois standpoint.[107]

Our reasoning on a bank charging interest to state enterprises is not altered in the least by whether or not this occurs according to a plan, nor by the fact that the interest rate is not set in a spontaneous fashion as under capitalism. Because in assessing interest on such loans, the bank is charging for the use of money that does not belong to it, an action that is typical of the functioning of a private bank.

When socialist banks lend out money at interest, they carry out an operation with the hallmarks of fetishism, since they are lending money that belongs to another enterprise. In this regard, Che pointed out:

If Marx expressed the view, as we have seen, that the abolition of private property deprives credit as such of any meaning, then what can be said about interest? Marx says:

"In interest-bearing capital, the capital relationship reaches its most superficial and fetishized form. Here we have *M-M′*, money that produces more money, self-valorizing value, without the process that mediates the two extremes. In commercial capital, *M-C-M′*, at least the general form of the capitalist movement is present, even though this takes place only in the circulation sphere, so that profit appears as merely profit upon alienation; but for all that, it presents itself as the product of a social *relation*, not the product of a mere *thing*. The form of commercial capital still exhibits a process, the unity of opposing phases, a movement that breaks down into two opposite procedures, the purchase and sale of commodities. This is obliterated in *M-M′*, the form of interest-bearing capital."[108]

Che continues:

Keeping in mind that, technically, interest is not a cost factor for enterprises, but instead a deduction from workers' social surplus labor, which should be counted as income in the national budget—is this not in reality the source, to a substantial degree, of the financing for the operational expenses of the banking apparatus?[109]

Concerning investment, Che had this to say:

What the bank does is distribute the resources of the national budget in the amounts set by the investment plan and place them at the disposal of the appropriate investment agencies.

This aspect of the financing and controls over investment—especially in the field of construction—along with the approach to banking credit and interest, marks a substantial difference between what is referred to in this article as the financial self-management system and the budgetary finance system. The financing and controls over investment will be the subject of an article by Compañero Alvarez Rom,[110] since the importance and scope of this subject merits separate treatment.

Nonetheless, we will indicate the fundamental

aspects of this procedure. . . . The Ministry of Finance came to the conclusion that the entire current muddle with regard to controls over investment stems from conceptions still surrounding it that have been carried over from commodity-producing society. That is, we still tend to think of the bank as the representative of the monopolies, their watchdog, carefully scrutinizing the type and effectiveness of the investment.

In a budgetary system, with properly functioning systems of controls and supervision, there is no need for the bank to be involved in investment decisions. These are political decisions concerning economic policy that are in the purview of the state's Central Planning Board. Nor should the bank concern itself with the physical overseeing of investments—this would require an enormous and senseless apparatus. Instead this should be done by the investment agency directly concerned—so long as the financial supervision is in the hands of the Ministry of Finance. The Ministry of Finance is responsible for the state budget, which is the only place that the social surplus product should accrue in order to ensure that it is effectively utilized. The bank should concern itself with scrutinizing fund withdrawals according to proper procedure, which is its specific function.[111]

Under the budgetary finance system, state enterprises are part of the one big enterprise that is the state. Under the financial self-management (or economic accounting) system, by contrast, each production unit constitutes an enterprise. In the financial self-management system, relations between enterprises are very similar to those that exist under capitalism: all transfers of products between state enterprises are carried out through the mechanism of buying and selling, with the result that the products of a state enterprise take on the characteristics of a *commodity*.

The budgetary finance system approaches enterprise management from two angles, a technical-economic angle and an ideological one: "An enterprise is a collection of factories or production units that have a similar technological base, possess a common destination for their output, or in some cases are located in the same geographic area."[112] As for the ideological angle, the basic points have been covered in the preceding pages.

Understanding the difference between the two systems noted above is essential to grasping their contrasting conceptions of financing enterprises. Che stated:

> We believe that the budgetary finance system makes both banking credit and the buying and selling of commodities unnecessary in the state sector.
>
> To understand the difference between the two systems . . . it is necessary to keep in mind that all these categories derive from an individual consideration of independent economic entities. Now that property is in the hands of the entire people, these economic categories are retained solely as instruments of control and supervision over the national economy. The fiction that manages to dominate the minds of men . . . is eliminated with the application of the budgetary finance system.[113]
>
> An enterprise is financed, on the other hand, in order to enable it (for the purpose of overall social accounting and controls) to compensate another enterprise for materialized labor in the form of supplies. On the other hand, state financing repays the living labor added in each process of social production. The first of these operations is purely formal, an act of compensation without economic content. The second amounts to paying the worker his wages *after* having used his labor power in the production of use-values. In effect, therefore, it is the worker who is actually providing the credit.[114]

Starting from the above assumptions, Che examined the mechanisms of setting prices. It became immediately evident to him that market mechanisms—through prices seeking an equilibrium between supply and demand for each commodity—end up leaving a margin of profit for the enterprise. It is the plan that yields to the law of value, not the reverse. The market, therefore, continues to operate on a competitive capitalist basis, only now with the peculiar "inconvenience" of also being the victim of state interference in its functioning.

A centralized system offers other solutions:

A. Economic imbalances can be avoided through precise mathematical calculations based on a study of production data and fluctuations in demand, along with the state of monetary circulation and purchasing power. With this data, we can proceed to a *pricing policy* that is both based on political and social criteria and whose end product is economically rational.

B. The system of taxes imposed on the circulation of commodities (characteristic of the financial self-management system) can be replaced. Instead, a scale of wages and prices can be established that maintains the desired overall equilibrium. Such a scale can be constructed through a detailed analysis of the total wage fund and the circulation and total value of output (understood here as the sum total of prices). In this regard, Che said:

> The "circulation tax" is an accounting fiction through which an enterprise is assured of maintaining certain levels of profitability. The price of the product to the consumer is raised in such a way as to balance the supply of goods and effective demand. We believe that such a tax, although imposed by the system, is not an absolute necessity, and we are working on other formulas that take all these aspects into account.[115]

C. Overall stabilization of the supply of goods and effective demand can be attained through directives from the bodies in charge of regulating domestic trade. The fact that a series of basic necessities of life are made available at prices below their cost does no harm to the country's economy so long as the prices of another series of nonessential articles are raised above their cost. Under socialism, a particular price can be set as far from an item's actual value as is considered necessary. *It is the overall proportions that are decisive.*

D. The system can be rounded out with sociological studies

to determine which types of products are needed and in what quantities. Such data, collected from daily life, can then be centrally processed together with figures on productive capacity, costs, the plan for distribution of national income, and so forth; all this can then be integrated into the plan. As the plan is being drawn up and implemented, the mechanisms of the party, the unions, and other organizations can serve as channels between the government and the masses to communicate concerns, complaints, and suggested corrections to the plan.

E. The budgetary finance system rejects using financial compulsion ("because financial self-management is in reality nothing more than financial compulsion"[116]) as a guiding principle in establishing control mechanisms to be used by the bodies responsible for managing and supervising the economy. The budgetary finance system establishes compulsion of an administrative type and concentrates efforts on planning and technological development, pointing to the latter as the key to improving the operations of both the state and economic production. These considerations are closely related to the process of setting prices, since the budgetary finance system does not include this among its methods to stimulate production, as a market economy would do.

F. Price differentials can be set for agricultural products, taking into account the wide variation in costs depending on the yield of the soil. This avoids differentiation of agricultural collectives into rich and poor. Application of the principles set forth in point C above would produce notable results in this economic sector.

While the phenomena of supply and demand need to be studied, it is essential to oversee and guide demand toward objectives in accordance with social rationality. Economists who support use of the market as the only way to automatically resolve the thousands of equations implicit in individual consumer "choices" forget that theories of "consumer sovereignty"—of the consumer as dictator over production—have lost all respectability even in bourgeois economic theory. It is common knowledge that consumer desires and trends are *created and channeled* through advertising.

In a socialist society, consumer behavior can and should be watched carefully and guided in order to avoid coming into conflict with the principles and goals of society as a whole. Just as for the sake of enabling people to live together, society holds in check an entire series of natural human instincts, so too must the habits of consumption be subject to regulation. A society that allows itself to be guided by spontaneous consumer desires will systematically reduce its resources, diverting them from their main purposes in order to use them to satisfy needs that reproduce themselves and multiply with each passing minute.

The point, then, is to establish an overall balance of supply and demand by using the plan to set prices at levels determined by political and social criteria. But a serious problem must still be resolved: what basis should be used to set *real* prices for the purpose of economic analysis? Che sought an initial solution:

> In putting the plan into practice, one of the many problems the socialist economy confronts is how to evaluate the performance of enterprises, in light of the new conditions created by the development of the socialist revolution.
>
> The capitalist market functions on the basis of the law of value, which in turn is directly expressed in the market. It is impossible to analyze the law of value separate from its natural medium, the market. In fact, the capitalist market is itself the expression of the law of value. During the process of building socialist society, many of the relations of production change as changes occur in ownership of the means of production. They change as the market is no longer characterized by free competition (leaving aside previous limits already imposed by monopolistic practices), and acquire other, new characteristics as market operations are restricted by the influence of the socialist sector, which consciously regulates the commodity sector.

Normally, a shortage of commodities would have immediately produced an increase in market prices to bring supply and demand into equilibrium. Instead we instituted a strict price freeze and established a system of rationing. The real value of commodities could no longer be expressed through the market, which now possesses different characteristics. Although rationing is a temporary situation, as the years go by the dynamics of a planned economy within the borders of a single country diverge more and more from those of the rest of the world.

In the complex process of producing and distributing goods, the costs of raw materials and many other factors come into play in determining prices. When the prices of all these products are set in relationship to each other, on a different basis from their relations in the capitalist market, then a new price structure is brought about that has no counterpart in the world market.

How can prices be made to coincide with value? How can we consciously use our understanding of the law of value to attain, on the one hand, a balance in the supply and demand of goods and, on the other, a true reflection of costs in prices? This is one of the most serious problems confronting the socialist economy. . . .

We emphasize cost analysis because our conception is based, in part, on the fact that in the socialist sector there is no necessary or close connection between an item's cost of production and its price. (For Cuba, a less-developed country that engages in a great deal of foreign trade, it is relations with the rest of the world that are of fundamental importance.)

That is why we say, in general, that the domestic price structure can in no way be severed from that of the world market. It is understood, of course, that we are referring solely to prices in the socialist sector, where their fundamental role is as money of account—that is, as a form of measurement.

Numerous difficulties are caused by distortions that already exist with regard to prices on the world market.

In addition, technological advances, seasonal factors, and monopoly manipulations of the market all lead to daily price fluctuations in the international market. Even though we have not yet completed our analysis of this problem, we believe a way can be found to deal with it.

A general system can be established based on a kind of historical average of prices in the capitalist market, corrected as needed to take account of price movements in the market among the socialist countries. (Prices on the socialist market are today very close to prices in the capitalist market.) This system would also take into account freight costs. Prices set in this way would remain fixed over a certain period of time.

If the prices of the most basic items in our economy are taken as the basis to estimate the prices of other goods, we would arrive at a weighted, historical level of world market prices. This would enable us to measure automatically the relative efficiency of every branch of the economy in reference to the world market.

It should also be noted that such a price structure offers a distorted picture of the national productivity of labor, since it measures only average world efficiency. This could unleash dangerous consumption trends, based on enticingly low prices for domestically produced goods in which much more labor has been expended than comparison with the world market price would suggest.

This is a valid objection. To plan correctly, certain index numbers need to be established so that products can be designated according to their profitability. Since this system is based on centralized control of the economy and greater centralization of decision making, relative profitability would be merely one indicator in setting prices. What is really of interest is the overall profitability of the entire productive apparatus. If at all possible this should be measured—and this is the permanent goal—in terms of world market values. If, unavoidably, that is not possible, it should be measured in terms of the domestic price level.

On January 1, 1959, Cuban working people, led by the Rebel Army and July 26 Movement, overthrew the U.S.-backed dictatorship of Fulgencio Batista and established the first "free territory of the Americas."

Top, Fidel Castro, and Camilo Cienfuegos, standing in jeep, right to left, during the Rebel Army's "caravan of liberty" from Santiago de Cuba to Havana, January 2–8, 1959. **Bottom**, people of Havana greet arrival of Rebel Army, January 8, 1959. They are carrying a flag of the July 26 Movement, with Fidel Castro's portrait on it.

Carrying through the historic program of the July 26 Movement, the May 1959 agrarian reform act expropriated foreign landlords and the vast plantations of Cuban landowners and gave hundreds of thousands of peasants title to the land they worked.

Top, sugar farmers in Camagüey, holding up their deeds, demonstrate support for revolution, 1961. **Bottom,** as the strength of the workers and peasants grew, the revolutionary government took control over more and more key positions in the economy. In November 1959, Che Guevara replaced bourgeois economist Felipe Pazos as president of National Bank. From left, Osmany Cienfuegos, Osvaldo Dorticós, Guevara, unknown, Pazos, Enrique Oltusky, Faustino Pérez.

In order for working people to lead the economic and social transformation, "the continual upgrading of skills at all levels is now a question of fundamental importance," Guevara stated. In 1961, one hundred thousand Cuban youth fanned out to teach workers and peasants to read and write, virtually eliminating illiteracy in one year and transforming the political and social consciousness of a generation of young people.

Top, peasants learning to read and write. **Bottom,** Guevara speaking at rally in Holguín celebrating transformation of dictatorship's military garrison into a school, February 24, 1960.

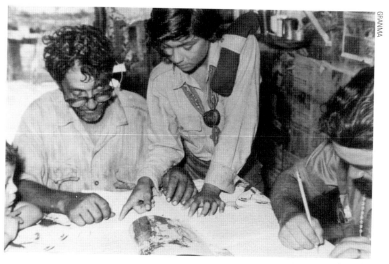

GRANMA

NATIONAL INSTITUTE OF AGRARIAN REFORM

RAUL CORRALES

GRANMA

Top, in October 1959, following air attack on Havana that killed 2 and wounded 47, bus drivers from Havana suburb demand weapons to defend revolution. **Bottom,** one of the first peasant militias is issued weapons, 1960, in response to armed attacks by U.S.-backed forces opposed to land reform and other revolutionary measures.

AIN

Top, on March 4, 1960, in the midst of mounting U.S. attacks against Cuba, the Belgian ship La Coubre, carrying weapons to defend the revolution, blew up in Havana harbor, killing over eighty. **Bottom,** revolutionary leaders head march to honor victims of La Coubre explosion and protest U.S.-sponsored aggression. Left to right, Conrado Béquer, Octavio Louit, Luis Buch, Pedro Miret, William Gálvez, David Salvador, Fidel Castro, Osvaldo Dorticós, Che Guevara, Augusto Martínez Sánchez, Antonio Núñez Jiménez.

As working people mobilized massively in defense of the measures taken, Cuba's revolutionary government nationalized most domestic- and foreign-owned industry between August and October 1960, creating the economic foundation for the transition to socialism.

This page top, Fidel Castro reads the decree expropriating the main U.S.-owned companies in Cuba, August 6, 1960. **Above,** workers militiamen guard recently nationalized oil refinery.

Facing page, top, march in Havana with symbolic burial of coffins representing U.S.-owned companies nationalized by the revolution, August 1960. **Bottom,** department store workers in Havana. Sign reads, "We support the nationalization of enterprises."

"Building socialism is based on the work of the masses, on the capacity of the masses to be able to organize themselves to better guide industry, agriculture, and the country's economy," Guevara said in August 1962.

Top, Che addressing 1962 union meeting to present awards to vanguard workers. **Bottom,** Guevara inspects work at Cuban factory. To right of him are Pablo Rivalta (with cigar), Orlando Borrego, Aleida March.

Guevara, as minister of industry, visiting nickel factory in Nicaro in eastern Cuba, January 1961, where the workers maintained production after the U.S.-dominated management fled in protest against the nationalization.

"Voluntary work," Che wrote in 1965, is "based on the Marxist appreciation that man truly reaches his full human condition when he produces without being compelled by physical necessity to sell himself as a commodity."

Top, volunteer cane cutters take part in 1963 sugar harvest. **Bottom,** Guevara doing voluntary work at José Martí housing project, February 27, 1961.

As minister of industry, Guevara devoted major energies to increasing the productivity of labor. His efforts led to automation of sugar harvest, releasing hundreds of thousands of Cuban workers from back-breaking work of cutting cane by hand. Guevara tests prototype of sugarcane-cutting machine, Camagüey, February 1963.

UNITED NATIONS

NEW YORK DAILY NEWS

"A victory by any country over imperialism is our victory, just as any country's defeat is a defeat for all of us. The practice of proletarian internationalism is not only a duty for the peoples struggling for a better future, it is also an inescapable necessity," Guevara said in a February 1965 speech.

Top, Guevara speaking on behalf of revolutionary Cuba at United Nations General Assembly, December 14, 1964. **Bottom,** appearing on CBS's "Face the Nation" television program, December 13, 1964, New York City.

"Vietnam represents the aspirations and hopes for victory of all the world's disinherited," Guevara wrote in 1966.

Facing page, top, Vietnamese youth join war against U.S. occupation, 1960s. Banner at center reads, "Chi Lang village youth volunteer in anti-U.S. war of national salvation." **Bottom,** Cuban caravan of material aid destined for shipment to freedom fighters in southern Vietnam, 1960s.

"Che's ideas are absolutely relevant today, ideas without which communism cannot be built," Fidel Castro said in October 1987, on the 20th anniversary of Guevara's death. The economic and social course set by Guevara remains essential to meeting the challenges facing the Cuban revolution.

Left, Cuban volunteer troops defending Angola against South African attack, February 1990. Cuban troops helped defend Angolan sovereignty against South African aggression between 1975 and 1991. **Above,** members of a volunteer minibrigade, composed of workers temporarily released with pay from their normal jobs, build housing in Havana, 1988.

Facing page, top, mechanics at La Esperanza sugarcane cooperative in Cienfuegos who, despite parts shortages, have kept tractors and combines running for the sugar harvest, April 1997. **Bottom,** May Day 1997 march in Havana in support of revolution.

"Imperialism considered us a weak and submissive flock and now it begins to be terrified of that flock . . . in whom Yankee monopoly capitalism now sees its gravediggers," Guevara said at the United Nations in December 1964. He was quoting the 1962 Second Declaration of Havana. Today capitalism's gravediggers have grown more numerous around the world.

Top, members of Movement of Landless Rural Workers (MST) march to presidential palace to demand land, Brasilia, Brazil, July 1995. **Bottom,** members of Teamsters union in Atlanta during national strike of 185,000 workers against United Parcel Service, August 1997.

This does not mean, even remotely, that we have now come up with surefire criteria for evaluating new investments. Nor does it mean that these investment decisions will be made purely on the basis of costs— either of our existing industries or the possible costs of that new investment—or on the basis of our possibilities for accumulation. This will not always be the case. For while the law of value is expressed in a relatively pure form in the world market, in our domestic economy its operation will be greatly influenced by the impact of the socialist sector and by the amount of socially necessary labor required locally to produce a given article. Moreover, it is quite possible that we might be much more interested in an investment to develop some type of product that is not the most profitable, but would nonetheless be more desirable from a strategic point of view or, simply, more beneficial for the population.

We stress once again that the price charged to the population may bear little relation to the price indicated by the internal accounting systems of enterprises governed by this system. With this approach we would immediately get a mirror of the overall direction of the economy at any given time. With this type of organization we can begin to apply— not necessarily to the country as a whole, but to some branches of industry—an increasingly accurate system of economic analysis.

Cost must be the real barometer of the performance of an enterprise. It is not important whether costs are higher or lower than prices of goods exchanged among enterprises in the socialist sector or even, in certain isolated cases, than the prices at which products are sold to the consumer. *What is important is constant evaluation of the management of an enterprise, over a given period, measured by its success in lowering costs.* Insofar as we succeed in establishing prices in relationship to costs, this will enable us to automatically analyze profitability in relation to world market prices. In short, it is necessary to work more seriously on these problems, which are still treated in a schematic form and without serious analysis.[117]

This lengthy quotation is cited to again make clear that the budgetary finance system is not synonymous with wasteful spending, lack of financial controls, or economic bankruptcy, and that it can control the use of resources just as well as the financial self-management system.

Ten months after publishing the article cited above, Che again put forward his conception of setting prices in his essay "On the Budgetary Finance System."

[The two management systems] also have profound disagreements regarding the theory of setting prices. Under financial self-management, prices are set "in relation to the law of value," but what is not explained, to our knowledge, is which expression of the law is used. The starting point is to calculate the socially necessary labor required to produce a given article, but what has been overlooked is the fact that socially necessary labor is an economic and historical concept. Therefore it changes not only on the local (or national) level but in world terms as well. Continued technological advances, a result of competition in the capitalist world, reduce the expenditure of necessary labor and therefore lower the value of the product. A closed society can ignore such changes for a certain time, but it would always have to come back to these international relations in order to compare product values. If a given society ignores such changes for a long time without developing new and accurate formulas to replace the old ones, it will create internal interrelationships that will shape its own value structure in a way that may be internally consistent but that would be in contradiction with the tendencies of more highly developed technology (for example, in steel and plastics). This could result in relative reverses of some importance and, in any case, would produce distortions in the law of value on an international scale, making it impossible to compare economies. . . .

We feel that an overall equilibrium between the supply of commodities and effective demand is essential. The Ministry of Domestic Trade would be in charge of bringing about a balance between the population's buying power and commodity prices, always bearing in mind that a whole series of necessities of life must be supplied at low prices, while we can go overboard in the other direction with less-important goods, openly ignoring the law of value in each concrete case.

Here, a big problem arises. What basis for setting real prices should the economy adopt in analyzing the relations of production? It could be an analysis of necessary labor in Cuban terms. This would bring with it immediate distortions, and cause us to lose sight of world problems, because of the automatic interrelationships that would necessarily be created. On the other hand, the world-market price could be used. This would cause us to lose sight of national problems, since in no branch of industry is our productivity up to world standards.

We propose, as a first approximation to solving the problem, that consideration be given to the creation of price indexes based on the following:

All imported raw materials would have a fixed, stable price based on an average international market price, plus a few points to cover the costs of transportation and the Ministry of Foreign Trade's administration costs. All Cuban raw materials would have a price based on real production costs in monetary terms. In both cases we would add planned labor costs plus depreciation of the means of production used to produce the raw materials. This would be the price of products supplied by domestic enterprises to each other and to the Ministry of Domestic Trade. However, these prices would be constantly affected by indexes reflecting the prices of those commodities on the world market plus the costs of transportation and of the Ministry of Foreign Trade.

Enterprises operating under the budgetary finance system would work on the basis of their planned costs and would make no profits. Instead, all profits would accrue to the Ministry of Domestic Trade. (Naturally, this refers to that part of the social product sold as commodities, the fundamental part of the consumption fund.) The indexes would continuously tell us (the central administration and the enterprise) how efficient we really are and would prevent our making wrong decisions. The population would not suffer at all as a result of all these changes, since the prices of the commodities they buy are established independently, in relation to the demand and essential need of each product.

For example, in order to calculate the amount of an investment, we would calculate the cost of raw materials and directly imported equipment; expenditure on construction and installation equipment; and planned wage costs—making allowances for contingencies and leaving a certain margin for administration costs. This would yield, upon completing the investment, three figures: (1) the real cost of the project in money terms; (2) what the project should have cost according to our plans; and (3) what it should cost in terms of world productivity. The difference between the first and the second would be chalked up to administrative inefficiency during construction; the difference between the second and the third would be the index of our backwardness in that particular sector.

This would allow us to make fundamental decisions regarding the alternative use of materials such as concrete, iron, or plastics; cement, aluminum, or zinc roofs; iron, lead, or copper piping; wood, iron, or aluminum window frames, etc.

All decisions could diverge from the mathematical optimum for political reasons, for foreign trade reasons, etc. But we would always have the real world as a mirror by which to compare our work. Prices would never be detached from their corresponding world market levels, which will fluctuate in given years according to advances in technology, and in which the socialist market and the international division of labor will increasingly gain preeminence, once a world socialist pricing system is achieved that is more logical than the one now used.

We could continue at length on this very interesting subject, but it is preferable to outline a few basic ideas here and point out that all this needs to be developed later.[118]

CHAPTER 7

Unequal exchange

COMMANDER IN CHIEF Fidel Castro, during a visit to the socialist countries, stated a principle of vital importance for our revolution:

> But there's something more. We think of our duty to the rest of the world. And to the extent that we have a people strongly educated in internationalist ideas, in solidarity, fully conscious of the problems of today's world, we will have a people better prepared to fulfill their international duty.
>
> You cannot speak of solidarity among the people unless at the same time you are creating that solidarity among all the peoples. Otherwise you fall into the trap of national self-centeredness.
>
> What did the bourgeoisie teach the peoples? Narrow, selfish nationalism. What did it teach the individual? Individual selfishness.
>
> Bourgeois ideology is the expression of individual selfishness, of national self-centeredness. Marxist-Leninist ideology is the expression of solidarity among individuals, of solidarity among peoples.[119]

In their writings and speeches, leaders of the Cuban revolution have laid out the theoretical and organizational basis for reducing the brutal impact of the law of value in international trade with *revolutionary* underdeveloped countries. Such an effort requires an effective international division of labor within the socialist market—a market different in conception from that of the world capitalist market. As Che explained:

We recognize the need for this trade to assume a higher form in countries of the new society, to prevent a widening of the differences between the developed and the more backward countries as a result of the exchange. In other words, it is necessary to develop terms of trade that permit the financing of industrial investments in the developing countries even if it contravenes the price systems prevailing in the capitalist world market. This would allow the entire socialist camp to progress more evenly, which would naturally have the effect of smoothing off the rough edges and of unifying the spirit of proletarian internationalism. (The recent agreement between Cuba and the USSR is an example of the steps that can be taken in this direction.)[120]

Che's ideas on unequal exchange are basically contained in the speech he gave at the World Conference on Trade and Development in Geneva, March 25, 1964, and in the speech he gave at the Second Economic Seminar of Afro-Asian Solidarity in Algiers, February 24, 1965. The best way of presenting Che's views on this subject is to reproduce the key parts of these speeches.

A conclusion must be drawn from all this: the socialist countries must help pay for the development of countries now starting out on the road to liberation. We state it this way with no intention whatsoever of blackmail or theatrics, nor are we looking for an easy way to get closer to the Afro-Asian peoples; it is our profound conviction. Socialism cannot exist without a change in consciousness resulting in a new fraternal attitude toward humanity, both at an individual level, within the societies where socialism is being built or has been built, and on a world scale, with regard to all peoples suffering from imperialist oppression.

We believe the responsibility of aiding dependent countries must be approached in such a spirit. There should not be any more talk about developing mutually beneficial trade based on prices forced on the backward countries by the law of value and the international relations of unequal exchange that result from the law of value.

How can it be "mutually beneficial" to sell at world market prices the raw materials that cost the underdeveloped countries immeasurable sweat and suffering, and to buy at world market prices the machinery produced in today's big automated factories?

If we establish that kind of relation between the two groups of nations, we must agree that the socialist countries are, in a certain way, accomplices of imperial exploitation. It can be argued that the amount of exchange with the underdeveloped countries is an insignificant part of the foreign trade of the socialist countries. That is very true, but it does not eliminate the immoral character of the exchange.

The socialist countries have the moral duty to put an end to their tacit complicity with the exploiting countries of the West.[121]

More than one distorted interpretation has arisen with regard to the point of view Che expressed above. One such interpretation tends to see it as a proposal for indiscriminate aid by the socialist countries to the underdeveloped countries and then sets out to refute it. This is accomplished by pointing to an undeniable fact: a number of underdeveloped countries that have received low-interest or interest-free loans and other development resources from the socialist camp have turned around and used such aid as a form of pressure on imperialism. Substantial funds have been obtained from the imperialist powers in this way. But a careful reading of Che's words, especially his speech in Algiers, indicates clearly that he set specific conditions and requirements for the policy he proposed for the socialist camp and the underdeveloped countries.

Each time a country is liberated, we said, it is a defeat for the world imperialist system. But we must agree that the break is not achieved by the mere act of proclaiming independence or winning an armed victory in a revolution. It is achieved when imperialist economic domination over a people is brought to an end. Therefore, it is a matter of vital interest to the socialist countries for a real break to take place. And it is our international duty, a duty determined by our guiding ideology, to contribute our efforts to make this liberation as rapid and deep-going as possible. . . .

For us there is no valid definition of socialism other than abolition of the exploitation of man by man. . . .

The proposed set of measures, however, cannot be implemented unilaterally. The socialist countries should help pay for the development of the underdeveloped countries, we agree. But the underdeveloped countries must also steel their forces *to embark resolutely on the road of building a new society— whatever name one gives it—where the machine, as an instrument of labor, is no longer an instrument for the exploitation of man by man. Nor can the confidence of the socialist countries be expected by those who play at balancing between capitalism and socialism,* trying to use each force as a counterweight in order to derive certain advantages from such competition. A new policy of absolute seriousness should govern the relations between the two groups of societies. It is worth emphasizing once again that *the means of production should preferably be in the hands of the state,* so that the marks of exploitation may gradually disappear.[122]

Other economists avoid making a fundamental analysis of the problem. They justify the existence of unequal exchange between the socialist countries and the underdeveloped countries of a socialist orientation by declaring that the former are not the cause of the situation. This is unquestionably true, but it in no way constitutes a sufficient reason to base trade relations on the rules of the capitalist market. In this respect, Che said:

Many underdeveloped countries, on analyzing their troubles, arrive at what seems a logical conclusion. They say that if the deterioration of the terms of trade is an objective reality and the cause of most of their problems, and if it is attributable to the fall in the prices of raw materials that they export and the rise in the prices of manufactured goods that they import on the world market, then, in the case of trade relations with the socialist countries based on existing market prices, the latter will also benefit from the situation since they are, in general, exporters of manufactured goods and importers of raw materials.

We should honestly and bravely answer that this is true, but with the same honesty we must also recognize that the socialist countries have not caused the present situation. They absorb barely 10 percent of the underdeveloped countries' primary commodity exports to the rest of the world. For historical reasons they have been compelled to trade under the conditions prevailing in the world market, which is the outcome of imperialist domination over the internal economy and external markets of the dependent countries. This is not the basis on which the socialist countries establish their long-term trade with the underdeveloped countries. . . .

On many occasions, these same countries demand unilateral preferential treatment from all the developed countries without exception, including the socialist countries in this category and putting all kinds of obstacles in the way of direct trade with them. There is a danger that, by seeking to trade through their national subsidiaries, companies from the imperialist powers could be given the opportunity to make spectacular profits by claiming that a given country is underdeveloped and therefore entitled to unilateral preferences.[123]

Che believed that the law of value did not necessarily have to govern commercial relations—and, therefore, political relations—between socialist countries and underdeveloped countries with a socialist orientation.

There are no borders in this struggle to the death. We cannot be indifferent to what happens anywhere in the world, because a victory by any country over imperialism is our victory, just as any country's defeat is a defeat for all of us. The practice of proletarian internationalism is not only a duty for the peoples struggling for a better future, it is also an inescapable necessity.[124]

The uneven development that has characterized the world capitalist system is well known. With Lenin and the October revolution, we learned that the outcome of the struggle against imperialism will not be decided in its initial stages, at least not in one final and frontal battle. Quite the contrary. Countries will continue to break away from the world capitalist system—as has been occurring—and will continue to take the only course possible to build a new social order: communism. It is an internationalist duty of the socialist camp—not to mention a contribution to its own survival—to accelerate this process and extend a hand to any country that makes an anticapitalist revolution, or at least displays some characteristics of an anticapitalist revolution.

From the days of Cuba's first confrontations with the United States, we received the timely aid of the Soviet Union. This helped our people resist the imperialist-imposed blockade, ensured that we would not die of hunger, and helped accelerate the radicalization of the Cuban revolutionary process. In his essay "On the Budgetary Finance System" and in many speeches, such as those given in Algiers, in Geneva, and at the United Nations, Che hailed the timely and fundamental solidarity that our country received from the socialist camp, and especially from the Soviet Union. During his visit to Chile in 1971, Commander Fidel Castro had this to say:

> I could describe our relations with the socialist camp as good, and with the Soviet Union as very good. Have we had disagreements? Yes, at times we have had a few disagreements. But we always keep in mind that at times that were decisive for our revolution, when it was a matter of life and death for our country, when our sugar quota was cut off, when our oil supply was cut off, when our people were threatened with death by

starvation or extermination, when invasions were being prepared against us, we had the Soviet market and a supply of fuel from the Soviet Union. . . .

The Soviet Union sent us all the weapons we needed. They have supported us in the political arena. Invariably and unfailingly, throughout these years, they have given us extraordinary aid in an unquestionably internationalist spirit. . . .

Apparently, some people would have preferred that no one would have helped us when the Yankee blockade was established, when our oil was cut off, and when we were invaded. How tragic, how painful it would have been for millions of Cubans if things had turned out that way! But instead we received aid and solidarity. This is what irritates the reactionaries so much. They discovered that for the first time in history, a small country could resist, a small country in this continent could stand up to all those aggressions and crimes.[125]

There is another reason, in addition to those noted by the revolution's leaders, that shows the correctness of the Cuban revolution's standpoint and that confirms the validity of its positions.

In his writings from the 1857–58 period, later published under the title *Outlines of the Critique of Political Economy* [*Grundrisse*], Karl Marx noted the possibility of two countries exchanging equivalents, with both obtaining advantages from the exchange, while nonetheless one was constantly robbing and exploiting the other.

> *Two nations may exchange according to the law of profit in such a way that both gain, but one is always defrauded.*
> From the fact that the profit may be *less* than the surplus value, and hence that capital [may] exchange at a profit without being valorised in the strict sense, it follows that not only individual capitalists, but nations too may continuously exchange with one another, and continuously repeat the exchange on an ever-growing scale, without gaining equally thereby. One nation may

continuously appropriate part of the surplus labour of the other and give nothing in exchange for it, except that here the measure is not as in the exchange between capitalist and worker.[126]

Also, in the third section of volume three of *Capital,* entitled "The Law of the Tendential Fall in the Rate of Profit," Marx dealt with this problem in passing.

There is a further question, whose specific analysis lies beyond the limits of our investigation: is the general rate of profit raised by the higher profit rate made by capital invested in foreign trade, and colonial trade in particular?

Capital invested in foreign trade can yield a higher rate of profit, *firstly, because it competes with commodities produced by other countries with less developed production facilities, so that the more advanced country sells its goods above their value, even though still more cheaply than its competitors.* In so far as the labour of the more advanced country is valorized here as labour of a higher specific weight, the profit rate rises, since labour that is not paid as qualitatively higher is nevertheless sold as such. The same relationship may hold towards the country to which goods are exported and from which goods are imported: i.e., *such a country gives more objectified labour in kind than it receives, even though it still receives the goods in question more cheaply* than it could produce them itself. In the same way, a manufacturer who makes use of a new discovery before this has become general sells more cheaply than his competitors and yet *still sells above the individual value of his commodity, valorizing the specifically higher productivity of the labour he employs as surplus labour. He thus realizes a surplus profit.*[127]

These paragraphs from Marx represent the strongest theoretical foundation for Che's views on unequal exchange.

Che held that by conducting foreign trade on the basis of market mechanisms and the law of value, the more developed socialist countries can contribute to the development of the dependent countries and, notwithstanding that fact, participate to one degree or another in their exploitation. The more backward country will benefit from trade with the developed socialist country, and yet part of its wealth will go to the socialist country without reciprocal and matching returns. What can happen, in effect, is that the dependent country transfers more materialized labor than it receives, even though it is obtaining goods more cheaply than it would have cost to produce them itself. That is, what can occur is an exchange of *equivalents*, but at the same time an *unequal* exchange. The solution Che saw, as we noted above, lay in a transformation, a genuine revolutionary change in international relations between the developed socialist countries and the underdeveloped countries with a socialist orientation. In Che's view:

> A great change of ideas will be involved in changing the order of international relations. *Foreign trade should not determine policy, but should on the contrary be subordinated to a fraternal policy toward the peoples.*[128]

In short, Che proposed making the new ethic put forward by Marx and Engels a permanent aspect of the relations between the developed, or more developed, socialist countries, on the one hand, and the underdeveloped countries with a socialist orientation that have begun to build a new social order, on the other. In Algiers Che cited the example of Cuba's trading relations with some of the socialist countries as an excellent precedent for a new way of setting prices.

> We have to prepare conditions so that our brothers can directly and consciously take the path of the complete abolition of exploitation, but we cannot ask them to take that path if we ourselves are accomplices in that exploitation. If we were asked what methods are used to establish fair prices, we could not answer because we do not know the full scope of the practical problems involved. All we know is that, after *political discussions,* the Soviet Union and Cuba have signed agreements advantageous to us, by means of which we

will sell five million tons of sugar at prices set above those of the so-called free world sugar market.[129]

For Che, however, this was in no way a definitive solution to the problem. World market prices are the basis of trade, but these prices themselves are influenced and regulated by unequal exchange. Even preferential terms, such as fixed prices over a period of years, do not eliminate unequal exchange; in the best of cases they simply mitigate it. Relations of this type help enrich the industrialized country at the expense of the raw-materials exporter.

The practice of a new ethic (proletarian internationalism) should govern not only setting prices of products destined for exchange, Che believed, but should also be extended to the question of loans.

> Let us briefly analyze the problem of long-term credits for developing basic industries. Frequently we find that beneficiary countries attempt to establish an industrial base disproportionate to their present capacity. The products will not be consumed domestically and the country's reserves will be risked in the undertaking.
>
> Our thinking is as follows: The investments of the socialist states in their own territory come directly out of the state budget, and are recovered only by the use of the products throughout the entire manufacturing process, down to the finished goods. We propose that some thought be given to the possibility of making these kinds of investments in the underdeveloped countries. In this way we could unleash an immense force, hidden in our continents, which have been exploited miserably but never aided in their development. We could begin a new stage of a real international division of labor, based not on the history of what has been done up to now, but rather on the future history of what can be done.
>
> The states in whose territories the new investments are to be made would have all the inherent rights of sovereign property over them with no payment or credits involved. But they would be obligated to supply agreed-upon quantities of products to the investor

countries for a certain number of years at set prices.

The method of financing the local portion of expenses incurred by a country receiving investments of this kind also deserves study. The supply of marketable goods on long-term credits to the governments of underdeveloped countries could be one form of aid not requiring the contribution of freely convertible hard currency.[130]

For all these reasons, the economic cooperation agreement between Cuba and the Soviet Union should be looked at, *for these accords are the precise embodiment of the ideas expressed by Che.*[131]

We should quote here Commander in Chief Fidel Castro's radio and television broadcast of January 3, 1973. At that time, he informed our people and the world of the economic agreements that had been reached with the USSR.

> Another problem faced by underdeveloped countries is the question of loans for development—not only loans to help cover their debt payments, but also loans for their further development. In general those loans are scarce in the capitalist world, and they are on a short-term, high-interest basis.
>
> Unfortunately there are times when we have to buy industrial plant and equipment on the capitalist market, and the loans are on a short-term and high-interest basis—five years, and in some exceptional cases, eight years. This is a field where imperialist pressure really makes itself felt everywhere, and for many years the imperialists were successful in preventing almost every capitalist country from granting loans of any sort to Cuba. Then, as their influence in the rest of the world declined, the doors of the capitalist lending agencies opened up to Cuba to a certain extent. But in general the credit terms for Cuba and for other countries are loans at high interest and for short periods of time.
>
> Another serious problem for the underdeveloped countries is the question of unequal exchange—the fact that the prices of products from the industrialized world are constantly increasing. This can be seen in any

item, from a bus or vehicle of any kind to all types of construction equipment and industrial installations.

All these products—the raw materials and other items from the industrialized world—become more expensive every year. If we compare prices now with prices ten years ago, we will see that they have practically doubled. Prices are now double what they were ten years ago for any of those products, especially industrial plant and equipment.

On the other hand, the products of the underdeveloped world, which are generally either raw materials or agricultural products, are becoming cheaper every year. . . .

This problem has become known as unequal exchange. It is a question that is discussed at all the international economic conferences and in the United Nations agencies. It is one of the subjects that is discussed most frequently.

Thus, the world is faced by a situation of a growing debt, high-interest loans, and stringent conditions; by short-term development loans at high interest rates, with difficult conditions attached. And finally it faces unequal exchange: higher prices for the products of the industrialized countries and lower prices for the products of the underdeveloped countries.

These are very serious problems that today are of deep concern to most of the world. So far, no solution has been found for them, and none is in sight.

In light of these facts we can appreciate the importance of the agreements we have signed with the Soviet Union. . . .

In our opinion, this constitutes an unprecedented example. We believe there is no precedent in history of such economic relations between a country like the Soviet Union and a small country like Cuba. These relations take into account the conditions in which Cuba has had to fight for its existence, only ninety miles from the United States, and subjected throughout these years—practically since the triumph of the revolution—

to a criminal blockade by the United States. . . .

I believe that relations between the Soviet Union and Cuba will always be spoken of as a model of truly fraternal, internationalist, and revolutionary relations.

Twelve days after Fidel's speech, an editorial entitled "The agreements with the USSR" appeared in the newspaper *Granma*, official organ of the Central Committee of the Communist Party of Cuba, underscoring the basic ideas Fidel had expressed. The editorial exemplified the unbroken continuity of our revolution's positions and demonstrated that the revolutionary thought and action of Che and Fidel are indivisible. It was a reaffirmation that the ideas Che expressed in 1964–65, as a representative of our country in international forums, remain the road forward for countries undertaking the task of building a communist society (and that these ideas hold true both for those countries that are economically developed, as well as for those that aspire to attain such development through socialism). The editorial said, in part:

In the agreements we signed the objective was not profit or the accumulation of wealth, but rather man. . . .

The contracting parties seek to help man to realize his full stature and dignity, to create a genuine sense of justice and equality, and to work with a new consciousness and spirit. . . .

Beyond their economic value, the importance of the accords lies in what they represent for the world in terms of principles, in the way they express the internationalist spirit of the Soviet Union, and in the way they demonstrate the generosity and selflessness of the Soviet people.[133]

Finally, it should also be noted that the socialist countries have announced in the United Nations Conference on Trade and Development their readiness to contribute 1 percent of their Gross National Product to the Fund for International Development. This unmasks the imperialist and colonialist powers who, despite being solely responsible for the backwardness of the developing nations, have not demonstrated the same political will. And how could it be otherwise? At the same time, it confirms the correctness of Che's ideas and offers a striking demonstration of socialist moral values in practice.

CHAPTER 8

Che and voluntary work

Ernesto Che Guevara was the originator of voluntary work in Cuba. For Che, its political impact on both the economy and morale was an important element of the system of economic management he developed.

> Socialism, in this stage of building socialism and communism, is not being built simply to have wonderful factories. It is being built for the sake of the whole man. Man must transform himself as production advances. We will not do an adequate job if we become simply producers of goods, of raw materials, without becoming at the same time producers of men.[134]

Voluntary work is of incalculable value in this process. Lenin was the first to note this fact, taking up the concept in his article "A Great Beginning."[135] Lenin's article is extremely important and timely in our decade and in decades to come until communism has been reached. Because in communist society all work will become voluntary, since it will cease to be an obligation and will become instead an inner necessity.

In this article, Lenin saw voluntary work as the seed of a revolutionary transformation of attitudes toward work, since it represents an effective means of struggle against petty-bourgeois self-centeredness, against the defects inherited from capitalism. In discussing voluntary work, Lenin stressed the creation of new social relations; of a new attitude toward work; of a new labor discipline, conscious and free, among workers. He spoke of a higher type of social organization of work than under capitalism—one that combines the scientific and technical advances of capitalism with the collective effort of conscious workers, an increase in the productivity of labor, and the importance of socialist emulation.

The ideas of Che Guevara are the logical continuation of those of Marx, Engels, and Lenin. Che offers us a rich source of ideas and solutions, of socialist formulas for building a new society. Voluntary work is unquestionably a major example.

For Che, voluntary work "is that done outside one's normal working hours, without additional economic payment. It can be done within or outside one's normal workplace."[136]

One of the most important tasks in the transition period—a task to be carried out simultaneously with the socialization of ownership of the means of production—is the creation of a new attitude toward work. And one of the most significant concrete aspects of the changes generated by socialist relations of production is the emergence of a new kind of work—voluntary work.

When private property in the means of production is abolished, socialist social ownership emerges. This form of property creates the conditions for a mode of production completely different from capitalism. The relationship between labor power and the means of production is no longer antagonistic, and the character of work is now stamped by a new principle: the elimination of the exploitation of man by man. Labor power ceases to be a commodity, and work objectively acquires the content of relations of mutual assistance and comradeship. Work begins to be done not just in the interest of the individual, but in the collective interest of society. While the social ownership of property in the means of production makes such a transformation possible, however, it is not in itself enough to bring about this change in individuals. As Che observed:

> The communist attitude toward work consists in the changes that occur in the mind of the individual. These changes will necessarily be prolonged and cannot be expected to be completed in a short period of time. Work must cease being what it still is today, a

compulsory social obligation, and be transformed into a social duty.[137]

Over time, voluntary work also contributes to creating an individual's identity with the tasks of daily work. It enhances the sense of individual fulfillment through labor.

Voluntary work is important economically, as well. As it develops, workers surpass the productivity records achieved in normal workdays.

The main importance of voluntary work lies in its role in communist education. It constitutes "a school that creates consciousness. It is an effort carried out both in society and for society, as an individual or collective contribution. And it shapes that high level of consciousness that allows us to speed up the transition process toward communism."[138] "Voluntary work is part of this educational task we talked to the compañeros about. In places where it can't be done, there's no point in inventing it."[139]

Che was not just concerned with the theoretical definition and importance of voluntary work; he dedicated equal effort to the problem of organizing it, implementing it, breaking it down into its component parts, and establishing systems of supervising it. In Che's view, good organization was an element of primary importance in voluntary work; he fought to keep time from being wasted. He stressed that voluntary work should not be done simply to burn up energy, but to incorporate that energy "into work that produces something and that helps to create consciousness."[140]

Che emphasized that in order to involve the masses in voluntary work, both its organization and content were important. People must feel that what they're doing is useful, Che maintained. "The goal we are after is for the individual to identify with his work. This is what must be organized."[141] He underscored the importance of supervising the performance of voluntary work, of rigorously checking on its results, without bureaucratism.

As acceptable types of voluntary work, Che included productive work in industry and agriculture, unpaid teaching and educational work, and technical work (under this category brigades of technicians were created from time to time to carry out a specific task).[142]

Che did not believe, however, that voluntary work should consist of carrying out uncompleted tasks in a workplace that has not been meeting its work norms. The character of voluntary work is distorted if it is used to cover up the inefficiency of cadres and indiscipline of workers. It was not Che's view that an enterprise could fail to make its quota, and then use voluntary work to make up for its previous lack of exactingness and discipline.

For Che, the impact of voluntary work on the creation of the new man was more important than its economic results.

> Our goal is that the individual feel the need to perform voluntary labor out of internal motivation, as well as because of the social atmosphere that exists. The two must go hand in hand. The atmosphere should help the individual feel the need to do voluntary work. But if it is simply the atmosphere, if it is simply moral pressure, then this just perpetuates what is known, for better or worse, as the alienation of man. Because then voluntary work is no longer something that comes from within oneself, something new, something done freely and no longer as a slave to work. It then loses a great deal, as we have seen—with some people wanting to know how many hours they have put in, or if so-and-so has as many hours or has completed the 240 hours. We have not been able to give voluntary work the content it should have.[143]

For that reason, Che began to examine the methods used to motivate man to give what is expected to society. Although this concern is evident in his earliest writings on the transition, it became stronger in 1964, especially at the end of that year.

CHAPTER 9

Incentive systems

T HE QUESTION of incentive mechanisms is an aspect of the budgetary finance system that is usually distorted in the vast literature on the Cuban revolution and Che's thought. Che's proposals are often viewed as romantic and idealistic. He is charged with ignoring the realities of the process of developing social consciousness during the transition period, thus opening the door to a voluntarist attitude in which communist consciousness is meted out by government decree.

The truth is quite the contrary. Che had unshakeable faith in man's capacity to transform himself. But he also recognized that forging the new consciousness would be the product of an ongoing process of transforming social structures, from which consciousness inevitably arises. Therefore, Che understood that more was needed than just appeals to consciousness. The possibilities of transforming man depended in large part on transforming the social relations of production, and on selecting the correct methods of motivation. For that reason, Che drew up a system based on the following pillars:

- a wage system;
- incentives;
- emulation.

Before turning to an analysis of these points, we should note that Che stressed three aspects in the overall effort to attain greater efficiency in work:

- improvements in economic planning;
- organization;
- rigorous supervision and controls.

It is not possible to examine here the concrete forms and system of management adopted under Che's leadership to carry out these norms. We should simply note the importance—both then and now—of being conscious of these factors.[144]

I. The wage system

Che believed the wage system should be an integral part of the overall political and ideological course of the socialist revolution, and that it should be based on Marxist-Leninist principles.

> Wages are an old evil born with the establishment of capitalism, when the bourgeoisie took power by dethroning feudalism. For that reason, wages will not die even under socialism. They will be done away with as the final remnant, when money ceases to circulate, when we reach the ideal stage: communism.
>
> Through wages—that is, money—we can measure the varying qualifications of all who receive something for working. Money can also be used as a measure of the quality of work by each individual, with their varying qualifications. Money is the sole yardstick that measures everything, and in the epoch of building socialism, where commodity relations still exist, we have to work with money.[145]

Later on, he had this to say:

> We live in an era in which injustice has not been uprooted, in which we cannot uproot it completely; we cannot provide to everyone according to their needs. We are building socialism, we have to provide to people according to their work, we have to correct injustices little by little, and we have to do it always in discussion with the workers.[146]
>
> Naturally, we are still in the stage of building socialism, in the period of transition, in which we have to provide to everyone according to their work, not according to their needs; that comes at a later stage.[147]

Che understood that pragmatists and technocrats are not the best sources of advice about revolutions. No lack of short-term technical solutions will arise. But some of them may mortgage the revolution's future and lead to steps backward in its ideological positions. For Che, the wage system and its implementation must be analyzed not just from the standpoint of their potential technical and economic advantages, but also in terms of their ideological implications.

As Che saw it, the wage system should be based on the principle of payment according to the quantity and quality of work. It should encourage the communist values that arise in the revolutionary process, as well as the use of moral incentives, while also using the existing material incentives inherited from capitalism. But the wage system in the transition period should not try *to develop* material incentives; quite the contrary.

Wage rates, the organization of work, work norms, and forms of payment are some of the most important elements that affect the equilibrium of the economic structure. In a socialist society, we associate the term *equilibrium* with the concept of the *rationality of the system*.

Under capitalism, however, equilibrium is expressed through specific laws that operate on the basis of what is rational within the framework of that economic system. Its framework is the market, which is precisely where the capitalist goes to obtain the elements required for the functioning of the profit system. He makes sure production will continue by acquiring as commodities the necessary means of production and labor power. Then he returns to the market to sell the product created and convert into money the surplus value that he has appropriated in the production process.

For the capitalist, therefore, what is rational is the appropriation of the worker's surplus labor. That is why, when the capitalist calculates his "cost of production," he does it in terms of capital disbursed; that is, for him the cost of production is equal to C + V, where C stands for constant capital (spent on means of production) and V stands for variable capital (spent on wages to purchase labor power).[148]

The capitalist does not count as part of the labor costs

necessary to obtain a commodity the unpaid part of the workers' labor that he appropriates in the form of surplus value. From the capitalist's point of view, the rationality of the system consists in achieving the lowest possible cost of production and appropriating the difference between his "cost price" and the price at which the commodity is sold on the market.

The capitalist, as we are well aware, is not interested in a commodity's use value as an end, but only as a means to get what does interest him: value. For that reason, he views efficiency in management solely in terms of the degree to which more surplus value is extracted from the workers. Under capitalism, rationality and efficiency have no genuine content in terms of social usefulness. The capitalist has no interest in producing to satisfy social needs. He engages in production solely to obtain more surplus value.

To attain these objectives, capitalism has developed its own methods of organization and supervision. Management of the modern capitalist enterprise requires an efficient organizational apparatus. The organizational techniques of capitalism reach down to the smallest elements of production and distribution. We must not overlook capitalism's traditionally rigorous methods of implementing controls and setting standards. Today these methods permit the most precise determination of productive inputs, inventories, and so forth, all aimed at promoting the rationalization and efficiency of the system. The wages and motivation of the worker constitute essential links in the system, with the goal of producing more surplus value.

Socialism obviously presents us very different conceptions of rationality and efficiency. In guaranteeing the best possible management, different methods must also necessarily be used.

When Marx laid out his ideas on value and labor costs, he pointed out that the real cost of production is not $C + V$, which is how the individual capitalist figures it. To the contrary, Marx held, the real cost of production is given by the formula $C + V + S$, where S also represents an expenditure of labor. It is precisely this expenditure of labor that the capitalist appropriates as surplus value when he sells his commodity.

When we study the rationality and efficiency of socialism as an economic system, we see that society's total production output, as a first approximation, is also represented by C + V + S. But here S is no longer surplus value but instead surplus product, created by the worker with a sense of its *social benefit,* a situation alien to capitalism. Here the expenditure of labor necessary to produce the item must be examined from a different perspective than the one we use to examine capitalism.

Since production under socialism is carried out for a different social purpose, it is clear that the elements involved are going to be qualitatively different from those in a capitalist economy governed by the law of value. These elements are determined by the economic policy set by the party and government. No longer does the law of value, through the spontaneous workings of the market, define rationality and efficiency on the basis of individual interest. Production now has a specific social content that is different from that under capitalism. Here management is conscious, and economic planning replaces the law of value.

Supervision and controls become extremely important, because they measure the *social results* of productive effort and of the labor expended. And they do so in a framework where the ongoing development of workers' consciousness does not yet in itself guarantee fulfillment of the conditions for the system's rational functioning. This will not happen until a later stage in the transition to communism. Here we come back to the fact that wages and motivation—with a different content than under capitalism—constitute merely two links in the chain that makes up the system. In this regard, Che stated:

> As we enter a new society, work cannot be considered the dark side of life but rather the opposite. Our educational task in the coming years is to transform work into a moral necessity, an internal necessity.
>
> We have to rid ourselves of the erroneous view—appropriate only to a society based on exploitation—

that work is a disagreeable human necessity. We have to bring out work's other aspect, as a human necessity within each individual.[149]

Because in considering the wages paid to a worker for meeting a work norm, we should not view them as payment for the sale of his labor power. We cannot simply say that the worker works because otherwise he wouldn't eat. In socialist society or in the building of socialism, the worker works because it is his social duty. He has to fulfill his duty to society. In this stage of socialist construction, in this period of transition, our duty is to turn in an average effort, according to one's level of skill, and to receive in return an individualized wage, in accordance with that level of skill. At the same time, everyone receives all the benefits the society provides.[150]

To use labor efficiently and in a socially useful way requires rigorous planning, organization, and supervision until even the least important elements in the productive process have been checked and double-checked.

On December 26, 1963, Che appeared on television to explain and respond to questions about work norms and the wage scale. He made the following point:

We inherited from capitalism an enormous quantity and variety of different wage rates for the same skills. As you know, under capitalism wages are a product of the sale of labor power and are influenced by the class struggle. In addition, Cuba, a semicolonial country dominated by U.S. imperialism, was at one time a field of investment for the U.S. manufacturing industry. Wage rates in these U.S.-owned workplaces were much higher than previously known in Cuba, despite being much lower than what workers in the United States would receive for the same work.

All this made the wage question more complex and increased the number of different wage rates. We have calculated there were some 90,000 different wage rates in Cuba and some 25,000 different job categories based on skill levels.[151]

The chaotic situation described by Che worsened from 1959 to 1961. Some unions carried out struggles for higher wages. And the bourgeoisie followed a policy of increasing wages, either out of fear of conflicts that might result in intervention by the revolutionary government or to destabilize the economy through inflation. Revolutionary administrative bodies helped deepen the chaos by setting wages arbitrarily. The result, by 1962, was a situation that can be summed up as follows:

• a great diversity of wages, including different wage rates for the same occupation;

• disproportionate wages among different branches of industry;

• different names for the same occupation;

• no job descriptions or clearly delineated skill requirements;

• various methods of payment for the same work;

• absence of work norms;

• a near total lack of personnel trained in the organization of work.[152]

In 1962 the Ministry of Industry and the Ministry of Labor undertook the task of drawing up a system of organizing and establishing work norms. This step was intimately linked with the creation of a wage system. The aim was to create a system that would encourage both economic development and communist consciousness. Such a system had to take account of the low average skill level in our labor force, from the standpoint of the technical advancement of agricultural and industrial expansion. So it was important that the new wage system encourage workers to raise their educational and technical level and, in this way, increase our people's overall cultural development. Among the most important tasks accomplished in that period were the following:

• drawing up a list of occupations, with a single title for each job classification;

• drawing up a list of job descriptions and skill requirements for each job; and evaluating, from the standpoint of complexity, more than 10,634 occupations, dividing them into 340 categories based on skill levels;

• reorganizing thousands of different wage rates into a total of 41 for the entire economy;

• classifying the country's workplaces according to their needs in leadership personnel;

• evaluating and classifying occupations involving abnormal working conditions;

• training some 5,000 technical personnel, and organizing an apparatus devoted to leading this effort;

• holding training courses throughout the country for leading political, administrative, and trade union cadres;

• drafting a single wage scale for the entire economy;

• establishing production norms in work centers where this was possible.

The elements of the wage system drawn up under Che's leadership can be summed up in the following points:

• the wage scale;

• job qualification categories; workers' skill levels;

• wage rates;

• work norms;

• forms and methods of payment.

A. The wage scale

By establishing the wage scale, Che introduced the principle of socialist distribution according to the quantity and quality of work. This task also involved establishing the varying degrees of complexity of all existing jobs in the country. The wage scale had two fundamental elements:

The first task was to break down and classify various jobs into a number of groups on the basis of their level of complexity. Here it was necessary to take account of the indispensable minimum of skill a worker needed to have, the required technology, and the complexity and organization of the production process.

Second, coefficients were established to indicate various degrees of complexity of each of these job groups. The job

group with the lowest level of complexity was given the co-
efficient *one;* the coefficients of the others expressed a multiple of complexity in comparison to the first. As Che indicated:

> The first task was to sort all wage rates into groups
> that reflected more or less the same characteristics, to
> boil down the enormous quantity of different wages
> and skills. . . . Concrete practice showed it was better,
> more logical, to classify wage rates into no more than
> eight levels. At the same time, however, differentials
> were applied for work carried out in dangerous or
> unhealthy conditions, taking as a yardstick the most
> dangerous and unhealthy, but on the basis of the same
> eight wage scales.[154]

A report written at the time on the implementation of the
new system noted:

> [This wage scale system] covered 98 percent of the
> workers, leaving only some 2 percent outside its reach.
> Moreover, the eight groups were sufficient to organize
> wages correctly. Unifying the various wage rates into
> eight groups not only established a noticeable incentive
> for a worker to raise his skill level, it also made it easier
> to compute and maintain payment records.[155]

B. Workers' skill levels; job qualification categories
   One of the greatest difficulties confronting the revolution in
its early years was the low skill level of our workers. Che
stressed the need to raise workers' technical capacities and
cultural level in order to move forward in building the new
society. Along these lines, Che stressed that in organizing
workers' wage rates and the salary levels of administrative,
technical, and leadership personnel, special emphasis should
be put on developing and increasing skills and capacities. The
wage system proposed by Che and the Ministry of Labor was
aimed at doing this. Training constitutes one of the fundamental principles of this system.
   As we have pointed out, the wage system was composed of

a scale of groups divided into eight levels or wage categories. The difference between one group and another on the scale depended not only on the basic wage rate but also on the skill level.

Through a system of bonuses, a worker who wanted to earn more than the wage corresponding to his wage group could do so, by producing more than the norm. But this system placed a cap on hourly wages plus bonuses; no one could be paid wages equal to those of a worker in the next higher group on the scale. Workers could pass on to the next wage level only by raising their skill level. Che explained this as follows:

> Questions have been raised precisely about this policy of not paying bonuses for all excess production above the norm. . . . Not only is there no payment for part of the overfulfillment, but overfulfillment itself has a limit. Its limit is the next highest wage category. . . . Why? Precisely to try to fight one of the great evils we believe the system has—a system that resembles piecework, paying hourly wages plus full bonuses. That evil is its lack of interest in raising skill levels.
>
> We call on workers to raise their skill level. We appeal to their consciousness—it is our duty to do so— and in general there is a response to this appeal. But we also have to take measures to ensure that raising skill levels becomes a genuine economic imperative. We have to take measures ensuring that a worker can never attain a wage higher than the rate immediately above his, based on his level of qualifications, no matter how much he surpasses production quotas. . . . We must do everything possible to convince workers of the importance of developing their skill levels if they want to receive a higher wage.[156]

In taking up the question of raising skill levels, Che underscored its connection with other elements of the system.

> The skill of a worker is directly related to his productive output. And production, in terms of

meeting work norms both for output and quality, is the social duty of each worker to the community as a whole. Because it is society that has given him work, guarantees food for his children, and guarantees him a minimal level of social well-being, of care and services. And society also sees to it that the level of such care and services will rise as we increase our capacity to produce.[157]

The wage system that was instituted had categories of skill levels that served to classify different jobs, and to determine which job group each worker belonged in. It provided for wage differentials in relation to a worker's skill level, that is, in relation to the quality of work. The categories of skill requirements included descriptions of the various jobs, the level of skill required, and the job group they belonged in, based on their degree of complexity. Two basic sets of categories of skill levels were drawn up: one for the most common jobs and one for occupations specifically related to each branch of industry.[158]

C. Wage rates

The wage rates determined the amount of the hourly or daily wage. The hourly wage rate (in pesos) was the following:

I	II	III	IV	V	VI	VII	VIII
0.48	0.56	0.65	0.76	0.89	1.05	1.23	1.49

The hourly wage of the first group was set at 48 centavos, on the basis of two factors. First, beginning from the bottom, this was found to be the wage of the first significant concentration of workers prior to the establishment of the new wage scale (19.11 percent of the workers received an hourly wage of between 45 and 49 centavos). Second, the minimum wage set by legislation, 85 pesos a month, corresponded to this hourly wage rate set for the first group on the scale. A wage differential was established based on working conditions. Three conditions were specified: normal, unhealthy, and dangerous. Work under normal conditions was paid at the regular scale; work under the second set of conditions at 20 percent above scale; and under the third at 35 percent above scale.[159]

D. Work norms

Che believed the wage system adopted should be consistent with the system of organizing and setting norms for work; at the same time, it should serve as one of the fundamental pillars of achieving these work norms. After he was named minister of industry, Che became involved in the task of establishing work norms. He discussed and promoted this task in the ministry, in his weekly visits to workplaces, in meetings with unions, and in other gatherings.

> We can draw a very important conclusion: that quality is an essential component of the norm. The norm is not just quantity, it is also quality. Therefore, the obligation of the worker is to meet the standard in both quantity and quality. If he does not meet the quality standard, he has not fulfilled his duty to society.[160]
>
> When we set our work norms for establishing wages, the minimum norm—what must be done by each worker every day—is one's duty to society. What is important is not what must be done to earn a wage. It is instead what must be done to fulfill one's duty to the community, which provides—through wages, and through social services that grow more abundant day by day—the opportunity to live, to clothe oneself, to educate one's children, to acquire culture, and to become an ever more rounded human being. This is perhaps a small and subtle difference. But it helps educate us and points the way forward toward a well-defined and permanent goal.[161]
>
> Work norms will produce no results for the country or even for the working class if we don't take organizational measures and maintain them vigilantly. If such controls go by the board, then the entire organizational apparatus that has been put together

will fall victim to the same distortions it suffered during the first five years of building the new society.[162]

Our system of norms has the merit of establishing compulsory professional training as a condition for promotion to a higher job category. Over time, this will bring about a significant increase in the level of technical skills.

Nonfulfillment of a norm means nonfulfillment of a social duty. Society punishes the offender by deducting a part of his income. The norm is more than a mere measuring stick marking a realizable or customary amount of labor. It is the expression of the worker's moral obligation, *it is his social duty*. Here is where the action of administrative controls and ideological controls must come together. The party's great role in the production unit is to be its internal driving force and to use the myriad examples set by its members to ensure that productive labor, training, and participation in economic matters of the unit become integral parts of the workers' lives, gradually becoming an irreplaceable habit.[163]

Besides pointing to the importance Che attached to work norms, we have sought through these quotations to highlight how Che saw the interconnection, in practice, between economic advancement—the expansion of production, the creation of a material base for socialism—and the creation of a new consciousness. This new consciousness itself becomes a fundamental material factor in the development of production and of socialist society. We have also tried to underscore the key role Che assigned to supervision and controls.

E. Forms and methods of payment[164]

The wage system established the forms of payment for workers and for administrative, technical, and leadership personnel. For workers, norms were set for work paid by the hour, with bonuses that linked wages to workers' productivity and skill level. Bonuses were paid for surpassing the norm and the production plan. The sum of the bonuses plus the base wage rate could not exceed the base wage of the next higher wage group. For hourly workers not directly involved in basic production, for whom it was practically impossible to set precise norms, bonuses were calculated on the basis of monthly work results. In both cases the bonus was computed on the basis of time actually worked. Bonuses were given for surpassing the production plan, so long as quality standards were also maintained. The bonus was paid out of the wage fund.

For administrative workers, technicians, and leadership personnel, calculations were based on the amount of time worked (eight hours). In the production sector, the productivity of these employees was measured by the final results of the work of the unit to which they were linked. Two forms of payment were established for these employees: hourly wages and hourly wages plus bonuses.

The first was used for those administrative personnel who work in the nonproduction sector and for those in the production sector who work in the ministries, middle-level offices, and central offices of an enterprise. Hourly wages were set at a fixed amount, in accordance with a scale.

Hourly wages plus bonuses were used for administrative personnel in the production sector. The fundamental indicator of the right to a bonus was surpassing the production plan with the requisite quality, along with reducing the cost of production.

All bonus payments were duly regulated, on the basis of established percentages and scales.

F. Stages of implementing the wage system

In 1963 the wage system was successfully instituted in an experimental form in 36 agricultural establishments and 247 units in the industrial and service sector. In June 1964 the second stage began, with the extension of the system to all units in the industrial sector.

The second stage was carried out along the same lines as the first. Guidelines were set for a study of occupations. Workforce rosters were drawn up by job category. Workers were assigned places on the roster. Wage levels were calculated. And meetings were held to publicize the work that had been carried out.

Once the wage system had been widely implemented, the Ministry of Labor issued Decree No. 1, April 24, 1965, governing the wages of workers who had been transferred or promoted.

On May 17, 1965, the issuance of Decree No. 2 opened the third stage of implementing the wage system, covering administrative workers. This designation included those who had previously been classified as working in the service sector. This third stage lasted from May 17, the date the decree was issued, until December of the same year.

G. Later evolution of the wage system

A report in *Cuba Socialista* on the new system stated:

> The wage system will respect existing incomes for every job and occupation. This means that some workers will receive wages that, according to the scale, are currently above the rate corresponding to their skill level. Such wages will be separated into two parts: the *base wage rate*, which will be the primary element; and *additional remuneration*, which is the excess over that base rate that has been preserved by the revolution as a conquest by workers in past struggles against the capitalists. As workers acquire higher skill levels, their wages will rise to the amount set by the scale for that level of skill, and the additional remuneration will decrease to the same extent. Such additional remuneration will be paid until the worker's total wage matches the wage rate corresponding to his skill level.[165]

In a television broadcast on the wage system, Che elaborated on this point:

> But another, very different phenomenon occurred. An entire series of industries had wages higher than those being considered at present. This was particularly true for the industries I referred to earlier—in general those owned by foreign capital, and those where struggles

over wages and salaries had been carried out by unions and various sectors. In some cases, the reductions would have been quite sizable under the new wage system. In general, it would naturally be extremely unpopular to reduce everyone to a single wage scale. This is especially true since this wage scale cannot be said to be fair, in absolute terms. It is the fair scale for Cuba today. But, given our conditions of underdevelopment, this means that it is a relatively low wage scale.

That's why we established the additional pay, which has come to be called the "plus" and is today known to all workers as the "plus. . . . " In other words, there is a group of workers who will receive a wage that is divided into two parts: their basic wage— corresponding to one of the eight categories, and the "plus," corresponding to their historic wage.

In considering bonuses for overproduction, only the basic wage is figured in. The entire wage, however, is taken into account for penalties for failure to meet the norm.[166]

This political decision was correct in the circumstances of Cuba in 1963, even though it did not strictly adhere to the socialist principle of payment according to work. The Cuban economy immediately experienced an increase in productivity, and the ratio between the average wage and productivity shifted in favor of productivity. Conscious of the importance of the socialist principle of payment, Che made these remarks to a meeting of administrators:

We are beginning a socialist revolution, we are building socialism. And socialism is built with work and sacrifice, by adhering to a series of norms.

We cannot build socialism with workers who make fifteen pesos a day for doing nothing. You can't build socialism this way! We could figure out how to survive, but we wouldn't be building socialism. There is one thing that is logical and of elementary political importance, and that is to try not to lower anyone's pay. Okay, so we don't cut anyone's pay. But what

about the new workers? Why should a new worker
come on the job and get the benefit of a union struggle
of the past that has nothing to do with today?[167]

Che advocated moving closer and closer to the socialist principle. But the wage system Che created suffered modifications
several times after April 1965. These modifications, along with
a failure to observe some of its stipulations, destroyed the system. It is important to understand this, because many people
confuse or erroneously identify this later stage with the system originally developed by Che. Among the later modifications were the following:

• the creation of new productive sectors with wage rates,
set by special decrees, that did not coincide with the established scales;

• promotions in cases where levels of training and other requirements specified under the system were not met;

• Decree No. 20, issued August 4, 1967, by the Labor and
Wages Department of the Ministry of Labor, which contained provisions regulating wage rates and living conditions of workers in youth and adult brigades mobilized for
two-year stints as agricultural laborers. The decree states:
"These wages are fixed and will not be affected by either
underfulfillment or overfulfillment of the norms. Nor will
these wages be altered should these workers carry out jobs
corresponding to other wage groups, whether they be above
or below the one taken as the basis for setting the wage
rate";

• Decree No. 20A of the same department, dated August 10,
1967, modified Decree No. 20 and stipulated that the wage
rate of the brigade members would be set to equal the wages
of permanent agricultural workers and would be subject to
meeting work norms, although free room and board would
be maintained;

• the Revolutionary Offensive of 1968, in which large
numbers of workers agreed not to accept overtime pay or
tips;[168]

• Decree No. 50 of the Labor and Wages Department of
the Ministry of Labor, dated October 17, 1968, which con-

tained regulations for applying the system of hourly wages and production norms in the industrial sector. They included eliminating wage deductions as a penalty for not fulfilling norms.

It should be stressed that the deterioration of the administrative apparatus began in 1966 with errors made in applying the measures against bureaucratism.[169] The situation grew worse around 1968, with the loss of economic controls—including work norms—and the loss of statistical capabilities and discipline. It became impossible to obtain the overall indicators needed to analyze the performance of administration and management. In his main report to the First Congress of the Communist Party, Fidel stated in this regard:

> In 1968, the connection between wages and work norms was severed. Encouragement was given to work schedules based on consciousness, and on workers renouncing overtime pay. . . .
>
> The failure to link payment to work performance led to a significant increase in the amount of excess currency in circulation. This excess of money, combined with the shortage of goods and services, created a breeding ground for absenteeism and a lack of labor discipline.[170]

This situation meant that the system based on hourly wages and production norms could not be accurately applied; the lack of controls made it difficult to determine whether or not the norms had been met. On the other hand, these same circumstances opened the door to grave financial indiscipline, such as undue wage payments to absentee workers and to workers on leave without pay.

The absence of economic controls created a situation that can be summed up as follows: The income of the country's labor force remained constant, no longer linked to fluctuations in production and productivity, or to labor discipline. At the same time, the volume of consumer goods within their reach declined. This in turn reduced the possibilities of absorbing the excess currency in circulation and set off an acute financial imbalance.

II. Incentives

The system of incentives is another element of the budgetary finance system developed by Che that is either unknown or mistakenly identified with the form it took later, after his departure from Cuba. The key aspects of this question will be summarized, letting Che himself explain his position.

A. The search for incentive mechanisms different from those used under capitalism is based on an understanding that socialism is not only a question of economics, but of consciousness as well.

Socialism does not just aim to create a system characterized by an abundance of consumer goods. Socialism also seeks to instill in human beings a new attitude toward society and toward the well-being society provides. If this is overlooked and socialism is analyzed only from the economic and pragmatic point of view, then concepts as antagonistic as "consumer society" and "communism" can be mistakenly identified with each other.

In his main report to the First Congress of the Communist Party of Cuba, Fidel expressed the following idea:

> In creating our communist consciousness, raising the material standard of living is, and must be, a noble and just objective of our people, to be attained through selfless work, in the natural environment in which we live. But at the same time we have to be aware that this environment is limited, that each gram of wealth has to be wrested from nature through human effort. We must keep in mind that material goods are created to satisfy the real and reasonable needs of the human being, and that superfluous things should be discarded. Our society cannot guide itself by the absurd concepts, habits, and deviations with which the decadent capitalist system of production has infected the world. . . .
>
> Socialism means not only material enrichment but also the opportunity to create an extraordinary cultural

and spiritual wealth among the people and to create an individual with deep feelings of human solidarity, free from the selfishness and meanness that degrade and oppress the individual under capitalism.[171]

It is clear, therefore, that material well-being does not automatically create a new social conciousness. Systematic and concrete work is required to create a new human sensibility, and this work parallels and is closely linked with building the economy of the new society. This task is both an ideological task and one that involves essential structural reforms. To carry it out, socialism must create its own *instruments,* its own mechanisms of change.

B. For a time, the slow and complex ideological transformation carries with it a contradiction between production and consciousness. During this period the habits of thought instilled under capitalism (individual ambition, selfishness, and so forth) weigh negatively on production. Changes in property relations, or the suppression of private property in the means of production, take place in an instant; the process of adapting the mind to the new state of affairs requires much more time. The problem is posed by Che as follows:

> Does this mean that giving priority to the development of consciousness retards production? In comparative terms, in a given period, that may be, although no one has made the relevant calculations. We maintain that in a relatively short time, however, the development of consciousness does more for the development of production than material incentives do.[172]

It is in this critical period that the great temptation could arise to unleash capitalist mechanisms — competition, material incentives, free enterprise, and so forth — especially since any application of these would demonstrate their efficiency in the *economic* sphere. Che stated:

> As for the presence of material interest in an individualized form, we recognize it (although fighting it and attempting to speed up its elimination through

education) and apply it in our norms of hourly work plus bonuses, and wage penalties for nonfulfillment of these norms.[173]

We believe that in economics this kind of lever quickly takes on an existence of its own and then imposes its strength on the relations between men. . . .

In our view, direct material incentives and consciousness are contradictory terms.[174]

C. An intelligent balance must be established, nonetheless, between the use of both material and moral incentives.

The process should be directed more toward the *withering away* of material incentives than toward *suppressing* them. Establishing a policy of moral incentives does not imply a total rejection of material incentives. The aim is simply to reduce their field of operation, and to do so through intensive ideological work rather than by bureaucratic means. Che commented:

We must make one thing clear: *we do not deny the objective need for material incentives,* although we are reluctant to use them as the main lever. . . . It should not be forgotten that it comes from capitalism and is destined to die under socialism.[175]

We have already often said that material incentives should not be viewed as having been eliminated, but rather as something to be eliminated. What we are doing is to present them not as an indispensable lever, but rather as a lever we unfortunately have to use, a remnant of the old society.[176]

The stage of building socialism is one of transition. Material incentive still plays an important role, but it is also slated to die. For the moment, however, we have to recognize the importance it has. We stress the moral incentives of socialist society. We believe that material incentives should decline until they disappear in classless society.[177]

On May 2, 1962, Che met with workers from abroad who attended the May Day celebration at the Plaza of the Revolution. The delegate from Canada asked him, "What incentives will the Cubans use with the workers? Are there some incentives aimed at increasing production?" Che responded in part:

> I don't know if you were at the annual meeting April 30 where we gave away forty-five houses to the best workers in each branch of industry. It turned out that forty-four were given away, because one worker declined his prize.
>
> We believe that we must use both moral and material incentives in the stage of building socialism. In this stage of revolutionary enthusiasm, we give great importance to moral incentives, but we are also concerned about workers' material interests.[178]
>
> Material incentives are a remnant of the past. They are something that *must be taken into account.* At the same time, as the process advances, their preponderance in people's consciousness must be eliminated. . . . Material incentives will play no part in the new society that is being created; they will wither away along the way.[179]
>
> The role of the vanguard party is precisely that of raising as high as possible the opposing banner, the banner of moral interest, of moral incentive, of the men who fight and sacrifice themselves and expect nothing more than the recognition of their compañeros. . . .[180]

D. Thus, for a period of time the historical process compels us to use a lever we know to be harmful. Given this fact, the task is to seek the least harmful variants, including those that will contribute to the self-destruction of this lever. Che studied the possible variants and applied some of them. The following ones can be noted:

• material incentives, based on the wage scale plus bonus payments, for fulfilling and surpassing work norms and/or the production plan;

• material disincentives for failure to meet norms for output and quality, as well as failure to meet the production plan;

• material incentives in the form of collective rewards;

• improvement in the quality of life.

The first variant consisted in applying a wage scale that gave higher pay to jobs requiring greater skill. The aim was to use material incentives to encourage an aspiration for self-improvement in a country with a low educational level, where the great mass of workers were unaccustomed to study. On the other hand, the wage scale itself placed a limit on material incentives, since payment for additional hours of work could never exceed the wage rate of the next higher wage and skill level.

The second variant, material disincentives, flowed from an understanding of work norms as a social duty—"duty" not only in an ethical but an economic sense, as well. Che stated in this regard:

> Each job will have a norm for quantity and quality. Therefore, an evaluation will be made of the quality and quantity of the work that is done. Payment will be made according to a lower scale if the work is poor in terms of quality or quantity, and according to a higher scale if the work is extraordinarily good in quality and quantity.[181]

Material disincentives were not intended for use only with workers. The system also envisioned reducing the pay of technicians and managers when the output of an enterprise failed to meet planning goals, or when production costs increased.

Let us start from the fact that money remains a means of exchange (a situation that will logically prevail for a considerable period). If we do not subtract something from the wages of a worker who does not meet the work norms, then this enables him to receive a quantity of values and social benefits that he has contributed very little toward creating.

No worker receives the entire fruit of his labor. Marx himself pointed out in the *Critique of the Gotha Programme* that from the total values created by society, the following must be deducted.

> *First,* cover for replacement of the means of production used up.

Secondly, an additional portion for expansion of production.

Thirdly, reserve or insurance funds to provide against accidents, dislocations caused by natural calamities, etc. . . .

There remains the other part of the total product, intended to serve as means of consumption.

But before this is divided among the individuals, there has to be deducted, again, from it:

First, the general costs of administration not belonging to production. . . .

Secondly, that which is intended for the common satisfaction of needs, such as schools, health services, etc. . . .

Thirdly, funds for those unable to work, etc. . . .

Only now do we come to the "distribution" which the programme, under Lassallean influence, alone has in view in its narrow fashion, namely, to that part of the means of consumption which is divided among the individual producers of the co-operative society.

The "undiminished proceeds of labour" have already unnoticeably become converted into the "diminished" proceeds, although what the producer is deprived of in his capacity as a private individual benefits him directly or indirectly in his capacity as a member of society.[182]

Work norms are an effective measure of productivity and of the productive apparatus as a whole. When a worker in a socialist society fails to meet them, yet still draws full wages and free social benefits—such as education, health care, sporting and cultural events, retirement, and so forth—he becomes a parasite on the collective effort. An additional economic consequence, if the situation becomes widespread, is inflation. Che commented:

The production norm is the average amount of labor that creates a product in a certain time, given average skill and under the specific conditions of equipment utilization. It is the contribution of a set amount of labor to society by one of its members. *It is the fulfillment of his social duty.*[183]

Production and wage norms and wage scales were not set simply to produce more, nor were they set simply to equalize basic wage patterns. The aim was also to be able to detect and reward the best, and to detect and punish, through lower wages, the worst, those who are incapable of fulfilling their duty.[184]

Each work norm must be combined with the consciousness that the norm is a social duty, not the minimum required to fulfill a contract between the enterprise and the union. No such contract exists, because there is no distinction between the enterprise and the worker when there is collective ownership.[185]

As for the presence of material interest in an individualized form, we recognize it (although fighting it and attempting to speed up its elimination through education) and apply it in our norms of hourly work plus bonuses, and wage penalties for nonfulfillment of these norms.[186]

In regard to the third variant, collective bonuses, in 1964 studies were begun on the possibilities of applying these in some industries. The tendency was to move cautiously in this area. The idea was that the bonus, instead of being cash, would take the form of some social service that was both necessary and useful to the workers collectively.

When a group of workers had proven themselves to be a vanguard detachment by surpassing the plan's goals, steps would then be taken to deal with one or more of a series of social problems. These improvements would in turn further benefit production. Examples might be the construction of a child-care center, or a new school for the workers' children, a lunchroom, improved working conditions, free work clothes, vacation facilities, and even small-scale investment in technology to attain greater productivity with less effort.

Finally, the most legitimate, sound, and always valid material incentives are those received by society as a whole. These gains come about when the economic plan has scientifically established a ratio of investment and consumption that gradually but steadily increases the population's historical standard of living. Through the quantitative and qualitative improvement in their living standards, the workers see the palpable results of their revolutionary commitment and their efforts in the field of production.

At the same time, all of the above is based on the most complete and realistic Marxist understanding that during the period of transition to communism, everyone has to receive payment according to their work, that is, according to the fulfillment of their social duty. It is true that this policy creates a series of injustices. There are workers who, due to their greater skill level, make high wages, even though they may not have a big family to provide for. Meanwhile there are other workers—with a lower educational level—who make less even though they may have many dependents. As Marx explained:

> But these defects are inevitable in the first phase of communist society as it is when it has just emerged after prolonged birth pangs from capitalist society. Justice can never be higher than the economic structure of society and the cultural development thereby determined.[187]

E. We have seen Che's views on material incentives and disincentives. Let us turn now to what Che said about the role and importance of *moral incentives*, and the way he put them into practice.

In the pages above, Che's overall conception of the period of transition to communism, particularly its first phase, socialism, was examined, including:

• his position that it is impossible to separate the creation of the material base from the emergence of a new consciousness in men about the society they are building;

• his rejection of the way some theoreticians subordinate the development of consciousness to a "gradual increase in consumer goods for the people. . . . This concept seems too mechanical, too rigid. 'Consumer goods'—that is the slogan and definitely the great molder of consciousness for the defenders of the other system";[188]

• his clear understanding that both aspects must go hand in hand, and that the development of consciousness would accelerate the creation of the economic base.

Moral incentives are the vehicle best suited for molding a new consciousness. This is put well in Fidel's main report to the First Congress of the Communist Party of Cuba:

> Under socialism there is no system that can substitute for politics, ideology, or the consciousness of the people. The factors that determine efficiency in a capitalist economy are different and can never operate under socialism, where the political aspect, the ideological aspect, and the moral aspect continue to be the main and decisive factors.[189]

In a meeting of the Ministry of Industry, Che stated:

> We should not fall into the illusion of viewing moral incentives as the centerpiece of the budgetary finance system. Its centerpiece is the sum total of its activities, among which the organizational capacity to lead and simultaneously develop consciousness is fundamental. And the key to developing consciousness—above all at the level of the masses, at the most general level—is the combination of material incentives, correctly applied, and moral incentives, with increasing stress on the latter as conditions improve. . . .[190]
>
> Discussion of "moral incentives" is becoming the centerpiece of all questions. But moral incentive is not in itself the centerpiece of the question—far from it. Moral incentives are the form, shall we say, the predominant form that should be adopted for incentives in this stage of building socialism. But to say that it is the predominant form means that it is not the only form.[191]

Having set forth Che's views on the matter, we will anticipate our conclusions and state that what is necessary during the transition period is an intelligent and revolutionary combination of moral and material incentives.

III. Emulation

In developing a model of economic management, Che viewed socialist emulation as a fundamental element in the structure of the entire system. As against the competition generated by the law of value, Che counterposed a fraternal competition based on socialist comradeship that favored emulation.

The Cuban revolution was characterized from the outset by broad mass participation. The style of leadership and work of Fidel and the vanguard in Cuba has always been based on participation by the masses in complex as well as simple decisions.

Che worked to establish the same approach in the economic sphere, in the process of laying the material and technical basis for socialism. He gave careful attention to ensuring that emulation did not become cold and formal. He constantly reviewed the system to ensure that its mechanisms did not become obstacles to the goals being pursued. He was interested not only in the system's concepts and procedures, but also in how well they were grasped by the workers. During his visits to workplaces in the production and service sectors, Che saw firsthand how revolutionary leadership was put into practice on the shop floor. And he found an ideal vehicle for this in emulation.

Che was one of the first to promote socialist emulation in our country. He personally helped organize it in the Ministry of Industry, involving other groups of workers who were officially attached to other ministries or to the Central Organization of Cuban Trade Unions.

He organized and participated in dozens of assemblies that marked the conclusion of emulation campaigns, handing out certificates and awards to vanguard workers and groups of workers. In working meetings of the Ministry of Industry, he discussed the concepts that should govern emulation and its mechanisms. He saw emulation as a magnificent incentive mechanism that linked the production of goods with the creation of communist consciousness. Below are some of Che's remarks at various meetings of workers:

> Emulation has to fulfill the great task of mobilizing the masses.[192]
>
> Every worker should take an interest in emulation. Every worker should understand the importance of the results of emulation, which is to produce more and better, increase production, increase productivity, improve the quality of products, and save raw materials. . . .
>
> Building socialism is based on the work of the masses, on the capacity of the masses to be able to organize themselves to better guide industry, agriculture, and the country's economy. It is based on the capacity of the masses to increase their knowledge day by day . . . on their capacity to create more products for all our people; on their capacity to see the future that is coming closer—closer in historical terms, not in the life of any one man—and to enter onto the road toward that future with enthusiasm.[193]
>
> Emulation must be the fundamental basis for developing socialist consciousness and for making gains in production and productivity.
>
> What is emulation? Emulation is simply a competition directed toward the noblest of aims, which is to improve the functioning of each work center, each enterprise, each unit, and place it in the front ranks of building socialism. . . . For this, we must necessarily turn to the masses. There is practically no need for any force other than the motor that the leadership by the masses provides. All we provide is technical help—a way to evaluate the results of emulation—so that different undertakings can be assessed in terms of common criteria and thus compared with one another.
>
> At the same time, when we organize emulation, we also have to establish incentives. This means moral incentives, such as those that individually or collectively recognize workers in a workplace as the

best among the best. It also means material incentives suited to the moment in which we live.[194]

Emulation is a fraternal competition. What is its purpose? To get everyone to increase production. It is a weapon for increasing production. But it is not only that. It is also a tool for deepening the consciousness of the masses. The two should always go together.

We have always stressed this dual aspect of the construction of socialism. Building socialism is neither a matter of work alone nor of consciousness alone. It combines work and consciousness—expanding the production of material goods through work and developing consciousness. Emulation has to fulfill both of these goals, both of these functions.[195]

These comments by Che also show how, in his day-to-day practice, he made no distinction between the technical work of managing the economy and the task of promoting the political and ideological development of the masses.

CHAPTER 10

Problems of leadership, organization, and management of

social production under the budgetary finance system

I n the pages above, a number of themes that express, directly or indirectly, the importance Che attached to the principles, functions, and methods of organization and management have been taken up.

Che's theoretical and practical work from 1959 through 1967[196] in the process of eliminating capitalism and creating a socialist system in Cuba led him to conceive and develop the budgetary finance system. The budgetary finance system in turn was made up of subsystems that included economic planning, organizing and setting production norms, accounting and costs, finances, prices, controls and supervision, incentive mechanisms, administrative and technical personnel policies, skill training, scientific and technical development, information, statistics, and workers' participation in management.

After he became involved in organizing and managing the economy, Che took up other questions as well. These included the struggle against bureaucracy, the establishment of socialist economic institutions and the relations among them, relations between the party and the state, relations between management and the unions, use of the principle of democratic centralism, social-psychological studies of organization and management, and the use of computers and mathematical-economic methods in socialist enterprises.

In this section the sole aim is to briefly indicate the importance Che assigned to establishing controls and supervision.

Beginning in October 1959, when he was named head of the Department of Industrialization of the National Institute of Agrarian Reform, and later, when he took charge of the National Bank and the Ministry of Industry, Che took on the task of developing a subsystem that would subject all levels of management and administration to strict controls. It can safely be said that he was the first to establish a system of rigorous controls and supervision in the tumultuous first five years of our revolution. In one sense, the technical side of the budgetary finance system emerged from, was shaped by, and owes its establishment to this subsystem of controls and supervision.

Che conscientiously studied, among other materials, the writings of Marx, Engels, and Lenin on the science of organizing, supervising, and managing social production. In Marx and Engels he found the main laws that govern the transition from capitalism to communism, the general characteristics of socialism and communism, as well as certain fundamental principles, some of which have been noted.

Che made a detailed study of Lenin's works. The leader of the October revolution was the first Marxist to take up in practice the question of organizing and managing a socialist society. In addition to learning the Leninist principles of organization and management, Che studied and adopted the best of the techniques that the capitalist monopolies had instituted in their Cuban subsidiaries.

The subsystem created by Che stretched from the national level to the smallest establishment. The way in which he implemented it in the Ministry of Industry is worthy of study. "Without controls, we cannot build socialism," Che said.[197]

Che believed the budgetary finance system had to be based, in part, on subsystems of general accounting and cost accounting. This was needed to ensure the best possible management of our enterprises and the entire state apparatus. Accurate accounting and rigorous cost analysis would help make the best use of our material, labor, and financial resources.

> Costs concern us greatly today; we have to work on this relentlessly. When prices are kept at fixed levels, costs become our basic tool for evaluating the

management of units or enterprises. And once the cost has been determined—whether figured on the basis of the overall costs of the production process, or the cost per unit of output—any administrator can quickly detect problems even of a technological character.

These might include, for example, excessive consumption of steam; defects in the bottling machine that is perhaps ejecting too many bottle caps; a machine that might be moving the bottles before they've been filled; or an automatic scale that puts too much of a product in a container. Any of these things can be detected simply through an analysis of costs.

This does not mean we do not still need all the types of technical controls, but simply that we need a well-executed analysis of costs, something that will enable the director of any enterprise or the administrator of any unit to master completely his area of responsibility.[198]

The great importance accorded by Che to accounting and cost analysis led him to pay attention to the details necessary to guarantee the accuracy of the data recorded and collected. He took an interest not only in technical matters, but also in the personnel who worked in the economic apparatus. He thought those responsible for keeping financial records in a factory or any state-managed enterprise should be compañeros of absolute discipline. They are the steadfast guardians of the nation's property, including against the directors of enterprises.

The problem is that people are not perfect, far from it. We have to improve systems of controls to detect the very first infraction, because the first one leads to all the others. People might be very good the first time. But when, through indiscipline, they commit the error of taking something for personal use, intending to replace it in two or three days, this can then spread to the point of their becoming thieves, becoming traitors, falling increasingly into crime.[199]

In the Ministry of Industry's leadership bodies, in the enterprises, in his regular visits to production units, in meet-

ings with unions and workers, Che used every opportunity
to stress the importance of organization, controls, and management.

Rigorous controls are needed throughout the entire
organizational process. These controls begin at the
base, in the production unit. They require statistics that
one can feel confident are exact, as well as good habits
in using statistical data. It's necessary to know how to
use statistics. These are not just cold figures—although
that's what they are for the majority of administrators
today, with the possible exception of output figures. On
the contrary, these figures contain within them an
entire series of secrets that must be unveiled. Learning
to interpret these secrets is the task of the day.

Controls should also be applied to everything related
to inventories in a unit or enterprise: the quantity on
hand of raw materials, or, let's say, of spare parts or
finished goods. All this should be accounted for
precisely and kept up to date. This kind of accounting
must never be allowed to slip. It is the sole guarantee
that we can carry on work with minimal chance of
interruption, depending on the distance our supplies
have to travel.

To conduct inventory on a scientific basis, we also
have to keep track of the stock of basic means of
production. For example, we must take inventory of all
the machinery a factory possesses, so that this too can
be managed centrally. This would give a clear idea of a
machine's depreciation—that is, the period of time over
which it will wear out, the moment at which it should
be replaced. We will also find out if a piece of
machinery is being underutilized and should be moved
to some other place. . . .

We have to make an increasingly detailed analysis of
costs, so that we will be able to take advantage of the
last particle of human labor that is being wasted.
Socialism is the rational allocation of human labor. . . .

You can't manage the economy if you can't analyze

it, and you can't analyze it if there is no accurate data. And there is no accurate data without a system of collecting reliable data, without a statistical system with men accustomed to collecting data and transforming it into numbers. This is an essential task.[200]

In the sections above we have noted the important role Che assigned to finances. Stressing the importance of employing accurate financial data in implementing controls, Che stated:

Financial discipline is one of the most important aspects of managing an enterprise or a factory. . . . The books must be kept up to date. This includes expenditures and income, all questions relating to contracts—for example, a negotiated adjustment concerning the delivery of a defective product. All these things are part of financial discipline, of financial controls.[201]

Che did not view the task of implementing controls as limited solely to various administrative bodies. He believed it should be accompanied by careful efforts by the workers, the unions, and the party. Che believed building socialism and communism involved production, organization, and consciousness. It is not just an administrative, technical, and economic task. It is also an ideological and political task.

Che believed, like Fidel, that we must try to produce more goods, more efficiently, with better quality and—at the same time—to produce the new man who will build the new socialist society, the man who produces, leads, checks, and supervises. To do that, controls are necessary to produce with efficiency and prevent man from being corrupted.

CHAPTER 11

Cadre policy: political leadership and the development of administrative and technical personnel

D URING THE FIRST YEARS of the revolution, what was the situation in terms of cadres to help lead the reorganization of the economy, society, and the state?

It is not necessary to dwell on the characteristics of our revolution, on the original way, with strokes of spontaneity, that the transition took place from a revolution of national liberation to a socialist revolution. Nor on the accumulation of rapidly passing stages in the course of its development, led by the same people who participated in the initial epic of the attack on the Moncada garrison, proceeding through the *Granma* landing, and culminating in the declaration of the socialist character of the Cuban revolution. New sympathizers, cadres, and organizations joined the weak organizational structure of the early movement, until it became the flood of people that today characterizes our revolution.

When it became clear that a new social class had definitively taken command in Cuba, we also saw the great limitations that would be faced in the exercise of state power because of the conditions in which we found the state. There were no cadres to carry out the enormous number of jobs that had to be filled in the state apparatus, in the political organization, and on the entire economic front. . . .

But with the acceleration of the process beginning

with the nationalization of the U.S. enterprises and later of the large Cuban enterprises, a real hunger for administrative technicians came about. On the other hand, an urgent need was felt for production technicians because of the exodus of many who were attracted by better positions offered by the imperialist companies in other parts of Latin America or in the United States itself. While engaged in these organizational tasks, the political apparatus had to make intense efforts to provide ideological attention to the masses who had joined the revolution eager to learn.[202]

In these lines, Che emphasized the urgency of the situation in those days: cadres forged in struggle without sufficient knowledge to become administrators; the accelerating confrontation with the Yankees and its consequences; the exodus to the United States and Latin America of middle-level personnel with training in the theory and practice of management; people taking on responsibilities that until then had been off-limits to them. No pool of trained administrators existed outside the imperialist corporations.

The need for cadres became one of the revolution's biggest and most difficult problems. Four kinds of cadres were needed simultaneously: political, military, economic, and administrative.

Cadre policy—based on Che's ideas of what a revolutionary cadre should be—forms another subsystem in the budgetary finance system. This is a question of fundamental importance because of its multiple and complex connections with all the internal mechanisms that enable the revolution to develop and advance.

Here, in outline form, are some of the characteristics Che thought a cadre should possess, cultivate, and develop, in order to assume leadership responsibilities in the Cuban revolution.

A. Leadership by example
This is an extremely important quality to Che. In the ceremony where he presented Certificates of Communist Work

to outstanding workers who had fulfilled their moral duty, he
noted:

> We try to be faithful to the principle that leaders
> must set an example, as Fidel has said so often.
> We have also come to this gathering, along with
> Compañero Borrego,[203] to receive our certificates. This
> is not a childish gesture and it is not a gesture of
> demagogy. It is simply the necessary demonstration
> that we—who constantly talk about the urgent need to
> create a new consciousness to develop the country so it
> can defend itself against the enormous difficulties it
> has and the great dangers that threaten it—can show
> our certificates, that we are conscious of and true to
> what we say, and that we therefore have the right to
> ask something more of our people.[204]

B. The leader must view work as a human necessity

> The leader who goes to work expecting to put in eight
> hours and, if he can, wastes one of them daydreaming
> about quitting time, is not a leader. He has no leadership
> qualities and is of no use now or in the future. Tomorrow
> this kind of man will disappear, because under
> communism this type of control mechanism will
> disappear. They will have to disappear. Such mechanisms
> for checking on whether or not a man works won't exist,
> since work will become a human necessity.[205]

C. Spirit of sacrifice

> The idea that socialism will be made without anybody
> making any sacrifices, in the midst of capitalist reaction,
> is a fairy tale. It's impossible, because someone has to
> sacrifice. In order for us to continue developing,
> everyone has to sacrifice something he might otherwise
> have had. Above all, those in the vanguard today must
> at all times be making sacrifices, until this becomes a
> way of life. At the risk of appearing to go a bit

overboard, I'd like to take as an example someone who is constantly involved in work, who has made work the only thing in his life.

This person does not go for a swim in the summer, or to the movies, because he is truly interested in his work, he is involved in his work, and sees it as something much more interesting than a momentary distraction. What is involved here is actually a choice between two distractions, between two views of life. After a while it's really no longer even a choice, it's simply a way of life.

We don't need to go to the extreme of saying that we all have to become people who never go anywhere, or who become bookworms and office mice. But even for those in the vanguard it will at first take a powerful effort to work this way. Later, however, it must become something natural, as work becomes a habit. The moment must come when work is no longer a burdensome obligation, but a genuinely creative act.[206]

D. An austere life

Of course there are dangers in the present situation, and not only that of dogmatism, not only that of freezing the ties with the masses midway in the great task. There is also the danger of the weaknesses we can fall into. If a man thinks that dedicating his entire life to the revolution means that in return he should not be distracted by such worries as that his child lacks certain things, that his children's shoes are worn out, that his family lacks some necessity, then with this reasoning he opens his mind to infection by the germs of future corruption.

In our case, we have maintained that our children should have or should go without those things that the children of the common man have or go without, and that our families should understand this and struggle for it to be that way. The revolution is made through man, but man must forge his revolutionary spirit day by day.[207]

E. Human sensitivity

I'll tell you one thing, when I visit a factory I systematically encounter a large number of criticisms of all kinds. Some of these criticisms really indicate there is something in the apparatus as a whole that has to be corrected. In one visit to a shoe factory in Matanzas, a worker told me, "Look how I'm covered with dust. I told them I needed a fan, some way of fixing this problem, or else I'll have to change jobs. Look at me. My asthma is killing me."

So I spoke with the head of the factory and said to him: "Hey, take a look at this poor fellow. These things cause asthma. A man with asthma can't stay where there's dust like this around. This is barbaric. It can't continue."

"But he can't change jobs."

"Well, either change his job or get him a fan."

"But the thing is, he doesn't really have asthma; he's got tuberculosis."

How on earth could something like this happen? What a lack of human sensitivity![208]

F. Constant and permanent contact with the masses

We must be in constant and permanent contact with the masses. In addition, compañeros, we must take part in physical labor, which is not only very good for us but also puts us in closer contact with the masses. It cuts across the somewhat natural tendencies of a man who sits here in this chair, especially if he inherited the office of a former big industrialist and has air conditioning—or at least one thermos with hot coffee and another with cold water—and thus has a certain tendency to keep his door shut so the hot air won't bother him. This type of leader is of no use. We have to get rid of them.[209]

G. Continual upgrading of skills

The continual upgrading of skills at all levels is now a question of fundamental importance. This is one of the country's essential tasks. . . . We have to understand that in the age of technology a sixth-grade education will be the equivalent of illiteracy.[210] This is not yet the case. But in the years to come a high school diploma will be the minimum requirement for an administrator not to be considered an illiterate.

In addition—and this is directed to all administrators who are listening now, or who have the misfortune to read or find out about this tomorrow—we are going to continue in every way to make you study. You are going to continue studying as long as you are administrators.[211]

H. Collective discussion and individual accountability in decision making

Some time ago an article was written on the tasks of the revolutionary administrator. These are concepts you are all more or less familiar with, so I won't repeat them. But there is one concept that is very important— the concept of collective discussion. This we've insisted on, along with accountability for decisions, individual accountability.

Whenever you are about to make a decision in accordance with the guidelines of the ministry or enterprise in charge, you should always keep these two things in mind. You must know how to distinguish between these two functions, compañeros.

You must know what should be discussed, what should be learned from the discussion, and how to discuss intelligently to gather all the ideas necessary to make a decision.

But this decision, be it good or bad, is going to be

your responsibility. Whatever happens in any
workplace, you will be the ones held ultimately
accountable. So you have to learn how to work
collectively, but with a concept of leadership.[212]

I. Administrators as political cadres: the ongoing need for
ideological and political development

Some time ago, I had to make a public correction of
something I had said (although of course people don't
remember much of what you say). At a congress of the
Central Organization of Cuban Trade Unions I said
something that I now consider totally absurd. I said,
"The administrator should not be, nor is he, a political
leader in the way that you are; he is an administrative
leader." This statement is not only absurd, it goes
against the principles we defend in the budgetary
finance system. We have to transform the administrator
into a political-administrative cadre with the qualities
of a leader.[213]

Throughout the writings and speeches of Fidel, Raúl
[Castro], Che, and other leaders of the revolution, another series of leadership qualities are pointed to: leadership means
to guide and to educate; to possess and cultivate modesty, sim-
plicity, courage, firmness, and honesty; it means to be both
disciplined and combative; to know how to respond correctly
when errors are pointed out.

The revolution opened a number of schools for administrators to train cadres, technically and culturally, to manage the
nationalized capitalist enterprises. To help make up for the
administrators' lack of experience and knowledge, Che ordered
the publication of a looseleaf manual for administrators of factories and workshops. He personally took part in drawing it
up and gave careful attention to the periodic revising of obso-
lete sections. [See Appendix.]

Both in its structure and in its contents, this manual provided the administrator with the knowledge necessary for his
work. Its pages reflect the nature and depth of Che's thinking,

his incomparable way of uniting theory and practice, his way of subjecting theory to the test of practice, and, in the tradition of Lenin and Fidel, his genuine enrichment and development of theory.

CHAPTER 12

Conclusions

AT THE RISK OF repetition, I would like by way of conclusion to summarize the ideas put forward in this book.

Studying Che's economic thought makes it possible to grasp in a fully rounded way the importance of the dialectical combination of three factors: the inviolable general laws that govern building a communist society and economy, the experiences of the sister socialist countries, and concrete national or regional characteristics. To fail to take into account the first of these factors would be to fall into idealism and voluntarism. To fail to take into account the latter two would be to sink into dogmatic, antidialectical ignorance.

Socialism is not a finished, perfect system, in which all the details and answers are known. Our system has flaws, shortcomings, and aspects requiring further development. In the economic, political, and ideological realm, Che sought solutions, on the basis of socialist principles, to concrete problems of establishing socialism in Cuba, and to the flaws that emerged in our system. Following Fidel's guidelines, Che sought "socialist formulas rather than capitalist formulas to solve problems, because before we realize it capitalist formulas can begin to corrupt us and contaminate us. . . ."[214]

In his writings and speeches on the transition period, Che synthesized two elements that appear inseparably linked, as a unified whole, in the works of Marx and Engels: economic production, and the mode by which economic production is carried out—that is, the production and reproduction of the social relations men establish inside and outside the process of production.

Che's originality lies in having defended the principles of Marxist-Leninist economic theory regarding the period of transition to communism, and doing so from the standpoint of the new conditions that emerged from the social, economic, and political system he lived under.

There is a dialectical link between the model of economic management in socialist society and the forms of social consciousness that accompany it. The economic relations that emerge from the structures of the management system determine and shape the possibilities for developing social consciousness. The effectiveness of the transitional model *cannot* therefore be evaluated solely on the basis of how well it maximizes use of the resources at its disposal. Nor can it be measured solely by the quantitative amount of revenues and profits obtained by its enterprises. Instead, it should be evaluated according to its capacity to harmonize strategic and tactical, social and economic, objectives.

The budgetary finance system created by Che "is part of a general conception of the development of building socialism and must therefore be studied as a whole."[215] For Che:

> A socialist economy without communist moral values does not interest me. We fight poverty, but we also fight alienation. One of the fundamental aims of Marxism is to eliminate material interest, the factor of "individual self-interest," and profit from man's psychological motivations.
>
> Marx was concerned with both economic facts and their reflection in the mind, which he called a "fact of consciousness." If communism neglects facts of consciousness, it can serve as a method of distribution but it will no longer express revolutionary moral values.[216]

Che thought the transformation of human consciousness should begin in the opening phase of the period of transition from capitalism to communism. He thought creation of the new social consciousness required as much effort as that devoted to developing socialism's material base. He saw consciousness as an active element, a material force, an engine for developing the material and technical base.

He believed socialist society had to be built by men who were fighting to escape from the bourgeois muck, not by subjecting them to the motivations of the past. The old and new had to be joined together in a dialectical way, on the basis of socialist principles.

As a revolutionary economist, Che never lost sight of the fact that under socialism the formation of a new type of human relations would have to be the central objective of every effort. All other factors should be judged positive or negative to the degree they advance or hinder this process. Any other approach would run the grave risk that the need to overcome centuries of accumulated poverty might lead the revolutionary vanguard to make advances in production the sole central goal, losing sight of the revolution's very reason for being. Seeking purely economic gains could lead to the application of methods that produce short-term economic results at the expense of mortgaging the revolution's future, through steady erosion of the process of developing consciousness. In this regard, Fidel has stated:

> The way I see it, in the development of communist society wealth and the material base must grow hand in hand with consciousness, because it can even happen that as wealth increases consciousness diminishes. . . . I'm convinced that it's not only wealth or the development of the material base that will develop consciousness—far from it. There are some countries much richer than ours—there are some. I don't want to make comparisons of any kind; that would not be correct. But we do know of revolutionary countries where wealth has advanced more than consciousness, leading even to counterrevolutionary problems and things of that sort. But you can have a great deal of consciousness without much wealth. . . .[217]

With a clear vision of these problems, Che carefully selected the elements that would make up the budgetary finance system, including its institutional forms, controls, and mechanisms of motivation. Ninety miles from the shores of imperialism, socialism did not have the luxury of failing to see the forest for the trees and taking the wrong road.[218] For Che

> . . . communism is a phenomenon of consciousness and not solely a phenomenon of production. We cannot arrive at communism through the simple mechanical accumulation of quantities of goods made available to the people. By doing that we would get somewhere, to be sure, to some peculiar form of socialism.
>
> But what Marx defined as communism, what is aspired to in general as communism, cannot be attained if man is not conscious. That is, if he does not have a new consciousness toward society. . . .[219]

For Che "productivity, more production, consciousness—these are the foundations upon which the new society can be built."[220]

Without doubt, one of Che's main theoretical merits is his understanding of the complex relations between the material base and the superstructure in the socialist transition. The way in which each of the new economic structures and institutions influence, express, and condition men's motivations is a vital aspect to be studied in any work on the transition period. Che's understanding of the relationship between the base and superstructure made it possible for him to take a revolutionary position in regard to the socialist economy. He understood that economic rationality per se was not a foolproof barometer of the revolutionary transformation of society.

Che thought that preserving and developing the economic laws and categories of capitalism would perpetuate the social relations of bourgeois production and, along with them, the habits of thought and the motivations of capitalist society. This would occur even if those laws and categories had been fundamentally changed under socialist forms. This view of Che's was not the product of dogmatic extremism, nor of fear of capitalist "contagion." At the same time that he vehemently denounced the dangers implicit in the attempt by some economists to view the socialist economy through the categories of capitalist political economy, he also envisioned the possibility of taking over capitalism's latest economic and technical advances in controls, organization, and accounting.

But Che was not an advocate of using the categories of capitalist political economy—such as market, interest, direct material incentive, and profit. He did not think it was possible to use the elements of capitalism to construct socialism without really changing its meaning. Taking that road would lead to a hybrid system requiring new concessions to capitalist economic levers and, therefore, to new steps backward.

In this regard we should also note Che's insistence that terms taken from capitalist political economy not be used to describe or express the phenomena of the transition period. He stressed this not only because of the confusion the use of such categories brings into analysis, but also because it sets a logic in motion that distorts Marxist thought.

The budgetary finance system was the way in which Cuban industry was organized in a very early phase of the socialist revolution. In putting the system together, Che drew upon:

• advanced accounting techniques that permitted more effective controls and more efficient centralized management; also, studies and practical application of the methods of centralization and decentralization used by the capitalist monopolies;

• computer techniques applied to the economy and to management, and the application of mathematical methods to the economy;

• techniques of programming and controlling production;

• budgetary techniques as instruments of planning and supervision through finances;

• administrative techniques of implementing economic controls;

• the experiences of the socialist countries.

Planning marks humanity's first opportunity to control economic forces. It characterizes and defines the entire period of transition and of communist society as a whole. Che thought it was a mistake to reduce planning to an economic notion; he felt this twisted and limited its possibilities from the very outset. In Che's view, the economic plan encompasses *material* relations as a whole (in the way Marx used the term). For that reason, planning should include and combine two elements:

• creating the foundations for developing the new society's economy, together with systems of regulation and controls;

• creating a new type of human relations, a new man.

The effectiveness of the plan cannot be judged solely by how it improves economic management, nor, therefore, by the economic goods society possesses or the profits made in the production process. The plan should be judged by its potential for improving economic management in terms of the objective being pursued: building a communist society. That is, it should be evaluated both according to how well it helps the economic apparatus create the material basis for the new society; and, at the same time, how well it contributes to transforming the habits and values of the men who participate in the productive process and to creating and instilling the new communist values.

Che rejected a dominant role for the law of value in the period of the transition to communism. It is one thing to acknowledge the existence during the transition period of a series of capitalist relations that have necessarily survived. This explains, for example, the continued existence of the law of value, given its character as an economic law, that is, as an expression of certain economic tendencies. But the period of the transition to communism, even in its earliest moments, does not have to be dominated by the law of value and the commodity categories implied by its use.

There was a contrasting point of view, however, that argued that in managing a socialist economy it was possible to make use of both the law of value and the other categories that necessarily go along with it. Some not only favored using the law of value and monetary-commodity relations among enterprises in the state sector during the transition period, but went so far as to affirm the necessity of developing capitalist relations as a vehicle for reaching communist society.

Che rejected this point of view. Free rein for the law of value in the period of transition to communism implies the impossibility of fundamentally restructuring social relations. It means perpetuating the "umbilical cord" that under capitalism binds alienated man to society. It produces at best a hybrid system in which deep-going change in the social nature of man and society will never be brought about.

What relation should exist between planning and the categories and mechanisms through which the plan is expressed? Che's position on this important question was as follows: the continued existence of commodity production for some time in the transition period does not mean that the plan must function on the basis of capitalist mechanisms, nor that it has to be expressed through capitalist categories.

> Why *develop*? We understand that the capitalist categories are retained for a time and that the length of this time cannot be determined beforehand. But the characteristics of the transition period are those of a society throwing off its old bonds in order to arrive quickly at the new stage.
>
> The tendency must be, in our opinion, to eliminate as vigorously as possible the old categories, including the market, money, and, therefore, the lever of material interest—or, to put it better, to eliminate the conditions for their existence. Otherwise, one would have to assume that the task of building socialism in a backward society is something in the nature of a historical accident and that its leaders, in order to make up for the "mistake," should set about consolidating all the categories inherent in the intermediate society. All that would remain as foundations of the new society would be the distribution of income according to work and the tendency toward elimination of man's exploitation of man. These things by themselves seem inadequate to bring about the gigantic change in consciousness necessary to tackle the transition. That change must take place through the multifaceted action of all the new relations, through education and socialist morality—with the individualistic way of thinking that direct

material incentives instill in consciousness acting as a brake on the development of man as a social being.[221]

Money is a product of commodity relations and, therefore, expresses certain definite relations of production. It is a social category historically conditioned by those relations. It is not possible to destroy commodity relations overnight. They continue to exist in the transition period. The length of time they continue to exist depends on the rhythm of development of the new relations of production and on the policy that is adopted toward them. But no matter how long or short this period may be, these relations have to be combated. The tendency should be for them to steadily wither away until they have totally disappeared.

Of the five functions of money under commodity production analyzed by Marx, only two should exist in the transition period. The first is as money of account, that is, as a measure of value. The second is money as a means of circulation and/or distribution between the state and the remaining small private producers, and between the state and individual consumers. Che's conviction that money could function as money of account was reinforced, among other things, by the modern techniques of economic organization, controls, management, and analysis that had been developed by the imperialist system.

The budgetary finance system gives finance a different role and content. It ceases to be the mechanism for reviewing, directing, analyzing, and organizing the economy. Financial compulsion is replaced by technical-administrative compulsion.

The budgetary finance system views enterprises as parts of a whole, of one big enterprise—the state. No enterprise has, or needs, its own funds. The enterprises maintain a separate bank account for deposits and for withdrawals.

The banking system will disappear, over the long term, in the period of transition to communism. It will survive as long as commodity relations continue, because "it is dependent on commodity relations of production, however developed they may be."[222] The fact that the budgetary finance system encourages centralization does not necessarily mean that the banking system will assume the primary responsibility for the state's accounting and economic review, nor that it will dictate the country's economic policy.

Under the budgetary finance system the banking system does not grant loans, much less gather dividends by collecting interest. When the state bank collects interest from state enterprises for funds advanced, it is charging for the use of money that the bank itself does not own—a function typical of a private bank. The fact that this may be done according to an economic plan, and that the rate of interest is not set spontaneously as under capitalism, does not make the slightest difference. Socialist banks carry out a fetishistic operation when they lend out money at interest. They are lending money that belongs to another enterprise. At bottom, it is the worker who is actually making the loan.

Starting from the premises noted above, Che looked into the mechanisms of setting prices. It became immediately evident to him that if market methods were used to set prices, the result would be to pursue an equilibrium between supply and demand in each product or commodity, ensuring a margin of profit for the enterprise. In practice the plan would yield to the law of value, not the other way around. The market would continue to operate on a competitive capitalist basis, only now with the inconvenience of also being the victim of state interference in its administration and management. In a centralized system, on the other hand, other solutions are possible. The stimulation of production through prices, as in a market economy, is not among the methods used by the budgetary finance system.

Che was among the first to denounce the injustice of unequal exchange and to advocate a fundamental revision of the international economic order. Che was the exponent, in that early stage of the revolution, of Fidel's ideas that have today developed into his proposals to cancel the foreign debt and establish a new international economic order.

Che understood that forging a new consciousness would be the result of a steady process of transforming the social structures from which ideas and attitudes inevitably arise. He rec-

ognized that the transformation of social relations of production and the correct selection of motivational levers—more
than simple appeals to consciousness—offered the best possibilities for transforming man. That's why he articulated a system based, among other things, on these three pillars: the wage
system, incentives, and emulation.

Che believed the wage system should be based on the principle of payment according to the quantity and quality of
work. At the same time, it should also help pave the way for
the communist values that will emerge in the revolutionary
process, encourage the use of moral incentives, and make
use of the material incentives inherited from capitalism in a
way that promotes their elimination rather than their development.

In collaboration with the Ministry of Labor, Che drew up a
wage system that put an end to the chaos that was inherited
from capitalism and deepened during the first three years of
the revolution. In doing so, Che applied Marxist-Leninist principles and developed them into formulas appropriate to the
period of the transition to socialism. In the period following
April 1965, the wage system that Che had created was subjected to a series of modifications that, combined with the failure to observe some of his provisions, ended up wrecking it.

Incentives comprise a part of Che's budgetary finance system that is generally either unknown, misunderstood, or mistakenly identified with what happened after Che had left Cuba.
Some essential aspects of the incentive methods proposed by
Che can be summed up as follows:

• The search for incentive mechanisms different from those
used by capitalism is based on the recognition that socialism
is not only a matter of economics but also of consciousness.
Personal interest should be a reflection of social interest. To
use personal interest as the main lever to increase production
is to retreat in the face of difficulties, encouraging capitalist
ideology.

• The slow and complex ideological transformation during
the transition period poses for a time a contradiction between
production and consciousness. During this period the habits
of thinking instilled by capitalism (personal ambition, selfish-

ness, and so forth) weigh negatively on productive effort. Change in ownership, or the elimination of private ownership in the means of production, takes but an instant. A much longer period is needed for people's consciousness to adjust to the new order of things.

• Both material and moral incentives should be used in an intelligent and balanced way. The process should lead to the withering away rather than suppression of material incentives. Putting forward a policy of moral incentives does not mean a total negation of material incentives. The point is to reduce their field of operation—through intensive ideological work rather than bureaucratic fiat.

• For a period of time material incentives must continue to be used. It is necessary to seek out the least harmful methods, including those that contribute to their own self-destruction. Che studied the possible options and implemented some of them. The transition period requires an intelligent and revolutionary combination of moral and material incentives.

Che viewed socialist emulation as a fundamental element in the structure of the entire system. As against competition generated by the law of value, Che counterposed fraternal competition based on the socialist comradeship engendered by emulation. Che was one of the originators of socialist emulation in Cuba. He saw emulation as an ideal vehicle for linking the system with the masses. In day-to-day work, Che made no distinction between the technical work of managing the economy and the work involved in the political and ideological advancement of the masses.

"Without controls, we cannot build socialism," Che said.[223] In leadership meetings of the Ministry of Industry, in regular visits to enterprises and production units, in meetings with unions and workers, Che never let pass an opportunity to stress the importance of organization, controls, and management.

Che was the driving force behind the implementation of planning in Cuba. He was the author of methods of establishing controls and supervision, and the originator of a system of training economic cadres that is well worth studying.

Che directed the industrial sector and paved the way for

implementing the socialist system of production. It was he who first organized Cuban industry under the principles of socialist management, applying these principles down to the level of the smallest workplace or production unit.

Che taught workers and leadership cadres the principles of socialist management, in this way applying the ideas of Fidel.

Havana
1969–1986

APPENDIX

Manual for administrators

To give the reader an overall picture of the manual Che helped prepare for administrators of factories and workshops, included below is most of its table of contents.

Section 1. Introduction

1. Table of contents
2. Aims of the manual
3. How the manual works
4. Responsibility for carrying out what is set down in the manual
5. Inspection procedures to check application and fulfillment of the guidelines in the manual
6. Compilation of administrators' suggestions for improving the manual
7. The planned economy
12. Selection from basic regulations governing Ministry of Industry provincial delegations
14. Basic regulations and organizational chart of the enterprise
15. Basic regulations and organizational chart of the administrative unit and production unit
Note: The directors of enterprises and institutes and the administrators of administrative or production units will place copies of regulations governing their enterprises and units in the spaces reserved for sections 14 and 15.
16. Basic regulations governing the administrative or production unit

17. Administrative councils and commissions: their functions, character, and objectives
18. The director
19. The administrator

Section 2. Fundamental concepts

2. Cost analysis
3. Economic analysis
4. Production assemblies
9. Training of administrative and technical personnel
10. Principles of socialist management
11. Discipline on the job
12. Financial discipline
15. Socialist emulation
17. Dangers and harm of liberalism
19. Productivity
21. Simplifying administrative work—methods of analysis and approach
22. Scope of application of labor law and violations of discipline on the job
24. Continuing technical, economic, and political education for the administrator
25. Key tasks of the year

Section 3. Plans: Technical-economic, operational, industrial perspectives, technical development

1. Technical-economic plan
2. Operational plan
3. Industrial perspectives plan
4. Technical development plan
5. Introduction to industrial maintenance

Section 4. Functions of the administrator; duties, rights, and responsibilities of administrative personnel and workers

1. Functions of the administrator
2. Duties, rights, and responsibilities of administrative

personnel in administrative or production units
3. Duties, rights, and responsibilities of workers in administrative or production units
5. Matters the administrator should personally approve
6. Matters the administrator should delegate
7. Matters the administrator should personally supervise
8. Levels of decision making and their relationships
9. On the need to find and select future administrative and technical cadres

Section 5. Technical-economic management by the administrator

1. Inventory control: fundamental task of the Ministry of Industry
2. International advances in technology and in new products
3. Productive capacity or potential of the administrative or production unit
7. The arbitration commission
10. Ongoing efforts to economize and reduce production costs
11. Investments
12. Fundamental indicators for technical-economic controls
17. Visits to workshops and other organizational divisions of administrative or production units
18. Bank accounts
19. Inspections—reports

Section 6. Qualities required of an administrator

1. Personal qualities an administrator should cultivate
2. Faults an administrator should overcome
3. The example the administrator should set
4. Proper use of the workday
6. Character development

Section 7. Organization, effective methods of work, and techniques of administration

1. The direction of work

2. Organization and methods of work by leaders
3. Organization of production flow
4. Glossary of terms used in organization
5. Guidelines—decision-making methods
6. Use of graphs in statistical reports
7. Art of delegating authority
8. Guidelines for delegating authority
9. Conventional formula of "1 + 1"
10. Principles of organization
11. Principles of leadership
12. Central administrative office
13. Keeping track of matters requiring study, reply, supervision, or decision
17. Statistics—concept and use
18. Methods of leadership in administration

Section 8. Training

2. Training of office managers and/or secretaries
3. Minimum study guide and reading list for the administrator
4. Planning, implementation, and supervision of training in the administrative or production unit—the education commission

Section 9. Technical development

2. Quality control
3. Inventions and innovations
4. Weights and measures
5. Technical standards
6. Development of machinery

Section 10. Communications

1. Communications
2. Minutes of meetings—general recommendations
3. Correspondence
5. Bulletin boards, notices on blackboards, etc.—proper use

6. The telephone
7. Organization and norms of functioning for board meetings

Section 11. Labor legislation and personnel matters

1. Purpose of this section on labor legislation and personnel matters
2. Relation between labor laws, decrees, and resolutions
4. Chief of personnel
5. The administrative disciplinary committee
7. Absenteeism—classification
8. Hiring—minimum education level
9. Dismissal of leadership personnel from administrative or production units and from other ministry bodies in the provinces
10. Regulations on filling or maintaining job openings

Section 12. Setting work norms

1. Introduction to work norms
2. Bonuses for surpassing work norms
3. Defective production—forms of payment
4. Payment during periods of interrupted production
5. Guidelines on work norms and wage scale

Section 13. Wage scales

1. Introduction to system of wage scales
2. Wage scale in effect for workers and administrative personnel
3. Pay for apprentices and their teachers

Section 14. Socialist emulation

Section 15. Voluntary work

1. Joint declaration on voluntary work by the Ministries

of Industry, Justice, and Sugar, and the Central Organization of Cuban Trade Unions-Revolutionary[224]

Section 16. *Council of Local Industries (CILO)*

1. Organization of CILOs
2. Penalties for absenteeism from CILO classes in administrative training

Section 17. *General relations*

2. Relations with revolutionary and mass organizations
3. Relations with the party
4. Relations with the trade union
5. Relations with provincial delegations of the Ministry of Industry
6. Relations with the CILO
8. Relations with higher bodies
9. Relations with administrative personnel of the enterprise

Section 18. *Work safety and cleanliness*

1. Introduction to work safety and cleanliness
2. Ministerial Decree No. 21—safety standards established by Law 1100
3. Industrial color-coding—implementation
4. Inspections of safety and cleanliness on the job

Section 19. *People's defense and protection of the factory*

1. Introduction to people's defense—its role, organization, and functioning in times of peace and times of war
2. Prevention of fires
3. How to divide up responsibilities in a program of accident prevention

NOTES

Notes to Preface

1. "At the Afro-Asian Conference," February 24, 1965, in *Che Guevara and the Cuban Revolution: Writings and Speeches of Ernesto Che Guevara* (New York: Pathfinder, 1987), p. 337.

2. "Che's Ideas Are Absolutely Relevant Today," p. 37 in this book.

3. Karl Marx and Frederick Engels, "The German Ideology," in *Collected Works*, vol. 5 (Moscow: Progress Publishers, 1976), p. 53.

4. *Granma International*, April 23, 1997, p 7.

5. See page 30 in this book.

6. "Che's Enduring Contributions to Revolutionary Thought," in *Che Guevara and the Cuban Revolution*, pp. 24–25.

7. "Speech given in La Plata, May 17, 1974, in *Granma Weekly Review*, May 26, 1974. See also "Land Reform and Farm Cooperatives in Cuba," three Cuban documents with introduction by Mary-Alice Waters, in issue no. 4 of *New International* magazine, distributed by Pathfinder.

8. See p. 39.

9. See p. 39.

10. See p. 61.

11. See p. 80.

12. See p. 80.

13. *Che Guevara and the Cuban Revolution*, p. 26.

14. Articles by Guevara from this debate in the early 1960s, together with discussions from the late 1980s and early 1990s of Che's views, appear in issue no. 8 of the magazine *New International*, entitled "Che Guevara, Cuba, and the Road to Socialism."

15. See p. 62.

16. See p. 39.

17. See p. 35.

18. See p. 36.

19. The speech was published in the May 15, 1996, issue of the weekly *Granma International*.

Notes to "Che's Ideas Are Absolutely Relevant Today"

1. On April 17, 1961, 1,500 Cuban mercenaries invaded Cuba at the Bay of Pigs on the southern coast. The mercenaries, organized and financed by Washington, aimed to declare a provisional government to appeal for direct U.S. intervention. However, the invaders were defeated within seventy-two hours by Cuba's militia and its Revolutionary Armed Forces. On April 19 the last invaders surrendered at Playa Girón (Girón Beach), which is the name Cubans use to designate the battle. The day before the abortive invasion, at a mass rally called to honor those killed or wounded in U.S.-organized air attacks on Havana, Santiago de Cuba, and San Antonio de los Baños, Fidel Castro had proclaimed the socialist character of the revolution in Cuba and called the people of Cuba to arms in its defense.

Amid escalating preparations by Washington for a new invasion of Cuba in the spring and summer of 1962, the Cuban government signed a mutual defense agreement with the Soviet Union. In October 1962 President Kennedy demanded removal of Soviet nuclear missiles installed in Cuba following the signing of that pact. Washington ordered a naval blockade of Cuba, stepped up its preparations to invade, and placed U.S. armed forces on nuclear alert. Cuban workers and farmers mobilized in the millions to defend the revolution. Following an exchange of communications between Washington and Moscow, Soviet premier Nikita Khrushchev, without consulting the Cuban government, announced his decision to remove the missiles on October 28.

In response to the escalation of aggression by U.S. imperialism, hundreds of thousands assembled in the Plaza of the Revolution on September 2, 1960, and adopted the First Declaration of Havana, reaffirming the course of the Cuban revolution and its deeply anti-imperialist character.

On January 31, 1962, the Organization of American States expelled Cuba from its ranks. All governments of Latin America except Mexico broke diplomatic relations with Cuba. Four days later, a mass rally of a million people proclaimed the Second Declaration of Havana, pointing to the Cuban revolution's socialist road as the way forward for the oppressed and exploited throughout Latin America.

2. Camilo Cienfuegos (1932–1959), a *Granma* expeditionary, became a Rebel Army commander and head of "Antonio Maceo" Column no. 2. He became Rebel Army chief of staff in January 1959. He was killed October 28, 1959, when the plane in which he was flying was lost at sea.

3. Jorge Ricardo Masetti was born in Buenos Aires, Argentina, in 1929. He interviewed Fidel Castro in the Sierra Maestra in early 1958. Following the revolution he was founding director of Prensa Latina news service. He was killed in 1964 while organizing a guerrilla nucleus in the Salta mountains of northern Argentina.

4. On April 17, 1967, the guerrilla unit was divided in two, with the main group led by Guevara and the rear guard of seventeen fighters under the command of Joaquín (Juan Vitalio Acuña). Although the separation was supposed to last for only a few days, the two groups lost contact with each other permanently. On August 31, the remnant of Joaquín's group fell into an ambush and was annihilated.

5. On June 25–26, 1987, directors of state enterprises in Havana Province and City of Havana Province met to assess what concrete progress the enterprises had made in the last year in the rectification process. Fidel Castro served as one of the co-chairs of the meeting. The First Congress of the Communist Party of Cuba, held in 1975, adopted the Economic Management and Planning System. This is based on the economic accounting system, discussed by Ernesto Che Guevara in the article "Planning and Consciousness in the Transition to Socialism (On the Budgetary Finance System)" in *Che Guevara and the Cuban Revolution*.

6. The minibrigades are composed of workers from a particular workplace who volunteer to be relieved of their normal responsibilities for a period of time in order to build housing, schools, and day-care centers. They were discontinued in the mid-1970s and launched again in 1986. Owing to the scarcity of materials in Cuba, however, beginning in 1991 only a few priority construction projects were continued, and even these with interruptions.

7. José Martí (1853–1895), Cuban national hero, was a noted poet, writer, speaker, and journalist. He founded the Cuban Revolutionary Party in 1892 to fight Spanish rule and oppose U.S. imperialist designs on Cuba. He launched Cuba's 1895 independence war against Spain and was killed in battle.

Notes to Chapter 1

1. Ernesto Che Guevara, "Socialism and Man in Cuba," March 12, 1965, in *Che Guevara and the Cuban Revolution*, p. 251.

2. Guevara, "Letter to José Medero Mestre," February 26, 1964, in *Che Guevara and the Cuban Revolution*, pp. 367–68.

3. Guevara, "Socialism and Man," in *Che Guevara and the Cuban Revolution*, p. 254.

4. The term "Our America" is often used by revolutionists in Latin America to refer to the America of the oppressed and exploited as opposed to the America of the Yankee imperialists. Cuban revolutionary José Martí first used the term in this sense in an 1891 essay titled "Nuestra América."

5. On July 26, 1953, some 160 fighters led by Fidel Castro took part in simultaneous attacks on the Moncada army garrison in Santiago de Cuba and the garrison in nearby Bayamo, Cuba, that marked the beginning of the popular revolutionary struggle against the dictatorship of Fulgencio Batista. After the attack's failure, Batista's forces massacred more than fifty of the captured revolutionaries. Castro and others were taken prisoner, tried, and sentenced to prison. They were released in May 1955 after a public defense campaign forced Batista's regime to issue an amnesty.

6. Guevara, *The Bolivian Diary of Ernesto Che Guevara* (New York: Pathfinder Press, 1994), p. 239. Entry for July 26, 1967.

7. Guevara, "Notes for the Study of the Ideology of the Cuban Revolution," October 8, 1960, in *Che Guevara and the Cuban Revolution*, p. 134.

8. Karl Marx, *Capital* (New York: Vintage, 1977), vol. 1, p. 90. (This edition is identical to the three-volume Penguin edition published in Britain.)

9. Marx, "Introduction: Economic Manuscripts of 1857–58" (Grundrisse), in Karl Marx and Frederick Engels, *Collected Works* (Moscow: Progress Publishers, 1986), vol. 28, p. 42. Hereafter *MECW*.

10. Marx and Engels, "Manifesto of the Communist Party," in *MECW*, vol. 6, p. 489.

11. Guevara, "Discurso pronunciado en el acto de entrega de los Certificados de Trabajo Comunista" (Speech given at ceremony for distribution of Certificates of Communist Work), January 11, 1964, in *El Che en la revolución cubana* (Che in the Cuban revolution) (Havana: Ed. Ministerio del Azúcar, 1966), vol. 5, pp. 9–10.

12. Cuba's revolutionary war for independence from Spain opened with a ten-year war that began in 1868.

13. Guevara, "Reuniones bimestrales del Ministerio de Industrias en las que participaban los directores de empresas, los delegados provinciales y los viceministros" (Bimonthly meetings of the Ministry of Industry with the participation of directors of enterprises, provincial delegates, and vice-ministers), October 12, 1963, in *El Che en la revolución cubana*, vol. 6, p. 387. Emphasis added.

14. Guevara, interview with Jean Daniel in Algeria, entitled "La profesía de Che" (Che's prophecy). Taken from the text as published in Buenos Aires in 1964 by Editorial Escorpión. First published in *L'Express* (Paris), July 25, 1963. It is also found in *El Che en la revolución cubana*, vol. 4, pp. 465–70.

15. "Our aspiration is for the party to become a mass party, but when the masses have reached the level of development of the vanguard; that is, when they are educated for communism." Guevara, "Socialism and Man," in *Che Guevara and the Cuban Revolution*, p. 258.

16. Marx and Engels, "The German Ideology," in *MECW*, vol. 5, pp. 52–53. Marx underscored the words "revolution," "ruling," and "overthrowing"; additional emphasis added by the author.

17. In 1845, in his *Theses on Feuerbach*, Marx rejected this false, anthropological notion of man. In the sixth thesis, he states quite correctly:

"Feuerbach resolves the essence of religion into the essence of *man. But the essence of man is no abstraction* inherent in each single individual. In its reality it is *the ensemble of the social relations*.

"Feuerbach who does not enter upon a criticism of this real essence, is hence obliged:

"1. *To abstract from the historical process* and to define the religious sentiment by itself, and *to presuppose an abstract—isolated —human individual.*

"2. Essence, therefore can be regarded only as "species", as an inner, mute, general character which unites the many individuals *in a natural way.*" Marx, "Theses on Feuerbach," in *MECW,* vol. 5., p. 4. Marx underscored the words "man," "isolated," and "in a natural way"; additional emphasis added by the author.

18. "Of all the instruments of production, the greatest productive power is the revolutionary class itself." Marx, "The Poverty of Philosophy," in *MECW,* vol. 6, p. 211.

19. Marx explained: "My view is that each particular mode of production and the relations of production corresponding to it at each given moment, in short 'the economic structure of society', [the base] is 'the real foundation, on which arises a legal and political *superstructure* and to which correspond definite forms of social consciousness', and that 'the mode of production of material life conditions the general process of social, political and intellectual life'." Marx, *Capital,* vol. 1, p. 175. Emphasis added.

20. Marx and Engels, "The German Ideology," in *MECW,* vol. 5, p. 54.

21. Marx, *Critique of the Gotha Programme* (New York: International Publishers, 1966), p. 10. Emphasis added.

22. Guevara, "Planning and Consciousness in the Transition to Socialism (On the Budgetary Finance System)," February 1964, in *Che Guevara and the Cuban Revolution,* p. 213.

23. Guevara, "Socialism and Man," in *Che Guevara and the Cuban Revolution,* p. 250.

24. Speaking at the Eleventh Congress of the Russian Communist Party in March 1922, Lenin said: "For a year we have been retreating. On behalf of the Party we must now call a halt. The purpose pursued by the retreat has been achieved. This period is drawing, or has drawn, to a close. We now have a different objective, that of regrouping our forces. We have reached a new line; on the whole, we have conducted the retreat in fairly good order." V.I. Lenin, "Eleventh Congress of the R.C.P.(B.): Political Report of the Central Committee of the R.C.P.(B.)," March 27, 1922, *Collected Works* (Moscow: Progress Publishers, 1976), vol. 33, p. 280.

25. We use and understand the term system to mean "a collection of elements, properties, and relations pertaining to objective reality and representing the object of the researcher's study or analysis. A system is a whole; as such it is capable of possessing properties or results not found in its components taken by themselves. This entire collection of elements, properties, relations, and results occurs in specific conditions of space and time." Orlando Borrego, "Acerca de los problemas del perfeccionamiento de la dirección económica en Cuba" (On the problems of perfecting economic management in Cuba), doctoral thesis in economic science, Moscow, 1979.

We take the term model to mean an arrangement of thought that sheds light on the functioning and subsequent development of the object of study—in our case, the country's economy. Creation of a model is a way of forming a link between reality and theory; seen in this way, a model is a representation of a system.

26. Guevara, published in English under the title "Planning and Consciousness in the Transition to Socialism (On the Budgetary Finance System)," in *Che Guevara and the Cuban Revolution*, p. 209.

27. Guevara, "Reuniones bimestrales" (Bimonthly meetings), December 21, 1963, in *El Che en la revolución cubana*, vol. 6, p. 421.

Notes to Chapter 2

28. In a January 1921 pamphlet, Lenin wrote: "I said again in my speech that politics is a concentrated expression of economics. . . . Politics must take precedence over economics. To argue otherwise is to forget the ABC of Marxism." Lenin, "Once Again on the Trade Unions," in *Collected Works*, vol. 32 (1977), p. 83.

29. Guevara, "Socialism and Man in Cuba," March 12, 1965, in *Che Guevara and the Cuban Revolution*, p. 250.

30. Guevara, "Socialism and Man," in *Che Guevara and the Cuban Revolution*, p. 258.

31. Guevara, "Discurso en la asamblea general de trabajadores de la 'Textilera Ariguanabo'" (Speech given at general assembly of workers at the Ariguanabo textile plant), March 24, 1963, in *El Che en la revolución cubana*, vol. 4, p. 389. Emphasis added.

32. Guevara, "Reuniones bimestrales del Ministerio de Industrias en las que participaban los directores de empresas, los delegados provinciales y los viceministros" (Bimonthly meetings of the Ministry of Industry with the participation of directors of enterprises, provincial delegates, and vice-ministers), December 21, 1963, in *El Che en la revolución cubana,* vol. 6, p. 423. Emphasis added.

33. Guevara, "A New Attitude Toward Work," August 21, 1962, in *Che Guevara and the Cuban Revolution,* p. 162.

34. Castro, "Discurso en la clausura del Cuarto Congreso de la Unión de Jóvenes Comunistas" (Speech at the fourth congress of the Union of Young Communists), April 4, 1982, in *Granma,* April 6, 1982. An English translation of major excerpts is found in Castro, *Our Power Is That of the Working People* (New York: Pathfinder, 1983), pp. 335–51.

Notes to Chapter 3

35. Lenin's views, in articles and speeches on the New Economic Policy, can be found in volumes 32 and 33 of his *Collected Works.*

36. The theory of Lenin's that Che refers to—and which he quoted in the essay "On the Budgetary Finance System"—is the following:

"Uneven economic and political development is an absolute law of capitalism. Hence, the victory of socialism is possible first in several or even in one capitalist country alone. After expropriating the capitalists and organising their own socialist production, the victorious proletariat of that country will rise *against* the rest of the world—the capitalist world—attracting to its cause the oppressed classes of other countries, stirring uprisings in those countries against the capitalists, and in case of need using even armed force against the exploiting classes and their states. The political form of a society wherein the proletariat is victorious in overthrowing the bourgeoisie will be a democratic republic, which will more and more concentrate the forces of the proletariat of a given nation or nations, in the struggle against states that have not yet gone over to socialism. The abolition of classes is impossible without a dictatorship of the oppressed class, of the proletariat. A free union of nations in socialism is impossible without a more or less prolonged and stubborn struggle of the socialist republics against the backward states." Lenin, "On the Slogan for a United States of Europe," in *Collected Works,* vol. 21 (1977), pp. 342–43.

37. Lenin, "Five Years of the Russian Revolution and the Prospects of the World Revolution: Report to the Fourth Congress of the Communist International, November 13, 1922," in *Collected Works*, vol. 33 (1976), pp. 419–22.

38. White hordes refers to the counterrevolutionary forces organized by the landlords and capitalists throughout the former Russian tsarist empire following the October revolution. They were backed by armed invasions by the major imperialist powers. German troops occupied territories containing one-third of the population of the former tsarist empire; the British and Japanese governments occupied the eastern port of Vladivostok; and the British and U.S. governments took the northern ports of Murmansk, Arkhangel'sk, and surrounding territory.

39. Guevara, "Planning and Consciousness in the Transition to Socialism (On the Budgetary Finance System)," February 1964, in *Che Guevara and the Cuban Revolution*, pp. 206–8. Emphasis added.

40. Wlodzimiers Brus was born in 1921 near Warsaw. He received his doctoral degree in 1950 at Warsaw's Central School of Planning and Statistics. He served as director of the department of political economy at the Institute of Social Sciences and at the Central School of Planning. From 1957 to 1962 he served as vice-president of the Economic Council of the Office of the President of the Council of Ministers.

Brus's influence on political economy was felt in the period of the Gomulka government. In March 1968 he was expelled from the Central Committee of the Polish Communist Party, and a few weeks later from the party itself. He was also dismissed from all his academic posts because of his revisionist positions.

41. Wlodzimiers Brus, *El funcionamiento de la economía socialista* (The workings of the socialist economy) (Barcelona: Editorial Oikos-Tau, 1969), p. 61.

42. Lenin's theses, "The Tasks of the Proletariat in the Present Revolution," drawn up immediately after his arrival in Russia in April 1917, oriented the Bolshevik Party toward leading the workers and peasants to take power. See *Collected Works*, vol. 24 (1980), pp. 21–26.

43. The Mensheviks originated as a minority faction of the Russian Social Democratic Labor Party at its second congress in 1903, in opposition to the majority (Bolsheviks) of the party led by Lenin. They opposed the workers and peasants taking power, under the ideological cover that only a bourgeois revolution was ripe in Russia. They moved increasingly to the right after 1907, participated in the procapitalist provisional government in early 1917, and opposed the October 1917 revolution. Sukhanov, to whom Lenin was replying, was a member of the Mensheviks from 1909 to 1919 and wrote the seven-volume *Notes on the Revolution*.

44. Assessing the prospects for a revolutionary upsurge in Germany, Marx wrote the following in an 1856 letter to Engels: "The whole thing in Germany will depend on the possibility of backing the proletarian revolution by some second edition of the Peasant War. Then the affair will be splendid." Marx, letter to Engels of April 16, 1856, in *Selected Correspondence* (Moscow: Progress Publishers, 1975), p. 86. The text of the letter in another translation is also found in *MECW*, vol. 40, pp. 37–41.

45. Lenin, "Our Revolution," January 16, 1923, in *Collected Works*, vol. 33 (1976), pp. 477–79.

46. The Ninth Congress of Soviets, meeting in December 1921, estimated the total number of persons directly affected by hunger at no less than 22 million.

47. Lenin, "Speech at a Plenary Session of the Moscow Soviet, November 20, 1922," in *Collected Works*, vol. 33 (1976), p. 438.

48. Lenin, "Report to Tenth Congress of the R.C.P.(B.) on the Substitution of a Tax in Kind for the Surplus-Grain Appropriation System, March 15, 1921," in *Collected Works*, vol. 32 (1977), p. 224.

49. Lenin, "Our Revolution," in *Collected Works*, vol. 33 (1976), p. 478.

50. Lenin, "Speech in Closing the Tenth All-Russia Conference of the R.C.P.(B.), May 28, 1921," in *Collected Works*, vol. 32 (1977), p. 436.

51. Lenin, "Fourth Anniversary of the October Revolution," October 14, 1921, in *Collected Works*, vol. 33 (1976), p. 59.

52. Lenin, "Eleventh Congress of the R.C.P.(B.): Political Report of the Central Committee, March 27, 1922," in *Collected Works*, vol. 33 (1976), p. 270. Emphasis added.

53. Lenin, "Report on the Substitution of a Tax in Kind for the Surplus-Grain Appropriation System," in *Collected Works*, vol. 32 (1977), p. 218.

54. *Smena Vekh* (Changing landmarks) was the name of a collection of articles published in Prague in 1921, and then of a journal published in Paris from October 1921 to March 1922. Alexander V. Kolchak was a tsarist admiral who, after the October revolution, established an anti-Bolshevik government in Siberia. The White armies he led in Siberia during the civil war were defeated by the Red Army. He was executed in February 1920 for his role in the armed counterrevolution.

55. Lenin, "Eleventh Congress of the R.C.P.(B.): Political Report of the Central Committee," in *Collected Works*, vol. 33 (1976), pp. 285–87. Emphasis added.

56. The Brest-Litovsk peace treaty ended Germany's war against the new Soviet government in March 1918. The highly unfavorable terms imposed by the German capitalists had to be accepted, Lenin argued, because to continue the war would tear apart the worker-peasant alliance on which rested the Soviet state and its capacity for self-defense.

57. Lenin, "Report on the Substitution of a Tax in Kind for the Surplus-Grain Appropriation System," in *Collected Works*, vol. 32 (1977), p. 218. Emphasis added.

58. Lenin, "The Role and Functions of the Trade Unions Under the New Economic Policy: Decision of the Central Committee of the R.C.P.(B.), January 12, 1922," in *Collected Works*, vol. 33 (1976), pp. 184–85. Emphasis added.

Notes to Chapter 4

59. The creation of the Department of Industrialization of the National Institute of Agrarian Reform was codified in Resolution No. 94, November 21, 1959.

On November 26, 1959, the Council of Ministers named Che president of the National Bank. This new responsibility did not lessen his attention to the Department of Industrialization or to other responsibilities he was later given.

When a separate Ministry of Industry was established in 1961, headed by Che Guevara, INRA remained in charge of industrial enterprises directly related to agriculture, such as sugar refineries. From 1962 through 1965, INRA was headed by Carlos Rafael Rodríguez.

60. A reference to the period of revolutionary war against the Batista dictatorship, when the Rebel Army under Castro's leadership was based in the Sierra Maestra mountains along

Cuba's southeastern coast.

61. The agrarian reform law of May 17, 1959, set a limit of 30 *caballerías* (about 1,000 acres) on individual landholdings. Implementation of the law resulted in the confiscation of the vast estates in Cuba—many of them owned by U.S. companies. These lands passed into the hands of the new government. The law also granted sharecroppers, tenant farmers, and squatters a deed to the land they tilled. A second agrarian reform law, October 3, 1963, reduced the limit on individual holdings to 5 *caballerías* (about 167 acres).

62. In November 1959 the revolutionary government approved a law authorizing the Ministry of Labor to "intervene" in an enterprise, assuming control of its management without changing its ownership. This action was often taken at the initiative of the workers in order to prevent decapitalization, production sabotage, antilabor policies, or other abuses by the owners. The private owners of "intervened" enterprises were still entitled to receive profits. In practice, most of the owners of these companies left the country. This procedure continued to be used by the revolutionary government until late 1960, when the major branches of the economy were nationalized.

63. Guevara, "Discurso pronunciado en una reunión con los directores y jefes de Capacitación de las Empresas Consolidadas y secretarios de Educación y de Trabajo de los veinticinco sindicatos nacionales de industrias" (Speech to a meeting with the directors and heads of training programs of consolidated enterprises, and with the secretaries of education and labor of the twenty-five national industrial unions), March 16, 1962, in *El Che en la revolución cubana*, vol. 4, pp. 105–6.

64. In *Nuestra Industria: Revista Económica*, published by the Ministry of Industry, articles by a number of compañeros take up the accounting and financial side of the budgetary finance system.

65. Guevara, "Yugoslavia, un pueblo que lucha por sus ideales" (Yugoslavia, a country that fights for its ideals), in *El Che en la revolución cubana*, vol. 1, pp. 33–35. Emphasis added.

66. INRA's Department of Industrialization was dissolved. Other legislation included the new law on the Cuban National Bank, which centralized the banking system, and laws establishing the Ministry of Finance and the Central Planning Board.

67. "The Consolidated Petroleum Enterprise, which was created by the merger of the three existing imperialist refineries (Esso, Texaco, and Shell), maintained and, in some cases, perfected their accounting systems and is considered a model in this ministry [of Industry]. In enterprises where neither the tradition of centralization existed nor the practical conditions for it, these systems were created on the basis of national experience. An example of this is the Consolidated Flour Enterprise, which merited first place among the enterprises in the Vice-Ministry of Light Industry." Guevara, "Planning and Consciousness in the Transition to Socialism (On the Budgetary Finance System)," in *Che Guevara and the Cuban Revolution*, p. 209.

68. In December 1959 Che began to study higher mathematics with Dr. Salvador Vilaseca. Dr. Vilaseca continued the classes until Che left Cuba in 1965 to carry out internationalist missions in Africa and Bolivia.

69. Guevara, "Reuniones bimestrales del Ministerio de Industrias en las que participaban los directores de empresas, los delegados provinciales y los viceministros" (Bimonthly meetings of the Ministry of Industry with the participation of directors of enterprises, provincial delegates, and vice-ministers), December 21, 1963, in *El Che en la revolución cubana*, vol. 6, p. 420.

70. On December 31, 1962, Law 1084 codified the interconnection between the financial operations and plans of enterprises and the national budget. On August 23, 1963, Law 1122 codified implementation of the budgetary finance system.

71. Lenin made this point on a number of occasions, including in his speech marking the first anniversary of the October revolution, where he said: "We have always realised that it was not on account of any merit of the Russian proletariat, or because it was in advance of the others, that we happened to begin the revolution, which grew out of world-wide struggle. On the contrary, it was only because of the peculiar weakness and backwardness of capitalism, and the peculiar pressure of military strategic circumstances, that we happened in the course of events to move ahead of the other detachments, while not waiting until they had caught us up and rebelled." Lenin, "Extraordinary Sixth All-Russia Congress of Soviets: Speech on the Anniversary of the Revolution, November 6, 1918," in *Collected Works*, vol. 28 (1977), pp. 137–38.

72. Guevara, "Reuniones bimestrales" (Bimonthly meetings), July 11, 1964, in *El Che en la revolución cubana,* vol. 6, pp. 506–7.

73. Guevara, "Planning and Consciousness in the Transition to Socialism (On the Budgetary Finance System)," February 1964, in *Che Guevara and the Cuban Revolution,* pp. 209–10.

74. Guevara, "Reuniones bimestrales" (Bimonthly meetings), December 21, 1963, in *El Che en la revolución cubana,* vol. 6, pp. 421–22.

75. Guevara, "Planning and Consciousness in the Transition to Socialism, (On the Budgetary Finance System)," in *Che Guevara and the Cuban Revolution,* pp. 227–28.

76. Guevara, "Reuniones bimestrales" (Bimonthly meetings), July 11, 1964, in *El Che en la revolución cubana,* vol. 6, p. 506.

Notes to Chapter 5

77. Guevara, "Notes for the Study of the Ideology of the Cuban Revolution," October 8, 1960, in *Che Guevara and the Cuban Revolution,* p. 135.

78. Guevara, "Planning and Consciousness in the Transition to Socialism (On the Budgetary Finance System)," February 1964, in *Che Guevara and the Cuban Revolution,* p. 220.

79. Marx, *Capital,* vol. 1, p. 169.

80. Marx, *Capital,* vol. 1, pp. 164–65. Emphasis added.

81. Marx, *Capital,* vol. 1, pp. 173–75. Emphasis added.

82. Guevara, "Planning and Consciousness in the Transition to Socialism (On the Budgetary Finance System)," in *Che Guevara and the Cuban Revolution,* p. 220.

83. Guevara, "Socialism and Man in Cuba," March 12, 1965, in *Che Guevara and the Cuban Revolution,* p. 250.

84. Guevara, "Socialism and Man," in *Che Guevara and the Cuban Revolution,* p. 249.

85. Guevara, "Reuniones bimestrales del Ministerio de Industrias en las que participaban los directores de empresas, los delegados provinciales y los viceministros" (Bimonthly meetings of the Ministry of Industry with the participation of directors of enterprises, provincial delegates, and vice-ministers), December 21, 1963, in *El Che en la revolución cubana,* vol. 6, p. 423. Emphasis added.

86. "In all previous revolutions the mode of activity always remained unchanged and it was only a question of a different distribution of this activity, a new distribution of labour to other persons, whilst the communist revolution is directed against the hitherto existing *mode* of activity. . . ." Marx and Engels, "The German Ideology," in *MECW*, vol. 5, p. 52.

87. The *Manual of Political Economy* was issued by the Institute of Economics of the Academy of Sciences of the USSR.

88. Guevara, "Planning and Consciousness in the Transition to Socialism (On the Budgetary Finance System)," in *Che Guevara and the Cuban Revolution*, pp. 218–20.

89. Guevara, "Consideraciones sobre los costos de producción como base del análisis económico en las empresas sujetas al sistema presupuestario" (Considerations on the costs of production as the basis of economic analysis in enterprises organized under the budgetary finance system), June 1963, in *El Che en la revolución cubana*, vol. 1, p. 156.

90. The reference is to an article by Alberto Mora, who was then minister of foreign trade, entitled "En torno a la cuestión del funcionamiento de la ley del valor en la economía cubana de los actuales momentos" (On the functioning of the law of value in the Cuban economy today), published in the Cuban magazine *Comercio Exterior* and reprinted in *Nuestra Industria: Revista Económica*, no. 3, Havana, October 1963.

91. The reference is to Guevara's article "Consideraciones sobre los costos de producción" (Considerations on the costs of production).

92. Guevara, "Sobre la ley del valor, contestando algunas afirmaciones sobre el tema" (On the law of value: a reply to some views expressed on the subject), October 1963, in *El Che en la revolución cubana*, vol. 1, pp. 170–71. For an English translation of this article, see *New International* no. 8 (1991), pp. 155–72.

93. Guevara, "Socialism and Man," in *Che Guevara and the Cuban Revolution*, p. 250.

Notes to Chapter 6

94. See *Capital* (in particular vol. 1, chapter 3, "Money, or the Circulation of Commodities," and vol. 3, part 5, chapters 21–36, "The Division of Profit into Interest and Profit of Enterprise"). Or see "La banca, el crédito y el socialismo" (Banking, credit, and socialism), March 1964, in *El Che en la revolución cubana*, or *Cuba Socialista*, no. 31, which presents Che's description of banking through an intelligent use of quotations from *Capital.*

95. Guevara, "La banca" (Banking), in *El Che en la revolución cubana,* vol. 1, p. 215.

96. The other three functions of money cited by Marx are hoarding, means of payment, and world money (foreign exchange). See "Money, or the Circulation of Commodities," in *Capital,* vol. 1, chapter 3, pp. 188–244.

97. Guevara, "Planning and Consciousness in the Transition to Socialism (On the Budgetary Finance System)," February 1964, in *Che Guevara and the Cuban Revolution,* p. 211.

98. Marx, *Capital,* vol. 1, p. 235.

99. Guevara, "Reuniones bimestrales del Ministerio de Industrias en las que participaban los directores de empresas, los delegados provinciales y los viceministros" (Bimonthly meetings of the Ministry of Industry with the participation of directors of enterprises, provincial delegates, and vice-ministers), January 20, 1962, in *El Che en la revolución cubana,* vol. 6, p. 151.

100. Guevara, "Reuniones bimestrales" (Bimonthly meetings), March 10, 1962, in *El Che en la revolución cubana,* vol. 6, pp. 180–81.

101. Luis Alvarez Rom, "Sobre el método de análisis de los sistemas de financiamiento" (On the method of analysis under different financial systems), in *Cuba Socialista,* no. 35, July 1964.

102. Guevara, "La banca" (Banking), in *El Che en la revolución cubana,* vol. 1, p. 215.

103. Guevara, "La banca" (Banking), in *El Che en la revolución cubana,* vol. 1, p. 217.

104. Guevara, "La banca" (Banking), in *El Che en la revolución cubana,* vol. 1, p. 232.

105. J.V. Stalin, "New Conditions—New Tasks in Economic Construction: Speech Delivered at a Conference of Business Executives, June 23, 1931," in *Works,* (Moscow: Foreign Languages Publishing House, 1955), vol. 13, pp. 76–77. Quoted by Che.

106. Guevara, "La banca" (Banking), in *El Che en la revolución cubana,* vol. 1, pp. 225–26. Emphasis added.

107. Marx, *Capital,* vol. 3, pp. 741–43. Marx underscored the words "never" and "crédit gratuit"; the remaining emphasis was added by Che. Cited in "La banca, el crédito y el socialismo" (Banking, credit, and socialism).

108. Marx, *Capital,* vol. 3, p. 515.

109. Guevara, "La banca" (Banking), in *El Che en la revolución cubana*, vol. 1, pp. 221–22.

110. Che refers to the article "Sobre el método de análisis de los sistemas de financiamiento" (On the method of analysis under different financial systems), later published in *Cuba Socialista*, no. 35, July 1964.

111. Guevara, "La banca" (Banking), in *El Che en la revolución cubana*, vol. 1, pp. 222–23.

112. Guevara, "Planning and Consciousness in the Transition to Socialism (On the Budgetary Finance System)," in *Che Guevara and the Cuban Revolution*, p. 211.

113. At this point, Che quotes from a study by Luis Alvarez Rom:

"In the [budgetary finance] system, the principle of commercial profit in the state sector is strictly formal and is dominated by the plan. Its only function is to facilitate economic accounting, bookkeeping, financial controls, and so forth. It will never come to predominate, in a fetishistic way, over the social content of production, since the enterprise does not possess any assets or property separate from the state and thus does not retain or accumulate as its own either the revenues from its output or funds for replacement costs.

"In the budgetary finance system the buying and selling of commodities takes place only when the state sells (without quotation marks) to other forms of ownership. And in conducting this operation—which has the character of commodity exchange—the enterprise transfers to the national budget (through depositing the revenues from all commodities sold to the non-state sector) both the complete costs and accumulated funds from the first to last act of production and sales. In this way, so long as the final exchange is transacted (which is the only operation with an essentially economic content), any failure due to disorganization or negligence to complete one or another intermediate operation between state enterprises of "paying and receiving" will have no serious negative impact on the national accumulation fund. This is because these operations among state enterprises are no more than bookkeeping functions with no economic effect in themselves.

"This system undercuts the concept that state factories have their own individual property and assets, and thus is objectively beneficial to the philosophic development of Marxism-Leninism. This makes it unnecessary to collect taxes from enterprises and lend them money at interest, since they do not retain or accumulate their own funds. In this way, we begin to eliminate categories that, both in form and content, would come into conflict with each other as the process unfolds."

114. Guevara, "La banca" (Banking), in *El Che en la revolución cubana,* vol. 1, p. 229.

115. Guevara, "Planning and Consciousness in the Transition to Socialism (On the Budgetary Finance System)," in *Che Guevara and the Cuban Revolution,* p. 221.

116. Guevara, "Reuniones bimestrales" (Bimonthly meetings), January 20, 1962, in *El Che en la revolución cubana,* vol. 6, p. 151.

117. Guevara, "Consideraciones sobre los costos de producción como base del análisis económico en las empresas sujetas al sistema presupuestario" (Considerations on the costs of production as the basis of economic analysis in enterprises organized under the budgetary finance system), June 1963, in *El Che en la revolución cubana,* vol. 1, pp. 155–60. Emphasis added.

118. Guevara, "Planning and Consciousness in the Transition to Socialism (On the Budgetary Finance System)," in *Che Guevara and the Cuban Revolution,* pp. 220–23.

Notes to Chapter 7

119. Castro, speech given at meeting in Katowice, Poland, June 7, 1972, in *GWR,* June 18, 1972.

120. Guevara, "Planning and Consciousness in the Transition to Socialism (On the Budgetary Finance System)," February 1964, in *Che Guevara and the Cuban Revolution,* p. 220.

121. Guevara, "At the Afro-Asian Conference," February 24, 1965, in *Che Guevara and the Cuban Revolution,* pp. 338–39.

122. Guevara, "At the Afro-Asian Conference," in *Che Guevara and the Cuban Revolution,* pp. 338–41. Emphasis added.

123. Guevara, "The Philosophy of Plunder Must Cease," March 25, 1964, in *Che Guevara and the Cuban Revolution,* pp. 310–11.

124. Guevara, "At the Afro-Asian Conference," in *Che Guevara and the Cuban Revolution,* p. 338.

125. Castro, "Conferencia de prensa ofrecida a los periodistas extranjeros, en Santiago de Chile, 3 de diciembre de 1971" (Press

conference with reporters of different countries in Santiago de
Chile, December 3, 1971), in *Cuba-Chile* (Havana: Ediciones
Políticas de la Comisión de Orientación Revolucionaria del Comité
Central del Partido Comunista de Cuba, 1972), pp. 507–8. An
English translation is found in *Fidel Castro on Chile* (New York:
Pathfinder, 1982).

126. Marx, "Outlines of the Critique of Political Economy: Economic Manuscripts of 1857–58," in *MECW,* vol. 29, p. 244. The
first sentence is missing from the English-language edition and
has been taken from the original German edition.

127. Marx, *Capital*, vol. 3, pp. 344–45. Emphasis added.

128. Guevara, "At the Afro-Asian Conference," in *Che Guevara
and the Cuban Revolution*, p. 340. Emphasis added.

129. Guevara, "At the Afro-Asian Conference," in *Che Guevara
and the Cuban Revolution*, pp. 339–40. Emphasis added.

130. Guevara, "At the Afro-Asian Conference," in *Che Guevara
and the Cuban Revolution*, p. 340.

131. For the contents of the five accords, see Castro, "Informe
al pueblo cubano sobre los acuerdos económicos suscritos con la
Unión Soviética" (Report to the Cuban people on the economic
accords reached with the Soviet Union), January 3, 1973, in *La
revolución de octubre y la revolución cubana* (The October revolution
and the Cuban revolution) (Havana: Ediciones del Departamento
de Orientación Revolucionaria del Comité Central del Partido
Comunista de Cuba, 1977). See also *Granma,* January 4, 1973. For
an English translation of this speech, see *GWR,* January 14, 1973.

132. Castro, "Informe al pueblo cubano" (Report to the Cuban
people), in *La revolución de octubre*, pp. 227–33.

133. *Granma Weekly Review,* January 21, 1973.

Notes to Chapter 8

134. Guevara, "Discurso pronunciado en la clausura del seminario 'La Juventud y la Revolución'" (Speech given at closing
session of seminar on 'youth and revolution'), published in *El
Mundo* (Cuba), May 10, 1964. In *El Che en la revolución cubana*, vol.
5, p. 150.

135. Lenin, *Collected Works,* vol. 29 (1977), pp. 411–34.

136. Guevara, "Voluntary Work Is a School for Communist Consciousness," August 15, 1964, in *Che Guevara and the Cuban Revolution*, p. 238.

137. Guevara, "Discurso pronunciado en la clausura del seminario 'La Juventud y la Revolución'" (Speech given at closing session of seminar on 'youth and revolution'), in *El Che en la revolución cubana,* vol. 5, p. 147.

138. Guevara, "Voluntary Work," in *Che Guevara and the Cuban Revolution,* p. 238.

139. Guevara, "Discurso pronunciado en la entrega de premios a los ganadores de la Emulación Socialista en el Ministerio de Industrias" (Speech given at ceremony presenting socialist emulation awards to winners in the Ministry of Industry), October 22, 1964, in *El Che en la revolución cubana,* vol. 5, p. 240.

140. Guevara, "Reuniones bimestrales del Ministerio de Industrias en las que participaban los directores de empresas, los delegados provinciales y los viceministros" (Bimonthly meetings of the Ministry of Industry with the participation of directors of enterprises, provincial delegates, and vice-ministers), July 11, 1964, in *El Che en la revolución cubana,* vol. 6, p. 510.

141. Guevara, "Reuniones bimestrales" (Bimonthly meetings), July 11, 1964, in *El Che en la revolución cubana,* vol. 6, p. 508.

142. Guevara, "Voluntary Work," in *Che Guevara and the Cuban Revolution,* p. 239.

143. Guevara, "Reuniones bimestrales" (Bimonthly meetings), December 5, 1964, in *El Che en la revolución cubana,* vol. 6, p. 563.

Notes to Chapter 9

144. Notes from a 1979 interview conducted by the author with Compañero Orlando Borrego Díaz, Che's first vice-minister in the Ministry of Industry.

145. Guevara, "Discurso pronunciado en el acto de entrega de premios a los 45 obreros más distinguidos del Ministerio de Industrias" (Speech at ceremony presenting awards to the forty-five most distinguished workers in the Ministry of Industry), April 30, 1962, in *El Che en la revolución cubana,* vol. 4, pp. 149–50.

146. Guevara, "Discurso pronunciado en el acto de entrega de premios a los obreros más destacados durante 1962" (Speech at ceremony presenting awards to the most outstanding workers of 1962), January 27, 1963, in *El Che en la revolución cubana,* vol. 4, p. 341.

147. Guevara, "Comparecencia ante la TV sobre las normas de trabajo y la escala salarial" (Television broadcast on work norms and wage scale), December 26, 1963, in *El Che en la revolución cubana*, vol. 4, p. 599.

148. For Marx's discussion of the production of surplus value, see *Capital*, vol. 1, especially "Part Two: The Transformation of Money into Capital" and "Part Three: The Production of Absolute Surplus-Value."

149. Guevara, "Discurso pronunciado en la entrega de premios a obreros más destacados del mes de julio" (Speech at ceremony presenting awards to the most outstanding workers of July), published in *Hoy* (Cuba), September 15, 1962. In *El Che en la revolución cubana*, vol. 4, p. 262.

150. Guevara, "Comparecencia ante la TV sobre las normas de trabajo" (Television broadcast on work norms), in *El Che en la revolución cubana*, vol. 4, p. 597.

151. Guevara, "Comparecencia ante la TV sobre las normas de trabajo" (Television broadcast on work norms), in *El Che en la revolución cubana*, vol. 4, p. 572.

152. Departamento de Orientación Revolucionaria, Comité Central del Partido Comunista de Cuba, *La organización salarial en Cuba (1959–1981)* (The structure of wages in Cuba, 1959–1981). From a 1983 conference held in Havana.

153. *La organización salarial en Cuba (1959–1981)* (The structure of wages in Cuba, 1959–1981).

154. Guevara, "Comparecencia ante la TV sobre las normas de trabajo" (Television broadcast on work norms), in *El Che en la revolución cubana*, vol. 4, p. 573.

155. Augusto Martínez Sánchez, "La implantación del nuevo sistema salarial en las industrias de Cuba" (Instituting the new wage system in Cuban industry), in *Cuba Socialista*, no. 26, October 1963.

156. Guevara, "Comparecencia ante la TV sobre las normas de trabajo" (Television broadcast on work norms), in *El Che en la revolución cubana*, vol. 4, pp. 598–99.

157. Guevara, "Discurso pronunciado en la clausura del Consejo Nacional de la Central de Trabajadores de Cuba" (Speech given at closing session, National Council of the Central Organization of Cuban Workers), April 15, 1962, in *El Che en la revolución cubana*, vol. 4, pp. 134–35.

158. Martínez Sánchez, "La implantación del nuevo sistema salarial" (Instituting the new wage system).

159. Martínez Sánchez, "La implantación del nuevo sistema salarial" (Instituting the new wage system).

160. Guevara, "Discurso pronunciado en una reunión con los directores y jefes de capacitación de las Empresas Consolidadas y secretarios de Educación y de Trabajo de los veinticinco sindicatos nacionales de industrias" (Speech to a meeting with directors and heads of training programs of consolidated enterprises and with the secretaries of education and labor of the twenty-five national industrial unions), March 16, 1962, in *El Che en la revolución cubana,* vol. 4, p. 109.

161. Guevara, "Discurso pronunciado en la graduación en la escuela de administradores Patricio Lumumba" (Speech at graduation ceremony, Patrice Lumumba School of Administration), December 21, 1962, in *El Che en la revolución cubana,* vol. 4, p. 321.

162. Guevara, "Comparecencia ante la TV sobre las normas de trabajo" (Television broadcast on work norms), in *El Che en la revolución cubana,* vol. 4, p. 602.

163. Guevara, "Planning and Consciousness in the Transition to Socialism (On the Budgetary Finance System)," February 1964, in *Che Guevara and the Cuban Revolution,* pp. 217–18.

164 The forms of payment are spelled out in detail in the pamphlet *Bases para la organización de los salarios y sueldos de los trabajadores,* published by the Ministry of Labor. We have taken the main points made in this document and summarized them in the section below.

165. Martínez Sánchez. "La implantación del nuevo sistema salarial" (Instituting the new wage system).

166. Guevara, "Comparecencia ante la TV sobre las normas de trabajo" (Television broadcast on work norms), in *El Che en la revolución cubana,* vol. 4, pp. 573–74.

167. Guevara, "Discurso pronunciado en una reunión con los directores y jefes de capacitación de las Empresas Consolidadas" (Speech to a meeting with directors and heads of training programs of consolidated enterprises), in *El Che en la revolución cubana,* vol. 4, pp. 100–101.

168. "In March 1968, a revolutionary offensive was carried out, as a result of which a large number of small enterprises passed into the hands of the nation. This step was not necessarily a question of principle in this stage of building socialism. It stemmed from the specific circumstances in our country resulting from the harsh economic blockade imposed by imperialism; from the need to make the utmost use of our human and financial resources; and, to top it off, from the negative political activity of a strata of urban capitalists who were obstructing the process. This does not, of course, exonerate the revolution from the responsibility for and consequences of the inefficient use of resources, which helped worsen the financial problems and the shortage of labor. The sole forms of private property that remained were peasant plots, covering 30 percent of the land; and a small number of vehicles, which remained in operation as the personal property of those who used them directly." Castro, "Informe del Comité Central del Partido Comunista de Cuba al Primer Congreso" (Report of the Central Committee of the Communist Party of Cuba to the first congress), December 17, 1975. In *Memorias: Primer Congreso del Partido Comunista de Cuba*, vol. 1, p. 39. For an English translation see *First Congress of the Communist Party of Cuba*.

169. Beginning in the mid-1960s, the Cuban leadership began a battle against bureaucratism, centering on the inflated number and poor work habits of administrative personnel. A description of this effort, contained in a March 1967 series of editorials in *Granma*, appeared in English in *GWR*, March 5 and March 12, 1967, under the title "The Struggle Against Bureaucracy: A Decisive Task." These editorials are also found in Castro, *Our Power Is That of the Working People* (New York: Pathfinder, 1983).

170. Castro, "Informe del Comité Central" (Report of the Central Committee), in *Memorias: Primer Congreso*, vol. 1, pp. 72–73.

171. Castro, "Informe del Comité Central" (Report of the Central Committee), in *Memorias: Primer Congreso*, vol. 1, p. 65.

172. Guevara, "Planning and Consciousness in the Transition to Socialism (On the Budgetary Finance System)," in *Che Guevara and the Cuban Revolution*, p. 213.

173. Guevara, "Planning and Consciousness in the Transition to Socialism (On the Budgetary Finance System)," in *Che Guevara and the Cuban Revolution*, pp. 215–16.

174. Guevara, "Planning and Consciousness in the Transition to Socialism (On the Budgetary Finance System)," in *Che Guevara and the Cuban Revolution*, p. 213.

175. Guevara, "Planning and Consciousness in the Transition to Socialism (On the Budgetary Finance System)," in *Che Guevara* *and the Cuban Revolution,* p. 213.

176. Guevara, "Reuniones bimestrales del Ministerio de Industrias en las que participaban los directores de empresas, los delegados provinciales y los viceministros" (Bimonthly meetings of the Ministry of Industry with the participation of directors of enterprises, provincial delegates, and vice-ministers), October 12, 1963, in *El Che en la revolución cubana,* vol. 6, p. 388.

177. Guevara, "Entrevista con visitantes latinoamericanos" (Interview with Latin American visitors), published in *Hoy* (Cuba), August 21, 1963. In *El Che en la revolución cubana,* vol. 4, p. 482.

178. Guevara, "Entrevista con los delegados obreros extranjeros asistentes al acto del Primero de Mayo" (Interview with international worker delegates attending May Day celebration), May 2, 1962, in *El Che en la revolución cubana,* vol. 4, p. 177.

179. Guevara, "Discurso pronunciado en el acto de presentación de los miembros del Partido Unido de la Revolución Socialista de la Textilera Ariguanabo" (Speech given at ceremony presenting members of United Party of the Socialist Revolution at the Ariguanabo textile plant), March 24, 1963, in *El Che en la revolución cubana,* vol. 4, p. 386. Emphasis added.

180. Guevara, "Discurso pronunciado en el acto de presentación de los miembros del Partido Unido de la Revolución Socialista de la Textilera Ariguanabo" (Speech given at ceremony presenting members of United Party of the Socialist Revolution at the Ariguanabo textile plant), in *El Che en la revolución cubana,* vol. 4, p. 385.

181. Guevara, "Entrevista con los delegados obreros extranjeros asistentes al acto del Primero de Mayo" (Interview with international worker delegates attending May Day celebration), in *El Che en la revolución cubana,* vol. 4, p. 178.

182. Marx, *Critique of the Gotha Programme,* pp. 7–8. Marx was criticizing the unnecessary concessions by his supporters in Germany in adopting the political program for the newly established Social Democratic Workers Party of Germany that was heavily influenced by the petty bourgeois conceptions of Ferdinand Lassalle.

183. Guevara, "Planning and Consciousness in the Transition to Socialism (On the Budgetary Finance System)," in *Che Guevara and the Cuban Revolution,* p. 216. Emphasis added.

184. Guevara, "Discurso pronunciado en el acto de homenaje a trabajadores y técnicos más destacados en el año 1962" (Speech at ceremony honoring the outstanding workers and technicians of 1962), April 30, 1963, in *El Che en la revolución cubana*, vol. 4, p. 425.

185. Guevara, "Discurso pronunciado en el acto de entrega de premios a los obreros más destacados del Ministerio de Industrias en los meses de noviembre y diciembre de 1962" (Speech at ceremony giving awards to the best workers in the Ministry of Industry for the months of November and December 1962), February 2, 1963, in *El Che en la revolución cubana*, vol. 4, p. 352. Emphasis added.

186. Guevara, "Planning and Consciousness in the Transition to Socialism (On the Budgetary Finance System)," in *Che Guevara and the Cuban Revolution*, pp. 215–16.

187. Marx, *Critique of the Gotha Programme*, p. 10.

188. Guevara, "Planning and Consciousness in the Transition to Socialism (On the Budgetary Finance System)," in *Che Guevara and the Cuban Revolution*, p. 213.

189. Castro, "Informe del Comité Central" (Report of the Central Committee), in *Memorias: Primer Congreso*, vol. 1, p. 76.

190. Guevara, "Reuniones bimestrales" (Bimonthly meetings), February 22, 1964, in *El Che en la revolución cubana*, vol. 6, p. 438.

191. Guevara, "Reuniones bimestrales" (Bimonthly meetings), February 22, 1964, in *El Che en la revolución cubana*, vol. 6, p. 435.

192. Guevara, "Discurso pronunciado en una reunión con los directores y jefes de capacitación de las Empresas Consolidadas" (Speech to a meeting with directors and heads of training programs of consolidated enterprises), March 16, 1962, in *El Che en la revolución cubana*, vol. 4, p. 98.

193. Guevara, "Discurso pronunciado en el acto de homenaje a los obreros, empleados y administradores de las fábricas que rompieron records de producción" (Speech at ceremony honoring workers, employees, and administrators in factories that broke production records), August 21, 1962, in *El Che en la revolución cubana*, vol. 4, pp. 248, 257–58.

194. Guevara, "Discurso pronunciado en la clausura del Consejo Nacional de la Central de Trabajadores de Cuba" (Speech given at closing session, National Council of the Central Organization of Cuban Trade Unions), April 15, 1962, in *El Che en la* *revolución cubana,* vol. 4, p. 127.

195. Guevara, "Discurso pronunciado en la Plenaria Nacional Azucarera" (Speech given at the national sugar conference), February 9, 1963, in *El Che en la revolución cubana,* vol. 4, p. 354.

Notes to Chapter 10

196. Che did not abandon his studies on the period of transition. He brought with him to the battlefield the books that were indispensable to his studies. Nor did he limit himself to this; he also taught classes in political economy to his compañeros in the Bolivian jungle.

197. Guevara, "Voluntary Work Is a School for Communist Consciousness," August 15, 1964, in *Che Guevara and the Cuban Revolution,* p. 241.

198. Guevara, "Comparecencia en el programa de TV 'Información Pública'" (Appearance on television program 'Public Information'), February 25, 1964, in *El Che en la revolución cubana,* vol. 5, p. 44.

199. Guevara, "Consejos de dirección: Informe de la Empresa Consolidada de Equipos Eléctricos" (Leadership councils: Report from consolidated electrical equipment plant), May 11, 1964, in *El Che en la revolución cubana,* vol. 6, pp. 106–7.

200. Guevara, "Comparecencia en el programa de TV 'Información Pública'" (Appearance on television program 'Public Information'), in *El Che en la revolución cubana,* vol. 5, pp. 36–38, 46.

201. Guevara, "Discurso pronunciado en la entrega de premios a los ganadores de la Emulación Socialista en el Ministerio de Industrias" (Speech given at ceremony presenting socialist emulation awards to winners in the Ministry of Industry), October 22, 1964, in *El Che en la revolución cubana,* vol. 5, p. 237.

Notes to Chapter 11

202. Guevara, "The Cadres: Backbone of the Revolution," September 1962, in *Che Guevara and the Cuban Revolution,* pp. 169–70.

203. Orlando Borrego Díaz was Che's first vice-minister in the Ministry of Industry.

204. Guevara, "Voluntary Work Is a School for Communist Consciousness," August 15, 1964, in *Che Guevara and the Cuban Revolution,* p. 233.

205. Guevara, "Reuniones bimestrales del Ministerio de Industrias en las que participaban los directores de empresas, los delegados provinciales y los viceministros" (Bimonthly meetings of the Ministry of Industry with the participation of directors of enterprises, provincial delegates, and vice-ministers), February 22, 1964, in *El Che en la revolución cubana,* vol. 6, pp. 453–54.

206. Guevara, "Reuniones bimestrales" (Bimonthly meetings), February 22, 1964, in *El Che en la revolución cubana,* vol. 6, p. 453.

207. Guevara, "Socialism and Man in Cuba," March 12, 1965, in *Che Guevara and the Cuban Revolution,* pp. 259–60.

208. Guevara, "Reuniones bimestrales" (Bimonthly meetings), February 22, 1964, in *El Che en la revolución cubana,* vol. 6, p. 443.

209. Guevara, "Comparecencia en el programa de TV 'Información Pública'" (Appearance on television program 'Public Information'), February 25, 1964, in *El Che en la revolución cubana,* vol. 5, p. 45.

210. Through a systematic campaign of adult education, Cuba has set itself the goal of raising the educational level of the entire population. In 1973 this effort was concretized in the Battle for the Sixth Grade, which met this target even before its 1980 goal. At that point, Cuba launched the Battle for the Ninth Grade.

211. Guevara, "Comparecencia en el programa de TV 'Información Pública'" (Appearance on television program 'Public Information'), in *El Che en la revolución cubana,* vol. 5, pp. 41–42.

212. Guevara, "Discurso en el acto de graduación de administradores del Ministerio de Industrias" (Speech at graduation ceremony for Ministry of Industry administrators), December 21, 1961, in *El Che en la revolución cubana,* vol. 3, p. 554.

213. Guevara, "Reuniones bimestrales"(Bimonthly meetings), December 5, 1964, in *El Che en la revolución cubana,* vol. 6, pp. 551–52.

Notes to Chapter 12

214. Castro, "Discurso en la clausura del Cuarto Congreso de la Unión de Jóvenes Comunistas" (Speech at the fourth congress of the Union of Young Communists), April 4, 1982, in *Granma,* April 6, 1982. Major English-language excerpts are found in Castro, *Our Power Is That of the Working People,* pp. 335–51.

215. Guevara, "Reuniones bimestrales del Ministerio de Industrias en las que participaban los directores de empresas, los delegados provinciales y los viceministros" (Bimonthly meetings of the Ministry of Industry with the participation of directors of enterprises, provincial delegates, and vice-ministers), October 12, 1963, in *El Che en la revolución cubana*, vol. 6, p. 387.

216. Guevara, interview with Jean Daniel in Algeria, first published in *L'Express* (Paris), July 25, 1963. In *El Che en la revolución cubana*, vol. 4, pp. 469–70.

217. Castro, "Discurso en la clausura del Cuarto Congreso de la Unión de Jóvenes Comunistas," (Speech at the fourth congress of the Union of Young Communists), April 4, 1982, in *Granma*, April 6, 1982.

218. Guevara, "Socialism and Man in Cuba," March 12, 1965, in *Che Guevara and the Cuban Revolution*, p. 250.

219. Guevara, "Reuniones bimestrales" (Bimonthly meetings), December 21, 1963, in *El Che en la revolución cubana*, vol. 6, p. 423.

220. Guevara, "A New Attitude Toward Work," August 21, 1962, in *Che Guevara and the Cuban Revolution*, p. 162.

221. Guevara, "Planning and Consciousness in the Transition to Socialism (On the Budgetary Finance System)," February 1964, in *Che Guevara and the Cuban Revolution*, p. 219.

222. Guevara, "La banca, el crédito y el socialismo" (Banking, credit, and socialism), March 1964, in *El Che en la revolución cubana*, vol. 1, p. 215.

223. Guevara, "Voluntary Work Is a School for Communist Consciousness," August 15, 1964, in *Che Guevara and the Cuban Revolution*, p. 241.

Notes to Appendix

224. For an English translation of this declaration, see *Che Guevara and the Cuban Revolution*, pp. 238–39.

FOR FURTHER READING

The following articles by Ernesto Che Guevara cited in this book are available in English in *Che Guevara and the Cuban Revolution: Writings and Speeches of Ernesto Che Guevara* (Pathfinder, 1987):
- At The Afro-Asian Conference
- The Cadres: Backbone of the Revolution
- Letter to José Medero Mestre
- A New Attitude Toward Work
- Notes for the Study of the Ideology of the Cuban Revolution
- Planning and Consciousness in the Transition to Socialism ("On the Budgetary Finance System")
- Socialism and Man in Cuba
- Voluntary Work Is a School for Communist Consciousness

The following articles, cited under their Spanish titles in the footnotes, are available in English in *Man and Socialism in Cuba: The Great Debate,* edited by Bertram Silverman (New York: Atheneum, 1971):
- La banca, el crédito y el socialismo (Banking, Credit, and Socialism)
- Consideraciones sobre los costos de producción como base del análisis económico en las empresas sujetas al sistema presupuestario (On Production Costs and the Budgetary System)
- Sobre la ley del valor, contestando algunas afirmaciones sobre el tema (On the Concept of Value)

The following articles, cited under their Spanish titles in the footnotes, are available in English in *Venceremos! The Speeches and Writings of Che Guevara,* edited by John Gerassi (New York: Simon and Schuster, 1968):
- Consideraciones sobre los costos de producción como base del análisis económico en las empresas sujetas al sistema presu-

puestario (On Production Costs)

- • Discurso pronunciado en el acto de presentación de los miembros del Partido Unido de la Revolución Socialista de la Textilera Ariguanabo (On Party Militancy)
- • Sobre la ley del valor, contestando algunas afirmaciones sobre el tema (On Value)

The following article, cited under its Spanish title in the footnotes, is available in English in *Che: Selected Writings of Ernesto Guevara*, edited by Rolando E. Bonachea and Nelson P. Valdés (Cambridge: MIT Press, 1969):

- • Discurso pronunciado en el acto de entrega de los Certificados de Trabajo Comunista (Volunteer Labor)

BIBLIOGRAPHY

Author's note

In preparing this investigation, innumerable books, documents, articles, etc., have been consulted, read, and studied. Only those that had a direct or indirect bearing on the present work are listed.

Items from *El Che en la revolución cubana* are listed respecting the order provided by its publisher. Although it has been studied, volume 7 is not listed because it deals with Guevara's views on guerrilla warfare.

Alvarez Rom, Luis. "Sobre el método de análisis de los sistemas de financiamiento." *Cuba Socialista* (Havana), no. 35 (June 1964).

Bekarevich, Anatoli Danilovich. *El gran octubre y la revolución cubana*. Havana: Editorial de Ciencias Sociales, 1982.

Berri, L. *Planificación de la economía socialista*. Moscow: Editorial Progreso, 1975.

Bettelheim, Charles. *Los marcos socio-económicos y la organización de la planificación social*. Havana: Publicaciones económicas, 1966.

—. *Formas y métodos de la planificación socialista y nivel de desarrollo de las fuerzas productivas*. Havana: Publicaciones económicas, 1966.

Brus, Wlodzimiers. *El funcionamiento de la economía socialista*. Barcelona: Colección OIKOS, 1966.

Castro Ruz, Fidel. Documents, speeches, letters, presentations, and books published for the period between 1953 and August 1985.

Castro Ruz, Raúl. Speeches published up to the present.

Cerniansky, V. *Economía del comercio exterior socialista*. Havana: Editora Universitaria, 1965.

Ciolkwna, Auna, and Strzoda, Joachim. *Planificación en la empresa industrial*. Havana: Editora Universitaria, 1965.

Darushenkov, Oleg. *Cuba, el camino de la revolución*. Moscow: Editorial Progreso, 1978.

Dobb, Maurice. *El cálculo económico en una economía socialista*. Barcelona: Ediciones Ariel, 1970.

Engels, Federico. "Carlos Marx." In Marx, Carlos, and Engels, Federico, *Obras escogidas*, 383–92. Moscow: Editorial Progreso.

—. *Anti-Dühring*. Montevideo: Ediciones Pueblos Unidos, 1960.

—. "Del socialismo utópico al socialismo científico." In *Obras escogidas*, 414–50.

—. "Discurso ante la tumba de Marx." Op. cit., 451–52.

—. "El origen de la familia, la propiedad privada y el estado." Op. cit., 471–613.

Guevara, Ernesto Che. *El Che en la revolución cubana* (7 vols.; Havana: Editorial Ministerio del Azúcar, 1966.)

Volume 1

International Questions

—. "La República Arabe Unida: Un ejemplo." Op. cit., 1:1–6.

—. "La India: país de grandes contrastes." Op. cit., 1:7–12.

—. "Recupérase Japón de la tragedia atómica." Op. cit., 1:13–18.

—. "Indonesia y la sólida unidad de su pueblo." Op. cit., 1:19–24.

—. "Intercambio comercial y amistad con Ceilán y Pakistan." Op. cit., 1:25–30.

—. "Yugoslavia, un pueblo que lucha por sus ideales." Op. cit., 1:31–36.

—. "América, desde el balcón afroasiático." Op. cit., 1:37–40.

—. "Cuba: Excepción histórica o vanguardia en la lucha anticolonialista." Op. cit., 1:41–58.

—. "Cuba y el plan Kennedy." Op. cit., 1:59–76.

—. "La Conferencia para el Comercio y Desarrollo en Ginebra." Op. cit., 1:77–85.

Problems in construction of socialism in Cuba

—. "Rumbos de la industrialización." (Previously unpublished.) Op. cit., 1:87–94.

—. "Discusión colectiva; decisión y responsabilidades únicas." Op. cit., 1:95–114.

—. "Tareas industriales de la revolución en los años venideros." Op. cit., 1:115–36.

—. "El cuadro, columna vertebral de la revolución." Op. cit., 1:137–44.

—. "Contra el burocratismo." Op. cit., 1:145–54.

—. "Consideraciones sobre los costos de producción como base del análisis económico en las empresas sujetas al sistema presupuestario." Op. cit., 1:155–66.

—. "Sobre la ley del valor, contestando algunas afirmaciones sobre el tema." Op. cit., 1:167–76.

—. "Sobre el sistema presupuestario de financiamiento." Op. cit., 1:177–212.

—. "La banca, el crédito y el socialismo." Op. cit., 1:213–34.

—. "La planificación socialista, su significado." Op. cit., 1:235–48.

—. "Cuba, su economía, su comercio exterior, su significado en el mundo actual." Op. cit., 1:249–66.

—. "El socialismo y el hombre en Cuba." Op. cit., 1:267–86.

Newspaper articles
—. "El francotirador." Op. cit., 1:287.

—. "El payaso macabro y otras alevosías." Op. cit., 1:289–92.

—. "El más peligroso enemigo y otras boberías." Op. cit., 1:293–96.

—. "El desarme continental y otras claudicaciones." Op. cit., 1:297–300.

—. "No seas bobo, compadre, y otras advertencias." Op. cit., 1:301–2.

—. "La democracia representativa sudcoreana y otras mentiras." Op. cit., 1:303–6.

—. "Cacareco, los votos argentinos y otros rinocerontes." Op. cit., 1:307–10.

—. "Los dos grandes peligros: los aviones piratas y otras violaciones." Op. cit., 1:311–14.

—. "El salto de rana, los organismos internacionales y otras genuflexiones." Op. cit., 1:315–16.

—. "Moral y disciplina de los combatientes revolucionarios." Op. cit., 1:317–22.

Advice to fighters
—. "Solidaridad en el combate." Op. cit., 1:323–27.

—. "El aprovechamiento del terreno." Op. cit., 1:329–38.

History of the revolution
—. "Camilo." Op. cit., 1:339–44.

—. "Un pecado de la revolución." Op. cit., 1:345–50.

—. "Notas para el estudio de la ideología de la revolución cubana." Op. cit., 1:351–62.

Introductions
—. "Al libro *Biografía del tabaco habano*." Op. cit., 1:363–66.

—. "Al libro *El partido marxista-leninista*." Op. cit., 1:367–78.

—. "Al libro *Guerra del pueblo, ejército del pueblo.*" Op. cit., 1:379–86.

Letters
Op. cit., 1:387–460.

Volume 2

Speeches

—. "Discurso pronunciado en el acto en su honor, organizado por el Colegio Médico." (Complete text, published in *Revolución,* January 16, 1959.) Op. cit., 2:1–4.

—. "Discurso pronunciado en el acto organizado por la Central de Trabajadores de Cuba para rendirle homenaje." (Summary account, published in *Hoy,* January 20, 1959.) Op. cit., 2:5–8.

—. "Conferencia pronunciada en la Sociedad Nuestro Tiempo titulada 'Proyecciones sociales del Ejército Rebelde.'" (January 27, 1959, stenographic account.) Op. cit., 2:9–22.

—. "Comparecencia en el programa de televisión 'Comentarios Económicos.'" (Summary account, published in *Revolución,* February 12, 1959.) Op. cit., 2:23–26.

—. "Discurso pronunciado en la conferencia organizada por Unidad Femenina Revolucionaria, en la Escuela Normal." (Summary account, published in *Hoy,* April 12, 1959.) Op. cit., 2:27–30.

—. "Breves palabras pronunciadas en el acto de clausura de la exposición de productos cubanos en la Escuela de Medicina de la Universidad de La Habana." (Summary account, published in *Hoy,* April 19, 1959.) Op. cit., 2:31–32.

—. "Discurso pronunciado en el acto de graduación del primer grupo de soldados que terminaron su entrenamiento militar en la Escuela de Reclutas de la Fortaleza de La Cabaña." (Summary account, published in *Hoy,* April 29, 1959.) Op. cit., 2:33–36.

—. "Comparecencia en el programa de televisión 'Telemundo Pregunta.'" (Summary account, published in *Revolución,* April 29, 1959.) Op. cit., 2:37–46.

—. "Discurso pronunciado en el acto del Primero de Mayo en Santiago de Cuba." (Stenographic account.) Op. cit., 2:47–56.

—. "Discurso pronunciado en el acto organizado por las milicias obreras y populares de Bejucal, May 3, 1959." (Summary account, published in *Hoy,* May 7, 1959.) Op. cit., 2:57–58.

—. "Conferencia pronunciada en el Salón Teatro de la Universidad de La Habana, organizada por la Asociación de Alumnos de la Facultad de Arquitectura." (Summary account, published in *Revolución,* May 26, 1959.) Op. cit., 2:59–62.

—. "Conferencia de prensa ofrecida en la República Arabe Unida, durante la visita de la delegación cubana de buena voluntad que presidió." (Summary account, published in *Hoy*, July 1, 1959.) Op. cit., 2:63–64.

—. "Conferencia de prensa ofrecida en Jakarta, Indonesia, durante la visita de la delegación cubana de buena voluntad que presidió." (Summary account, published in *Revolución*, July 31, 1959.) Op. cit., 2:65–68.

—. "Conferencia de prensa ofrecida en Belgrado, Yugoslavia, durante la visita de la delegación cubana de buena voluntad que presidió." (Translation of the account published in *Política*, Belgrade, August 22, 1959.) Op. cit., 2:69–72.

—. "Conferencia de prensa ofrecida al regreso del viaje por los países del Pacto de Bandung, el 8 de septiembre de 1959." (Stenographic account.) Op. cit., 2:73–86.

—. "Comparecencia en el programa de televisión 'Comentarios Económicos.'" (Summary account, published in *Revolución*, September 15, 1959.) Op. cit., 2:87–94.

—. "Entrevista con estudiantes extranjeros que visitaron La Habana, en su residencia en Santiago de las Vegas." (Summary account, published in *Revolución*, September 18, 1959.) Op. cit., 2:95–98.

—. "Palabras pronunciados en la despedida del duelo del comandante Juan Abrantes, y el teniente Jorge Villa, en la Necrópolis de Colón." (Text published in *Revolución*, September 26, 1959.) Op. cit., 2:99–100.

—. "Conferencia pronunciada en la Academia de la Policía Nacional Revolucionaria." (Summary account, published in *Hoy*, October 2, 1959.) Op. cit., 2:101–4.

—. "Discurso pronunciado en el acto organizado para dar inicio a una campaña de honradez y honestidad en la COA." (Summary account, published in *Hoy*, October 15, 1959.) Op. cit., 2:105–8.

—. "Discurso pronunciado en el acto de conmemoración del 10 de octubre, en el Tercer Distrito Militar 'Leoncio Vidal,' de Santa Clara." (Summary account, published in *Hoy*, October 18, 1959.) Op. cit., 2:109–10.

—. "Discurso pronunciado en el acto ofrecido ante el Palacio Presidencial, el 26 de octubre de 1959." (Stenographic account.) Op. cit., 2:111–14.

—. "Entrevista concedida a un periodista de *Revolución*, en su oficina del Departamento de Industrialización del Instituto Nacional de Reforma Agraria." (Published in *Revolución*, October 29, 1959.) Op. cit., 2:115–18.

—. "Entrevista grabada en La Habana y transmitida por 'Radio Rivadavia' de Argentina." (Summary account, published in *Revolución*, November 3, 1959.) Op. cit., 2:119–22.

—. "Entrevista con Carlos Franqui, al tomar posesión como presidente del Banco Nacional de Cuba." (Published in *Revolución*, November 27, 1959.) Op. cit., 2:123–26.

—. "Discurso pronunciado en el acto conmemorativo del fusilamiento de los estudiantes de medicina, en La Punta." (Summary account, published in *Hoy*, November 28, 1959.) Op. cit., 2:127–31.

—. "Entrevista concedida a un periodista del diario *Prensa Libre*, de Guatemala." (Summary account, published in *Revolución*, December 1, 1959.) Op. cit., 2:132.

—. "Discurso pronunciado en el encuentro de la Juventud Cívica Unida, en el Caney." (Summary account, published in *Hoy*, December 2, 1959.) Op. cit., 2:133–36.

—. "Discurso pronunciado en el acto organizado por la Universidad de Las Villas, donde se le entregó el título de Doctor Honoris Causa de la Facultad de Pedagogía." (Complete text, published in *Hoy*, January 1, 1960.) Op. cit., 2:137–42.

—. "Discurso pronunciado en la clausura de la Semana de la Liberación en Santa Clara." (Summary account, published in *Revolución*, January 5, 1960.) Op. cit., 2:143–46.

—. "Conferencia pronunciada en la clausura del ciclo de conferencias organizado por las organizaciones del Banco Nacional de Cuba, el 26 de enero de 1960." (Stenographic account.) Op. cit., 2:147–56.

—. "Discurso pronunciado en el acto de homenaje a Martí, en el Hemiciclo de la Cámara, Capitolio Nacional, el 28 de enero de 1960." (Stenographic account.) Op. cit., 2:157–62.

—. "Comparecencia en el programa de televisión 'Ante la Prensa.'" (Summary account, published in *Hoy*, February 6, 1960.) Op. cit., 2:163–76.

—. "Discurso pronunciado en el acto celebrado en la Central de Trabajadores de Cuba, organizado por la Federación Nacional de Trabajadores de la Industria Textil, el 7 de febrero de 1960." (Stenographic account.) Op. cit., 2:177–82.

—. "Discurso pronunciado en el acto de entrega de la Fortaleza Militar de Holguín al Ministerio de Educación, para una ciudad escolar, el 24 de febrero de 1960." (Stenographic account.) Op. cit., 2:183–84.

—. "Palabras pronunciadas a los delegados de la Asociación de Colonos de Cuba, que se hallaban reunidos en sesión permanente." (Text published in *Hoy,* February 28, 1960.) Op. cit., 2:185–90.

——. "Conferencia pronunciada en la Plaza Cadenas de la Universidad de La Habana, el 2 de marzo de 1960." (Stenographic account.) Op. cit., 2:191–202.

——. "Conferencia pronunciada en el programa de televisión 'Universidad Popular,' titulada 'Soberanía política e independencia económica,' el 20 de marzo de 1960." (Stenographic account.) Op. cit., 2:203–24.

——. "Discurso pronunciado en el acto conmemorativo del Primero de Mayo en Santiago de Cuba, el 1ro. de mayo de 1960." (Stenographic account.) Op. cit., 2:225–32.

——. "Discurso pronunciado en el acto de inauguración de la Exposición Industrial en Ferrocarril, el 20 de mayo de 1960." (Stenographic account.) Op. cit., 2:233–238.

——. "Comparecencia en el programa de televisión 'Cuba Avanza,' el 18 de junio de 1960." (Stenographic account.) Op. cit., 2:239–66.

——. "Conferencia pronunciada en la Escuela Técnica Industrial 'José B. Alemán,' el 1ro. de julio de 1960." (Stenographic account.) Op. cit., 2:267–80.

——. "Discurso pronunciado en el acto frente al Palacio Presidencial, el 10 de julio de 1960." (Stenographic account.) Op. cit., 2:281–86.

——. "Discurso pronunciado en la sesión inaugural del Primer Congreso Latinoamericano de Juventudes, el 28 de julio de 1960." (Stenographic account.) Op. cit., 2:287–302.

——. "Discurso pronunciado en el acto de inauguración de un ciclo de charlas, organizado por el Ministerio de Salud Pública, el 19 de agosto de 1960." (Stenographic account.) Op. cit., 2:303–16.

——. "Discurso pronunciado en el acto conmemorativo del 2do. aniversario de la partida de la columna 'Ciro Redondo,' en el Caney de las Mercedes." (Summary account, published in *Revolución,* August 28, 1960.) Op. cit., 2:317–20.

——. "Discurso pronunciado en la asamblea de los trabajadores tabacaleros, en la Central de Trabajadores de Cuba, el 17 de septiembre de 1960." (Stenographic account.) Op. cit., 2:321–32.

——. "Discurso pronunciado en la Asamblea General Popular, en respaldo de la Declaración de La Habana, en Camagüey, el 18 de septiembre de 1960." (Stenographic account.) Op. cit., 2:333–48.

——. "Declaraciones formuladas con motivo de la nacionalización de tres bancos norteamericanos." (Published in *El Mundo,* September 20, 1960.) Op. cit., 2:349–50.

——. "Discurso pronunciado en el acto de despedida a las Brigadas

Internacionales de Trabajo Voluntario, el 30 de septiembre de 1960." (Stenographic account.) Op. cit., 2:351–64.

—. "Comparecencia en el programa de televisión 'Ante la prensa,' para clausurar el ciclo de charlas organizado por los empleados del Banco Nacional de Cuba, el 20 de octubre de 1960." (Stenographic account.) Op. cit., 2:365–410.

—. "Declaraciones formuladas a su llegada a Checoslovaquia." (Summary account, published in *Hoy,* October 21, 1960.) Op. cit., 2:411–12.

—. "Entrevista concedida a periodistas del *Sovetskaya Rossia,* en Moscú." (Summary account, published in *Revolución,* November 2, 1960.) Op. cit., 2:413–16.

—. "Discurso pronunciado en el acto ofrecido en el Palacio de los Sindicatos de la URSS." (Summary account, published in *Hoy,* December 11, 1960.) Op. cit., 2:417–19.

Volume 3

—. "Discurso pronunciado durante su visita a la Planta de Nicaro." (Summary account, published in *Revolución,* January 1, 1961.) Op. cit., 3:1–2.

—. "Comparecencia ante las cámaras y micrófonos de la 'Cadena de la Libertad,' el 6 de enero de 1961." (Stenographic account.) Op. cit., 3:3–56.

—. "Discurso pronunciado en el acto organizado para recibir a las milicias, a su regreso de las trincheras, en Cabañas, Pinar del Río, el 22 de enero de 1961." (Stenographic account.) Op. cit., 3:57–66.

—. "Discurso pronunciado en el acto de clausura de la Convención Nacional de los Consejos Técnicos Asesores, en el Círculo Social Obrero 'Charles Chaplin,' el 11 de febrero de 1961." (Stenographic account.) Op. cit., 3:67–70.

—. "Discurso pronunciado en el acto de entrega de premios a los obreros que se han destacado en la producción, en el Salón de Actos del Ministerio de Industrias, el 22 de febrero de 1961." (Stenographic account.) Op. cit., 3:71–76.

—. "Entrevista concedida a un periodista del periódico *Revolución,* al ser designado Ministro de Industrias." (Published in *Revolución,* February 27, 1961.) Op. cit., 3:77–80.

—. "Conferencia pronunciada en el Cine-Teatro MINFAR, titulada 'El papel de la ayuda exterior en el desarrollo de Cuba,' el 9 de marzo de 1961." (Stenographic account.) Op. cit., 3:81–102.

—. "Discurso pronunciado en el Encuentro Nacional Azucarero, celebrado en el Stadium de Santa Clara, el 28 de marzo de 1961."

(Stenographic account.) Op. cit., 3:103–14.

—. "Discurso pronunciado en la inauguración de la fábrica de lápices 'José A. Fernández,' en Batabanó." (Summary account, published in *Revolución,* April 1, 1961.) Op. cit., 3:115–16.

—. "Declaraciones formuladas en la reunión sobre el problema de las piezas de repuesto, en el Salón de Actos del Ministerio de Industrias." (Summary account, published in *Revolución,* April 10, 1961.) Op. cit., 3:117–20.

—. "Palabras pronunciadas en el acto de entrega de los productos de la exposición china al Gobierno Revolucionario." (Summary account, published in *Hoy,* April 30, 1961.) Op. cit., 3:121–22.

—. "Conferencia pronunciada en el programa de televisión 'Universidad Popular' titulada 'La economía en Cuba,' el 30 de abril de 1961." (Stenographic account.) Op. cit., 3:123–82.

—. "Discurso pronunciado en el acto conmemorativo del asesinato de Antonio Guiteras, en los salones de la Industria Eléctrica, el 8 de mayo de 1961." (Stenographic account.) Op. cit., 3:183–202.

—. "Entrevista con 47 extranjeros que visitaron Cuba, junto con el Comandante Raúl Castro, en Santiago de Cuba." (Summary account, published in *Revolución,* May 24, 1961.) Op. cit., 3:203–4.

—. "Discurso pronunciado en el acto organizado con motivo de la visita del general Enrique Líster, en el Centro Gallego, el 2 de junio de 1961." (Stenographic account.) Op. cit., 3:205–12.

—. "Palabras pronunciadas en el acto de clausura del Campo Internacional de Trabajo Voluntario, en el que participaron los delegados de la Unión Internacional de Estudiantes, el 4 de junio de 1961." (Published in *Obra Revolucionaria,* no. 28–a, August 14, 1961.) Op. cit., 3:213–18.

—. "Conferencia pronunciada en el curso de adiestramiento para funcionarios y empleados del Ministerio de Industrias y sus Empresas Consolidadas, sobre el Plan de Desarrollo de la Economía Nacional, en el Teatro de la Central de Trabajadores de Cuba, el 23 de junio de 1961." (Stenographic account.) Op. cit., 3:219–38

—. "Entrevista con Adele Lauzon van Schendel, de *Le Magazine Maclean,* de Montreal, en junio de 1961." (Complete text.) Op. cit., 3:239–44.

—. "Discurso pronunciado en el acto de entrega de Diplomas de Mérito a cien obreros destacados en la producción." (Summary account, published in *Revolución,* June 23, 1961.) Op. cit., 3:245–48.

—. "Discurso pronunciado como delegado de Cuba ante el Consejo Interamericano Económico y Social (CIES), en Punta del Este, el 8 de agosto de 1961." (Stenographic account.) Op. cit., 3:249–90.

—. "Conferencia de prensa ofrecida en Punta del Este, el 9 de agosto de 1961." (Complete text, published in *Hoy,* August 11, 1961.) Op. cit., 3:291–306.

—. "Palabras pronunciadas ante una de las comisiones del CIES, en Punta del Este." (Summary account, published in *Hoy,* August 10, 1961.) Op. cit., 3:307–10.

—. "Discurso pronunciado en la séptima sesión del CIES en Punta del Este, el 16 de agosto de 1961." (Stenographic account.) Op. cit., 3:311–22.

—. "Discurso pronunciado en la Universidad de Montevideo, el 18 de agosto de 1961." (Stenographic account.) Op. cit., 3:323–42.

—. "Entrevista concedida a un periodista del periódico *El Popular,* de Montevideo." (Summary account, published in *Hoy,* August 19, 1961.) Op. cit., 3:343–44.

—. "Comparecencia en un programa especial de televisión y radio sobre la reunión del CIES, en Punta del Este, el 23 de agosto de 1961." (Stenographic account.) Op. cit., 3:345–80.

—. "Discurso pronunciado en la Primera Reunión Nacional de Producción, que se celebró los días 26 y 27 de agosto de 1961 en el teatro 'Chaplin.'" (Stenographic account.) Op. cit., 3:381–438.

—. "Discurso pronunciado en la clausura de la Asamblea de Producción de la Gran Habana, en el Centro Gallego, el 24 de septiembre de 1961." (Stenographic account.) Op. cit., 3:439–62.

—. "Discurso pronunciado en una reunión con funcionarios y empleados del Ministerio de Industrias, en el Salón de Actos del Ministerio de Industrias, el 6 de octubre de 1961." (Stenographic account.) Op. cit., 3:463–82.

—. "Palabras pronunciadas en la reunión celebrada para entregar las cifras de control del Plan Económico de 1962, en el Salón de Actos del Ministerio de Industrias." (Summary account, published in *Revolución,* October 26, 1961.) Op. cit., 3:483–84.

—. "Discurso pronunciado en el acto de inauguración de la planta de sulfometales 'Patricio Lumumba,' en el poblado de Santa Lucía, Pinar del Río, el 29 de octubre de 1961." (Stenographic account.) Op. cit., 3:485–92.

—. "Palabras pronunciadas en la reunión con Directores de Empresas Consolidadas y dirigentes sindicales sobre el Plan de Desarrollo de la Economía Nacional." (Summary account, published in *Revolución,* November 5, 1961.) Op. cit., 3:493–96.

—. "Discurso pronunciado en el acto de despedida a los becarios que parten a estudiar en los países socialistas, en el barco *Gruzia.*"

(Summary account, published in *Revolución*, November 7, 1961.) Op. cit., 3:497–98.

——. "Discurso pronunciado en el acto organizado en la fábrica de pinturas Klipper, al ganar la emulación de la alfabetización, el 15 de noviembre de 1961." (Stenographic account.) Op. cit., 3:499–508.

——. "Discurso pronunciado en el banquete ofrecido por el Ministerio de Industrias a los trabajadores de ese organismo que participaron como delegados en los congresos obreros, en la fábrica Cubana de Acero, el 25 de noviembre de 1961." (Stenographic account.) Op. cit., 3:509–14.

——. "Discurso pronunciado en el acto organizado en memoria de los estudiantes de medicina fusilados en 1871, en la escalinata de la Universidad de La Habana, el 27 de noviembre de 1961." (Stenographic account.) Op. cit., 3:515–24.

——. "Discurso pronunciado en el XI Congreso Nacional Obrero, el 28 de noviembre de 1961." (Stenographic account.) Op. cit., 3:525–48.

——. "Discurso pronunciado en el acto de graduación de administradores del Ministerio de Industrias, el 21 de diciembre de 1961." (Stenographic account.) Op. cit., 3:549–59.

Volume 4

——. "Discurso pronunciado en el acto de inauguración de la fábrica de galletas 'Albert Kuntz,' en Guanabacoa, el 3 de enero de 1962." (Stenographic account.) Op. cit., 4:1–6.

——. "Discurso pronunciado en la asamblea general de trabajadores portuarios, sección sindical de La Habana, en el espigón No. 1 'Margarito Iglesias,' el 6 de enero de 1962." (Stenographic account.) Op. cit., 4:7–20.

——. "Comparecencia en un programa especial de 'Ante la Prensa,' en relación con la II Zafra del Pueblo, el 27 de enero de 1962." (Stenographic account.) Op. cit., 4:21–70.

——. "Discurso pronunciado en el acto de entrega de premios a los vencedores en la emulación de círculos de estudios en el Ministerio de Industrias, el 31 de enero de 1962." (Stenographic account.) Op. cit., 4:71–82.

——. "Discurso pronunciado en el acto de inauguración de la Escuela de Capacitación Técnica para obreros, en la ciudad escolar 'Abel Santamaría,' en Santa Clara, el 1ro. de febrero de 1962." (Stenographic account.) Op. cit., 4:83–88.

——. "Discurso pronunciado en el acto de inauguración del curso académico 1962–1963 de la Universidad de Las Villas." (Summary account, published in *Hoy*, February 3, 1962.) Op. cit., 4:89–92.

—. "Discurso pronunciado en una reunión con los directores y jefes de Capacitación de las Empresas Consolidadas y secretarios de Educación y de Trabajo de los veinticinco sindicatos nacionales de industrias, el 16 de marzo de 1962." (Stenographic account.) Op. cit., 4:93–110.

—. "Discurso pronunciado en la Plenaria Nacional Azucarera, celebrada en el teatro 'Camilo Cienfuegos' de Santa Clara, el 13 de abril de 1962." (Stenographic account.) Op. cit., 4:111–20.

—. "Discurso pronunciado en el acto de clausura del Consejo Nacional de la Central de Trabajadores de Cuba, en la Ciudad Deportiva, el 15 de abril de 1962." (Stenographic account.) Op. cit., 4:121–38.

—. "Discurso pronunciado en el acto de entrega de premios a los 45 obreros más distinguidos del Ministerio de Industrias, en el teatro 'García Lorca,' el 30 de abril de 1962." (Stenographic account.) Op. cit., 4:139–58.

—. "Entrevista con los delegados obreros extranjeros asistentes al Primero de Mayo, en el salón de actos del Ministerio de Industrias, el 2 de mayo de 1962." (Stenographic account.) Op. cit., 4:159–88.

—. "Conferencia pronunciada en el Aula Magna de la Universidad de La Habana sobre 'El papel de los estudiantes de tecnología y el desarrollo industrial del país,' el 11 de mayo de 1962." (Stenographic account.) Op. cit., 4:189–214.

—. "Discurso pronunciado en un acto con los compañeros argentinos, el 25 de mayo de 1962." (Stenographic account.) Op. cit., 4:215–24.

—. "Discurso pronunciado en el acto de entrega de premios a los técnicos y obreros más destacados durante los meses de marzo y abril, en el salón de actos del Ministerio de Industrias." (Summary account, published in *Revolución*, June 8, 1962.) Op. cit., 4:225–28.

—. "Discurso pronunciado en el acto de entrega de premios a los obreros más destacados del mes de mayo, en el salón de actos del Ministerio de Industrias." (Summary account, published in *Revolución*, June 29, 1962.) Op. cit., 4:229–32.

—. "Entrevista con Vadim Listov." (Published in *Tiempos Nuevos*, no. 27, July 4, 1962.) Op. cit., 4:233–40.

—. "Discurso pronunciado en el acto de inauguración del astillero

'Chullima,' en La Habana." (Summary account, published in *Revolución*, August 16, 1962.) Op. cit., 4:241–44.

——. "Discurso pronunciado en el acto de homenaje a los obreros, empleados y administradores de las fábricas que rompieron records de producción; y para recibir las herramientas y equipos que donaron los trabajadores de la República Democrática Alemana, en el teatro de la Central de Trabajadores de Cuba, el 21 de agosto de 1962." (Stenographic account.) Op. cit., 4:245–58.

——. "Entrevista con el periodista Pedro Rojas, al terminar una jornada de trabajo voluntario en la textilera 'Camilo Cienfuegos.'" (Published in *Hoy*, September 11, 1962.) Op. cit., 4:259–60.

——. "Discurso pronunciado en el acto de entrega de premios a los obreros más destacados del mes de julio." (Summary account, published in *Hoy*, September 15, 1962.) Op. cit., 4:261–64.

——. "Discurso pronunciado en el acto conmemorativo del segundo aniversario de la integración de las organizaciones juveniles, en el teatro 'Chaplin,' el 20 de octubre de 1962." (Stenographic account.) Op. cit., 4:265–82.

——. "Discurso pronunciado en el acto conmemorativo de la muerte del General Antonio Maceo, en el Cacahual, el 7 de diciembre de 1962." (Stenographic account.) Op. cit., 4:283–90.

——. "Discurso pronunciado en el acto de graduación de alumnos en la Escuela de Superación Obrera 'Lenin.'" (Summary account, published in *Revolución*, December 15, 1962.) Op. cit., 4:291–94.

——. "Discurso pronunciado en la clausura de la Plenaria Nacional Azucarera, en el teatro 'Chaplin,' el 19 de diciembre de 1962." (Stenographic account.) Op. cit., 4:295–314.

——. "Discurso pronunciado en el acto de graduación de 296 administradores del Ministerio de Industrias, en el Círculo Social Obrero 'Cristino Naranjo,' el 21 de diciembre de 1962." (Stenographic account.) Op. cit., 4:315–28.

——. "Discurso pronunciado en el acto de clausura de la primera etapa de las Escuelas Populares, en el local del Sindicato del Comercio." (Summary account, published in *El Mundo*, January 27, 1963.) Op. cit., 4:329–34.

——. "Discurso pronunciado en el acto de entrega de premios a los obreros más destacados durante el año 1962, en el Hotel Habana Libre, el 27 de enero de 1963." (Stenographic account.) Op. cit., 4:335–46.

——. "Discurso pronunciado en el acto de entrega de premios a los obreros más destacados del Ministerio de Industrias en los meses de noviembre y diciembre de 1962." (Summary account, published in *Revolución*, February 2, 1963.) Op. cit., 4:347–52.

—. "Discurso pronunciado en la Plenaria Nacional Azucarera, celebrada en Camagüey, el 9 de febrero de 1963." (Stenographic account.) Op. cit., 4:353–74.

—. "Discurso pronunciado en el acto de inauguración de la primera etapa de la fábrica de alambre de púas, en Nuevitas." (Summary account, published in *Revolución*, February 11, 1963.) Op. cit., 4:375–76.

—. "Entrevista filmada para la televisión canadiense, en los campos de caña del central 'Ciro Redondo,' Camagüey." (Published in *Revolución*, February 12, 1963.) Op. cit., 4:377–80.

—. "Discurso pronunciado en el acto de presentación de los miembros del Partido Unido de la Revolución Socialista de la Textilera Ariguanabo, el 25 de marzo de 1963." (Stenographic account.) Op. cit., 4:381–96.

—. "Discurso pronunciado en la inauguración de la planta procesadora de cacao, en Baracoa." (Summary account, published in *Revolución*, April 2, 1963.) Op. cit., 4:397–98.

—. "Discurso pronunciado en el tercer chequeo nacional de la III Zafra del Pueblo, en el teatro 'Camilo Cienfuegos,' de Santa Clara, el 6 de abril de 1963." (Stenographic account.) Op. cit., 4:399–412.

—. "Discurso pronunciado en el acto de homenaje a trabajadores y técnicos más destacados durante el año 1962, el 30 de abril de 1963." (Stenographic account.) Op. cit., 4:413–36.

—. "Discurso pronunciado en el almuerzo ofrecido al personal del periódico *Hoy*, con motivo de su XXV aniversario, el 16 de mayo de 1963." (Stenographic account.) Op. cit., 4:437–42.

—. "Entrevista con el periodista Víctor Rico Galán, de la revista mexicana *Siempre*." (Published in *Hoy*, June 19, 1963.) Op. cit., 4:443–48.

—. "Intervención en el Seminario sobre Planificación, en Argelia, el 16 de julio de 1963." (Stenographic account.) Op. cit., 4:449–64.

—. "Entrevista concedida a Jean Daniel, en Argelia (Translated from *L'Express*, Paris, July 25, 1963.) Op. cit., 4:465–70.

—. "Entrevista con estudiantes norteamericanos que visitaron Cuba." (Published in *Revolución*, August 2, 1963.) Op. cit., 4:471–80.

—. "Entrevista con visitantes latinoamericanos que vinieron a Cuba." (Published in *Hoy*, August 21, 1963.) Op. cit., 4:481–92.

—. "Breves palabras al terminar una jornada de trabajo voluntario en la fábrica 'Antonio Cornejo' de la Empresa Consolidada de la Madera." (Summary account, published in *Revolución*, August 26,

1963.) Op. cit., 4:493–94.

—. "Discurso pronunciado en el acto de clausura del Primer Encuentro Internacional de Profesores y Estudiantes de Arquitectura, el 29 de septiembre de 1963." (Stenographic account.) Op. cit., 4:495–506.

—. "Discurso pronunciado en el acto de entrega de premios a los obreros más destacados durante los meses de enero, febrero y marzo." (Summary account, published in *El Mundo,* October 27, 1963.) Op. cit., 4:507–12.

—. "Entrevista concedida al periodista de la sección 'Siquitrilla,' publicada en el periódico *La Tarde* del 11 de noviembre de 1963." (Complete text.) Op. cit., 4:513–22.

—. "Discurso pronunciado en la clausura del seminario sobre documentación de obras para inversiones, en el Círculo Social Obrero 'Patricio Lumumba.'" (Summary account, published in *Revolución,* November 18, 1963.) Op. cit., 4:523–26.

—. "Discurso pronunciado en el acto de clausura del Fórum de la Energía Eléctrica, el 23 de noviembre de 1963." (Stenographic account.) Op. cit., 4:527–38.

—. "Discurso pronunciado en el acto de graduación de 400 alumnos de las escuelas populares de Estadística y de Dibujantes Mecánicos, en el teatro de la Central de Trabajadores de Cuba, el 16 de diciembre de 1963." (Stenographic account.) Op. cit., 4:539–60.

—. "Discurso pronunciado en el acto de clausura de la Semana de Solidaridad con Vietnam del Sur, el 20 de diciembre de 1963." (Stenographic account.) Op. cit., 4:561–70.

—. "Comparecencia en un programa especial de televisión, con otros compañeros, para informar sobre la aplicación de las normas de trabajo y la escala salarial, el 26 de diciembre de 1963." (Stenographic account.) Op. cit., 4:571–602.

—. "Discurso pronunciado en el acto de inauguración de la fábrica 'Plásticos Habana.'" (Summary account, published in *Revolución,* December 30, 1963.) Op. cit., 4:603–5.

Volume 5

—. "Discurso pronunciado en el acto de entrega de los Certificados de Trabajo Comunista, en el teatro de la Central de Trabajadores de Cuba, el 11 de enero de 1964." (Stenographic account.) Op. cit., 5:1–14.

—. "Comparecencia en el programa de televisión 'Información Pública,' pronunciando la charla titulada 'Necesidad para el desarrollo de nuevas industrias. Cómo juega esa política con el empleo pleno, automatización y mecanización,' el 25 de febrero de 1964." (Stenographic account.) Op. cit., 5:15–48.

—. "Discurso pronunciado en el acto de entrega de premios a los Trabajadores Vanguardia del Ministerio de Industrias." (Summary account, published in *Revolución,* March 5, 1964.) Op. cit., 5:49–52.

—. "Discurso pronunciado en el acto de entrega de premios a los ganadores de la Emulación en el Ministerio de Industrias, el 14 de marzo de 1964." (Stenographic account.) Op. cit., 5:53–76.

—. "Discurso pronunciado en la Conferencia Mundial sobre Comercio y Desarrollo, en Ginebra, el 25 de marzo de 1964." (Stenographic account.) Op. cit., 5:77–104.

—. "Intervención en la Conferencia Mundial sobre Comercio y Desarrollo, en Ginebra." (Summary account, published in *Revolución,* March 26, 1964.) Op. cit., 5:105–6.

—. "Conferencia de prensa celebrada en el Palacio de las Naciones, en Ginebra, el 25 de marzo de 1964." (Stenographic account, published in *Revolución,* April 1, 1964.) Op. cit., 5:107–12.

—. "Entrevista concedida a *Economía Mundial y Relaciones Internacionales,* órgano del Instituto de Economía Mundial y Relaciones Internacionales de la Academia de Ciencias de la URSS." (Published in no. 5 of 1964.) Op. cit., 5:113–22.

—. "Entrevista por la TV suiza, con motivo de la Conferencia Mundial sobre Comercio y Desarrollo, en Ginebra, el 11 de abril de 1964." (Prensa Latina account, April 12, 1964.) Op. cit., 5:123–26.

—. "Declaraciones formuladas en Argelia a publicaciones argelinas y a Prensa Latina, el 15 de abril de 1964." (Published in *Revolución,* April 16, 1964.) Op. cit., 5:127–30.

—. "Discurso pronunciado en la inauguración de la planta mecánica 'Fabric Aguilar Noriega,' en Santa Clara." (Stenographic account, published in *Hoy,* May 5, 1964.) Op. cit., 5:131–38.

—. "Discurso pronunciado en la clausura del Seminario La Juventud y la Revolución." (Stenographic account, published in *El Mundo,* May 10, 1964.) Op. cit., 5:139–52.

—. "Discurso pronunciado en la inauguración de la fábrica de bujías 'Neftali Martínez,' en Sagua la Grande, el 17 de mayo de 1964." (Stenographic account.) Op. cit., 5:153–60.

—. "Discurso pronunciado en el acto de apertura de la Plenaria Provincial de la Central de Trabajadores de Cuba de Camagüey, el 12 de junio de 1964." (Account published in *Revolución.*) Op. cit., 5:161–66.

—. "Discurso pronunciado en el acto de homenaje a los macheteros."

(Published in *Revolución,* June 27, 1964.) Op. cit., 5:167–70.

—. "Discurso pronunciado en el acto de inauguración de la segunda etapa de la fábrica de alambre de púas 'Gonzalo Esteban Lugo,' en Nuevitas, Camagüey, el 12 de julio de 1964." (Stenographic account.) Op. cit., 5:171–80.

—. "Discurso pronunciado en el acto de inauguración de la segunda etapa del combinado del lápiz 'Miatico Fernández,' en Batabanó, el 19 de julio de 1964." (Stenographic account.) Op. cit., 5:181–88.

—. "Discurso pronunciado en el acto de inauguración de la fábrica de bicicletas, en Caibarién, el 20 de julio de 1964." (Stenographic account.) Op. cit., 5:189–94.

—. "Discurso pronunciado en el acto de inauguración de la Industria Nacional Productora de Utensilios Domésticos (INPUD), en Santa Clara, el 25 de julio de 1964." (Stenographic account.) Op. cit., 5:195–212.

—. "Discurso pronunciado en el acto de entrega de los Certificados de Trabajo Comunista, a los trabajadores del Ministerio de Industrias que trabajaron voluntariamente más de 240 horas durante el primer semestre de 1964, en el teatro de la Central de Trabajadores de Cuba, el 15 de agosto de 1964." (Stenographic account.) Op. cit., 5:213–32.

—. "Discurso pronunciado en el acto de entrega de premios a los ganadores de la Emulación Socialista en el Ministerio de Industrias, en el teatro de la Central de Trabajadores de Cuba, el 22 de octubre de 1964." (Stenographic account.) Op. cit., 5:233–54.

—. "Discurso pronunciado en el acto de presentación de los militantes del Partido Unido de la Revolución Socialista Cubana en la refinería 'Ñico López.'" (Summary account, published in *Hoy,* October 24, 1964.) Op. cit., 5:255–56.

—. "Discurso pronunciado en el acto de homenaje a Camilo Cienfuegos, en la sala 'Granma' del Ministerio de la Construcción, el 28 de octubre de 1964." (Stenographic account.) Op. cit., 5:257–64.

—. "Discurso pronunciado en el acto de inauguración de la fábrica de brocas, escareadoras y fresas 'Alfredo Gamonal,' en el edificio del antiguo mercado 'La Purísima.'" (Summary account, published in *Hoy,* October 29, 1964.) Op. cit., 5:265–66.

—. "Entrevista en Moscú con un periodista uruguayo del periódico *El Popular.*" (Complete text, published in *Hoy,* November 13, 1964.) Op. cit., 5:267–72.

—. "Entrevista en Moscú con periodistas de la agencia Nóvosti, la revista *Tiempos Nuevos* y Radio Moscú." (Summary account, published in *Hoy,* November 18, 1964.) Op. cit., 5:273–76.

—. "Discurso pronunciado en la Plenaria de Industrias celebrada en Santiago de Cuba." (Summary account, published in *Hoy,* November 29, 1964.) Op. cit., 5:277–80.

—. "Discurso pronunciado en el acto de inauguración del combinado industrial de Santiago de Cuba, y de homenaje a los caídos en la jornada del 30 de noviembre, en Santiago de Cuba, el 30 de noviembre de 1964." (Stenographic account.) Op. cit., 5:281–98.

—. "Discurso pronunciado como delegado de Cuba ante la XIX Asamblea General de las Naciones Unidas, el 11 de diciembre de 1964." (Stenographic account.) Op. cit., 5:299–320.

—. "Discurso pronunciado en la XIX Asamblea General de las Naciones Unidas, usando el derecho de réplica, para responder a los pronunciamientos anticubanos de los representantes de Costa Rica, Nicaragua, Venezuela, Colombia, Panamá y Estados Unidos, el 11 de diciembre de 1964." (Stenographic account.) Op. cit., 5:321–36.

—. "Comparecencia en el programa de televisión 'Ante la Nación' de la Columbia Broadcasting System (CBS), el 14 de diciembre de 1964." (Translated from the English-language transcription.) Op. cit., 5:337–48.

—. "Entrevista concedida a periodistas del periódico *La Etancel,* de Ghana, y de Prensa Latina." (Summary account, published in *Revolución,* January 19, 1965.) Op. cit., 5:349–54.

—. "Declaraciones formuladas en Dar es-Salam, Tanzania, al completar su gira por siete países africanos." (Prensa Latina cable published in *Revolución,* February 19, 1965.) Op. cit., 5:355–56.

—. "Declaraciones formuladas en una reunión con dirigentes sindicales de Ghana." (Prensa Latina cable published in *Revolución,* January 20, 1965.) Op. cit., 5:357–58.

—. "Discurso pronunciado en el Segundo Seminario Económico de Solidaridad Afroasiática, en Argelia, el 24 de febrero de 1965." (Stenographic account.) Op. cit., 5:359–72.

—. "Discurso pronunciado en Egipto, el 10 de marzo de 1965." (Stenographic account.) Op. cit., 5:373–76.

—. "Charla pronunciada en el salón de actos del Ministerio de Industrias, al regreso de su viaje por los países afroasiáticos, marzo de 1965." (Stenographic account.) Op. cit., 5:377–97.

Volume 6

Comments made during visits to production centers:

—. "Visita a la Empresa Consolidada del Níquel." Op. cit., 6:3–4.

—. "Visita a la escuela 'Bernardo Ponce.'" Op. cit., 6:5.

—. "Visita a Tejidos Planos." Op. cit., 6:6.

—. "Visita a la fábrica No. 2 de la Química Liviana." Op. cit., 6:7.

—. "Visita a la fábrica de Productos Farmacéuticos." Op. cit., 6:8.

—. "Visita a la Empresa Consolidada de Servicios 'Dionisio San Román.'" Op. cit., 6:9.

—. "Visita a la fábrica de pintura 'Vicente Chavez Fernández.'" Op. cit., 6:10.

—. "Visita a Tabaco Torcido." Op. cit., 6:11.

—. "Visita a Suministros." Op. cit., 6:12–13.

—. "Visita a Fertilizantes." Op. cit., 6:14–15.

—. "Visita a Construcción Naval 'Astillero Chullima.'" Op. cit., 6:16–17.

—. "Visita a Licores y Vinos, fábrica No. 201." Op. cit., 6:18.

—. "Visita a Recuperación de Materias Primas." Op. cit., 6:19.

—. "Visita a la fábrica No. 601 de la Sal." Op. cit., 6:20.

—. "Visita al taller 202–19 Tejidos de Punto y Confecciones." Op. cit., 6:21.

—. "Visita a la fábrica No. 207 de Silicatos." Op. cit., 6:22.

—. "Visita a la Empresa Consolidada Automotriz." Op. cit., 6:23.

Leadership councils

—. "Informe de la Empresa Consolidada de Productos Farmacéuticos, el 21 de enero de 1963." Op. cit., 6:25–26.

—. "Informe de la Empresa Consolidada del Cemento, el 25 de marzo de 1963." Op. cit., 6:27–30.

—. "Informe de la Empresa Consolidada del Níquel, el 8 de abril de 1963." Op. cit., 6:31–34.

—. "Informe de la Delegación Provincial de Matanzas, el 15 de abril de 1963." Op. cit., 6:35–38.

—. "Informe de la Empresa Consolidada de la Metalúrgica no Ferrosa, el 29 de abril de 1963." Op. cit., 6:39–42.

—. "Informe de la Empresa Consolidada Automotriz, el 13 de mayo de 1963." Op. cit., 6:43–46.

—. "Informe de la Empresa Consolidada Convertidora de Papel y Cartón, el 27 de mayo de 1963." Op. cit., 6:47–50.

—. "Informe de la Empresa Consolidada de la Electricidad, el 13 de junio de 1963." Op. cit., 6:51–54.

—. "Informe de la Empresa Consolidada de Azúcar, el 5 de agosto de 1963." Op. cit., 6:55–58.

—. "Informe de la Empresa Consolidada del Fósforo, el 2 de septiembre de 1963." Op. cit., 6:59–60.

—. "Informe de la Delegación Provincial de Camagüey, el 16 de septiembre de 1963." Op. cit., 6:61–64.

—. "Informe de la Empresa Consolidada de Aguas Minerales y Refrescos, el 23 de septiembre de 1963." Op. cit., 6:65–67.

—. "Informe de la Dirección de Métodos y Sistemas, el 7 de octubre de 1963." Op. cit., 6:69–70.

—. "Informe de la Empresa Consolidada del Petróleo, 21 de octubre de 1963." Op. cit., 6:71–75.

—. "Informe del Instituto Cubano de Recursos Minerales, el 11 de noviembre de 1963." Op. cit., 6:77–82.

—. "Informe de la Empresa Consolidada de Recuperación de Materias Primas, el 18 de noviembre de 1963." Op. cit., 6:83–86.

—. "Informe de la Empresa Consolidada de la Minería, el 2 de diciembre de 1963." Op. cit., 6:87–90.

—. "Informe de la Empresa Consolidada de Suministros, el 9 de diciembre de 1963." Op. cit., 6:91–94.

—. "Informe del Instituto Cubano para el Desarrollo de Maquinarias, el 6 de enero de 1964." Op. cit., 6:95–96.

—. "Informe del Instituto Cubano para el Desarrollo de la Industria Química, el 13 de enero de 1964." Op. cit., 6:97–100.

—. "Informe del Instituto Cubano de Investigaciones de los Derivados de la Caña de Azúcar, el 24 de febrero de 1964." Op. cit., 6:101–2.

—. "Sesión Ordinaria, el 20 de abril de 1964." Op. cit., 6:103–4.

—. "Informe de la Empresa Consolidada de Equipos Eléctricos, el 11 de mayo de 1964." Op. cit., 6:105–8.

—. "Informe de la Empresa Consolidada de Construcción Naval, el 16 de junio de 1964." Op. cit., 6:109–10.

—. "Informe del Viceministerio para la Producción de la Industria Ligera, el 29 de junio de 1964." Op. cit., 6:111–12.

—. "Sesión Ordinaria, el 6 de julio de 1964." Op. cit., 6:113–16.

—. "Informe de la Empresa Consolidada de Productos Farmacéuticos, el 13 de julio de 1964." Op. cit., 6:117–20.

—. "Informe de la Empresa Consolidada de los Silicatos, el 20 de julio de 1964." Op. cit., 6:121–26.

—. "Informe del Viceministerio para la Construcción Industrial, el 3 de agosto de 1964." Op. cit., 6:127–28.

—. "Informe de la Empresa Consolidada de Tenerías, el 8 de agosto de 1964." Op. cit., 6:129–32.

—. "Informe de la Delegación de Matanzas, el 10 de agosto de 1964." Op. cit., 6:133–36.

—. "Informe de la Empresa Consolidada de Tejidos de Punto y sus Confecciones, el 14 de septiembre de 1964." Op. cit., 6:137–40.

—. "Informe del Viceministerio para el Desarrollo Técnico, el 28 de septiembre de 1964." Op. cit., 6:141–44.

Bimonthly meetings
—. "Enero 20 de 1962." Op. cit., 6:145–72.
—. "Marzo 10 de 1962." Op. cit., 6:173–252.
—. "Julio 14 de 1962." Op. cit., 6:253–306.
—. "Septiembre 28 de 1962." Op. cit., 6:307–34.
—. "Marzo 9 de 1963." Op. cit., 6:335–54.
—. "Agosto 10 de 1963." Op. cit., 6:355–80.
—. "Octubre 12 de 1963." Op. cit., 6:381–412.
—. "Diciembre 21 de 1963." Op. cit., 6:413–32.
—. "Febrero 22 de 1964." Op. cit., 6:433–68.
—. "Mayo 9 de 1964." Op. cit., 6:469–86.
—. "Julio 11 de 1964." Op. cit., 6:487–512.
—. "Septiembre 12 de 1964." Op. cit., 6:513–44.
—. "Diciembre 5 de 1964." Op. cit., 6:545–81.

Annual tasks of the ministry
—. "Tareas generales para 1963." Op. cit., 6:583–98.
—. "Orientaciones para 1964." Op. cit., 6:599–622.
—. "Tareas fundamentales para 1965." Op. cit., 6:623–64.

Report on Council of Ministers activities
Yearly reports 1961–62:
—. "Tareas y fines del Ministerio." Op. cit., 6:665–78.
—. "Conclusiones generales." Op. cit., 6:679–94.
—. "Calificación del personal dirigente del Ministerio." Op. cit., 6:695–700.
—. "Problemas fundamentales del Ministerio." Op. cit., 6:701–4.
—. "Autocrítica y sugerencias críticas." Op. cit., 6:705–8.
—. "Sugerencias de tipo general a los Organismos." Op. cit., 6:709–12.
Yearly reports 1963:
—. "Conclusiones." Op. cit., 6:713–18.

Other documents and writings
—. "Editorial en la revista *Nuestra Industria Tecnológica*, no. 1 de mayo de 1962." Op. cit., 6:719–22.
—. "Plan especial de integración al trabajo." Op. cit., 6:723–28.
—. "Opiniones del Ministerio sobre el Plan Perspectivo." Op. cit., 6:729–40.
—. "Prólogo del libro *Geología de Cuba* del ICRM." Op. cit., 6:741–43.

Huberman, Leo. Los bienes terrenales del hombre. Havana: Imprenta Nacional de Cuba, 1961.
Jantichy. "Análisis económico a nivel de empresa." *Nuestra Industria, Revista Económica* (Havana, 1963).

Jessin, Nicolás. "El concepto de cálculo económico y su significación
  metodológica para la economía política del socialismo." *Nuestra
  Industria, Revista Económica* (Havana, October 1964).
Kaganov, Gdali V. *Organización y planificación de la circulación monetaria
  en la URSS*. Havana: Editorial de Ciencias Sociales, 1977.
Lange, Oskar. *Problemas de la economía política del socialismo*. Havana:
  Publicaciones económicas, 1966.
Laptin, M. *V.I. Lenin. Acerca de los estímulos materiales y morales en el
  trabajo*. Moscow: Editorial Progreso.
Lavretski, I. *Ernesto Guevara*. Moscow: Editorial Progreso, 1975.
Lenin, Vladimir Ilich. "Carlos Marx." In V.I. Lenin, *Obras escogidas* (3
  vols.), 1:23–54. Moscow: Ediciones en Lenguas Extranjeras.
—. "Tres fuentes y tres partes del marxismo." Op. cit., 1:64–68.
—. "Marxismo y revisionismo." Op. cit., 1:70–78.
—. "¿Qué hacer?" Op. cit., 1:125–290.
—. "Dos tácticas de la socialdemocracia en la revolución democrá-
  tica." Op. cit., 1:499–609.
—. "Sobre la reorganización del partido." Op. cit., 1:610–18.
—. "Las enseñanzas de la insurrección de Moscú." Op. cit., 1:619–
  26.
—. "El imperialismo, fase superior del capitalismo." Op. cit., 1:723–
  834.
—. "Informe sobre la revolución de 1905." Op. cit., 1:846–62.
—. "Carta desde lejos." Op. cit., 2:23–32.
—. "Las tareas del proletariado en la presente revolución." Op. cit.,
  2:35–39.
—. "Las tareas del proletariado en nuestra revolución." Op. cit.,
  2:45–75.
—. "VII Conferencia—de abril—de toda Rusia del POSDR(b)." Op.
  cit. Within it, "Informe sobre el programa agrario," 2:119–23;
  "Resolución sobre el programa agrario," 2:124–26.
—. "I Congreso de Diputados Campesinos de toda Rusia." Op. cit.
  Within it, "Proyecto de resolución sobre el problema agrario,"
  2:145–46; "Discurso sobre el problema agrario," 2:147–64.
—. "La catástrofe que nos amenaza y cómo combatirla." Op. cit.,
  2:245–83.
—. "Uno de los problemas fundamentales de la revolución." Op.
  cit., 2:248–90.
—. "El estado y la revolución." Op. cit., 2:295–389.
—. "Los bolcheviques deben tomar el poder." Op. cit., 2:390–92.
—. "El marxismo y la insurrección." Op. cit., 2:393–98.
—. "La crisis ha madurado." Op. cit., 2:399–406.

—. "¿Se sostendrán los bolcheviques en el poder?" Op. cit., 2:409–51.

—. "Carta al CC, a los comités de Moscú y Petrogrado y a los bolcheviques miembros de los soviets de Petrogrado y Moscú." Op. cit., 2:452–53.

—. "Consejos de un ausente." Op. cit., 2:454–56.

—. "Carta a los camaradas bolcheviques que participan en el Congreso de los Soviets de la Región del Norte." Op. cit., 2:457–62.

—. "Segundo Congreso de los Soviets de Diputados Obreros y Soldados de toda Rusia." Op. cit. Within it, "Informe acerca de la tierra," 2:493–96; "Resolución sobre la formación del gobierno obrero y campesino," 2:497–98.

—. "Respuesta a las preguntas de los campesinos." Op. cit., 2:507–8.

—. "A la población." Op. cit., 2:509–11.

—. "Congreso extraordinario de los Soviets de Diputados Campesinos de toda Rusia." Op. cit., 2:517–20.

—. "La alianza de los obreros y de los campesinos trabajadores y explotados." Op. cit., 2:521–23.

—. "Informe sobre la situación económica de los obreros de Petrogrado y las tareas de la clase obrera, pronunciado en la reunión de la sección obrera del Soviet de Diputados Obreros y Soldados de Petrogrado." Op. cit., 2:525–26.

—. "Tesis sobre la Asamblea Constituyente." Op. cit., 2:527–31.

—. "Discurso sobre la nacionalización de los bancos pronunciado en la sesión del Comité Ejecutivo Central de toda Rusia." Op. cit., 2:523–34.

—. "Por el pan y la paz." Op. cit., 2:535–36.

—. "Proyecto de decreto sobre la puesta en práctica de la nacionalización de los bancos y las medidas indispensables derivadas de ella." Op. cit., 2:537–39.

—. "¿Cómo debe elaborarse la emulación?" Op. cit., 2:540–48.

—. "Declaración de los derechos del pueblo trabajador y explotado." Op. cit., 2:549–51.

—. "Acerca de la historia sobre la paz desdichada." Op. cit., 2:556–63.

—. "Epílogo a las Tesis sobre el problema de la conclusión inmediata de una paz separada y anexionista." Op. cit., 2:564–65.

—. "III Congreso de los Soviets de Diputados Obreros, Soldados y Campesinos de toda Rusia." Op. cit., 2:566–80.

—. "Posición del CC del POSD(b) de Rusia en el problema de la paz separada y anexionista." Op. cit., 2:584–86.

—. "Una lección dura, pero necesaria." Op. cit., 2:587–90.

—. "Peregrino y monstruoso." Op. cit., 2:592–99.

—. "Séptimo Congreso Extraordinario del PC(b) de Rusia." Op. cit., 2:603–47.

—. "La tarea principal de nuestros días." Op. cit., 2:648–52.

—. "Cuarto Congreso Extraordinario de los Soviets de toda Rusia." Op. cit., 2:655–73.

—. "Las tareas inmediatas del poder soviético." Op. cit., 2:677–711.

—. "Seis tesis acerca de las tareas inmediatas del poder soviético." Op. cit., 2:712–14.

—. "Borrador del plan de trabajos científico-técnicos." Op. cit., 2:715.

—. "Acerca del infantilismo izquierdista y del espíritu pequeño burgués." Op. cit., 2:716–41.

—. "Tesis sobre la situación política actual." Op. cit., 2:742–45.

—. "El hambre." Op. cit., 2:746–52.

—. "Discurso pronunciado en el II Congreso de Comisarios del Trabajo de toda Rusia." Op. cit., 2:753–57.

—. "Discurso pronunciado en el I Congreso de los Consejos de Economía Nacional de toda Rusia." Op. cit., 2:758–65.

—. "Discurso pronunciado en la reunión conjunta del Comité Ejecutivo Central de toda Rusia, del soviet de Moscú, de los comités fabriles y de los sindicatos de Moscú." Op. cit., 3:23–37.

—. "Carta a los obreros norteamericanos." Op. cit., 3:38–50.

—. "Resolución aprobada en la reunión conjunta del Comité Ejecutivo Central de toda Rusia, del Soviet de Moscú, de los comités fabriles y de los sindicatos." Op. cit., 3:51–52.

—. "Las preciosas confesiones de Pitirim Sorokin." Op. cit., 3:53–60.

—. "La revolución proletaria y el renegado Kautsky." Op. cit., 3:63–144.

—. "Primer Congreso de la Internacional Comunista." Op. cit., 3:145–59.

—. "VIII Congreso del PC(b) de Rusia." Op. cit., 3:163–209.

—. "Tesis del CC del PC(b) de Rusia en relación con la situación en el Frente Oriental." Op. cit., 3:210–12.

—. "Un saludo a los obreros húngaros." Op. cit., 3:213–16.

—. "Una gran iniciativa." Op. cit., 3:219–39.

—. "¡Todos a la lucha contra Denikin!" Op. cit., 3:240–57.

—. "Acerca del estado." Op. cit., 3:258–74.

—. "Carta a los obreros y campesinos con motivo de la victoria sobre Kolchak." Op. cit., 3:275–81.

—. "La economía y la política en la época de la dictadura del proletariado." Op. cit., 3:289–98.

—. "Informe en el II Congreso de toda Rusia de las organizaciones comunistas de los pueblos de Oriente." Op. cit., 3:299–309.

—. "Discurso pronunciado en el I Congreso de las comunas rurales y arteles agrícolas." Op. cit., 3:311–19.

—. "Carta a los obreros y campesinos de Ucrania a propósito de las victorias sobre Denikin." Op. cit., 3:320–25.

—. "IX Congreso del PC(b) de Rusia." Op. cit., 3:329–45.

—. "De la destrucción de un régimen secular a la creación de otro nuevo." Op. cit., 3:346–48.

—. "La enfermedad infantil del 'izquierdismo' en el comunismo." Op. cit., 3:351–434.

—. "II Congreso de la Internacional Comunista." Op. cit., 3:454–76.

—. "Tareas de las juventudes comunistas." Op. cit., 3:477–91.

—. "La cultura proletaria." Op. cit., 3:492–93.

—. "Discurso pronunciado ante la conferencia de los órganos de instrucción política." Op. cit., 3:494–502.

—. "VIII Congreso de los Soviets de toda Rusia." Op. cit., 3:503–31.

—. "Insistiendo sobre los sindicatos." Op. cit., 3:532–66.

—. "Sobre el plan económico único." Op. cit., 3:567–74.

—. "X Congreso del PC(b) de Rusia." Op. cit., 3:575–600.

—. "Sobre el impuesto en especie." Op. cit., 3:601–34.

—. "X Conferencia de toda Rusia del PC(b) de Rusia." Op. cit., 3:635–36.

—. "III Congreso de la Internacional Comunista." Op. cit., 3:637–53.

—. "Con motivo del cuarto aniversario de la revolución de octubre." Op. cit., 3:654–62.

—. "Acerca de la significación del oro ahora y después de la victoria completa del socialismo." Op. cit., 3:663–69.

—. "Acerca del papel y de las tareas de los sindicatos en las condiciones de la Nueva Política Económica." Op. cit., 3:670–80.

—. "Sobre el significado del materialismo militante." Op. cit., 3:681–89.

—. "XI Congreso del PC(b) de Rusia." Op. cit., 3:670–731.

—. "Acerca de la formación de la URSS." Op. cit., 3:732–33.

—. "IV Congreso de la Internacional Comunista." Op. cit., 3:734–46.

—. "Discurso pronunciado en el pleno del soviet de Moscú." Op. cit., 3:747–54.

—. "Carta al congreso." Op. cit., 3:757–72.

—. "Páginas del diario." Op. cit., 3:773–77.

—. "Sobre la cooperación." Op. cit., 3:778–85.

—. "Nuestra revolución." Op. cit., 3:786–89.

—. "Cómo tenemos que reorganizar la inspección obrera y campesina." Op. cit., 3:790–94.

—. "Más vale poco y bueno." Op. cit., 3:795–808.

Lowy, Michael. *El pensamiento del Che Guevara*. Mexico: Editorial Siglo XXI, 1971.

Maidanik, Kiva. "El revolucionario." *América Latina* (Moscow), no. 4 (1977): 185–213.

Martínez Sánchez, Augusto. "La implantación del nuevo sistema salarial en las industrias de Cuba." *Cuba Socialista* (Havana), no. 26 (October 1963).

Marx, Carlos. "Tesis sobre Feuerbach." In Marx and Engels, *Obras escogidas*, 24–26. Moscow: Editorial Progreso.

—. *La ideología alemana*. ("Prólogo," "Capítulo I," and "Apéndices.") Havana: Editorial Pueblo y Educación, 1982.

—. "Trabajo asalariado y capital." In *Obras escogidas*, 69–92. Moscow: Editorial Progreso.

—. "Manifiesto del Partido Comunista." Op. cit., 27–60.

—. *Fundamentos de la crítica de la economía política (Grundrisse)*. Havana: Editorial de Ciencias Sociales, 1970.

—. *Contribución a la crítica de la economía política*. Havana: Edición Revolucionaria, 1970.

—. "Salario, precio y ganancia." In *Obras escogidas*, 186–232. Moscow: Editorial Progreso.

—. *El capital*. 3 vols. Havana: Editorial Nacional de Cuba, 1962.

—. "Crítica del Programa de Gotha." In *Obras escogidas*, 325–46. Moscow: Editorial Progreso.

Mora, Alberto. "Sobre algunos problemas actuales de la construcción del socialismo." *Nuestra Industria, Revista Económica* (Havana, August 1965).

Oleinik, I. *Manual de economía política*. 3 vols. Havana, 1977.

Risquet, Jorge. Various speeches published in the Cuban press.

Roca, Blas. *Los fundamentos del socialismo en Cuba*. Havana: Ediciones Populares, 1960.

Rodríguez, Carlos Rafael. *La revolución cubana y el período de transición*. Havana, 1966.

—. *Letra con filo*. 2 vols. Havana: Editorial de Ciencias Sociales, 1983.

—. Various speeches published in the Cuban press.

Rumiantsev, A. *Categorías y leyes de la economía política de la formación comunista*. Moscow: Editorial Progreso.

Stalin, José. *Sobre el materialismo dialéctico e histórico*.

—. *Observaciones sobre cuestiones de economía relacionadas con la discusión de noviembre de 1951*.

—. *Respuesta al camarada Alexander Ilich Notkin*.

—. *Sobre los fundamentos del leninismo.*
—. *Otros errores del camarada Yarostrenko.*
Valdés, Ramiro. Speeches made at ceremonies commemorating Che.
Zaródov, K. *El leninismo y la transición del capitalismo al socialismo.* Moscow: Editorial Progreso, 1973.

Documents:
Declaración de la Conferencia de los Representantes de los Partidos Comunistas y Obreras celebrada en Moscú. Editorial Progreso.
Materiales del XXV Congreso del PCUS. Moscow, 1976.
Materiales del XXVI Congreso del PCUS. Moscow, 1981.
Pleno del Comité Central del PCUS. Moscow, 1982.
Primer Congreso del Partido Comunista de Cuba: Memorias. 3 vols. Havana: Departamento de Orientación Revolucionaria del PCC, 1976. (Includes "Plataforma Programática del Partido," "Informe Central," "Tesis y Resoluciones," and other documents.)
Programa del PCUS. Moscow, 1971.
Segundo Congreso del Partido Comunista de Cuba: Documentos y discursos. Havana: Editora Política, 1981.
Sixth, Seventh, Eighth, and Ninth Plenums of the Central Committee of the Communist Party of Cuba.

Publications:
América Latina.
Cuba Socialista.
Departamento de Orientación Revolucionaria (DOR), Central Committee of the Communist Party of Cuba. *La organización salarial en Cuba (1959–1981).*
Economía y Desarrollo.
Gaceta Oficial de la República de Cuba.
Nuestra Industria, Revista Económica.

INDEX

Absenteeism, 184, 227

Accounting, 99, 106, 131, 132, 143; cost accounting, 46–47, 197–201; fictitious, 102, 137, 138; modern techniques of, 74–75, 101–2, 104–5, 129–30, 215, 218

Acuña, Vilo (Joaquín), 29–30, 230

Administration, 146, 190, 198; centralization of, 75, 106–7; efficiency of, 77, 79–80, 146, 184; techniques of, 103–5, 129–31; workers' participation in, 179, 197

Administrative/technical personnel, 197, 199, 200, 209–10, 224–26; development of, 174, 203–10; shortage of, 74, 106, 204; and wages, 175, 179–80. *See also* Cadre policy

Africa, 241

Agriculture, 21, 73–74, 84, 93, 139, 165, 195; and unequal exchange, 160; wages in, 173, 180, 183. *See also* Land reform

Alienation, 62, 166, 212

Alvarez Rom, Luis, 135, 245

April Theses (Lenin), 86, 237

Arbitration, 225

"Banking, Credit, and Socialism" (Guevara), 127

Banks and banking system, 225; and commodity relations, 128, 131; role of, 130–37, 219. *See also* Credit; Interest; Investment; Money; National Bank

Batista, Fulgencio, 12, 18, 232, 239

Blockade, U.S., 51, 155, 159, 160–61, 251

Bolivia, 10, 30, 241, 254

Bolshevik Party, 15, 89

Bonuses and penalties, 41, 45, 182, 184, 186–87, 189, 191–92; ceilings, 176, 179–80; unearned, 35–36. *See also* Incentives, material

Borrego, Orlando, 235, 248

Brest-Litovsk treaty, 91, 93, 239

Brus, Wlodzimiers, 86, 117, 237

Budgetary finance system, 19–20, 82, 127, 212, 213–14, 215; and administrative compulsion, 130–31, 139, 218; and banking system, 128–37, 218–29; and cadre policy, 204–10; and centralization, 75, 97–99, 132, 138–44, 219; and communist consciousness, 129, 245–46; and construction of socialism, 61–62, 77–78, 94; and economic controls, 197–201, 221; emergence of, 97–107, 241; and emulation, 194, 196, 221; evaluating efficiency of, 78; and incentives, 185–94, 220; and law of value, 114–24; and prices, 137–47, 219; shortcomings in, 106–7; and wages, 167–83

Bureaucratism, 21, 22, 42, 187, 221; and budgetary finance system, 106–7; struggle against, 184, 197, 251; and voluntary work, 35, 40–41, 172

Cadre policy, 203–10

Canada, 188
Capital (Marx), 18, 109, 111–14, 129,
    133–34, 157, 233–34, 244
Capital, flight of, 79, 125
Capitalist categories, 41, 43, 80–81,
    112; Castro on use of, 36, 39, 45,
    95; Guevara on use of, 39, 69, 70,
    76, 79, 105, 114–16, 119–25, 211,
    214–18; Marx on use of, 59. *See
    also* Commodity relations; Inter-
    est; Law of value; Profit and
    profitability
Capitalist methods. *See* Market
    economy mechanisms
Capitalism, 58–59, 72, 122–24, 133–35,
    169–70, 242–43; legacy of, 64, 73–
    74, 163, 172, 185, 186, 220
Casa de las Américas, 38
Castro, Fidel: on Carlos Tablada, 14,
    38–39; on communist conscious-
    ness, 81–82, 193, 213; on economic
    errors, 81; on Guevara's economic
    thought, 38–39, 43–46; on Gue-
    vara's qualities, 9, 12, 27, 28–33,
    37, 38, 45; as Rebel Army com-
    mander, 232, 239–40; on rectifica-
    tion process, 39; on Soviet Union,
    11, 154–55, 159; on use of capital-
    ist formulas, 36, 39, 45, 82; on vol-
    untary work, 35
Castro, Raúl, 209
"Castroism," 57
Central Organization of Cuban Trade
    Unions (CTC), 24, 194, 209
Central Planning Board, 136, 240
Centralization, 60, 132; of accounting
    and management, 75, 101, 102, 106,
    215; and budgetary finance sys-
    tem, 97–99, 132, 137–44, 218–19; of
    planning, 110, 117, 122, 142
Chile, 154
Cienfuegos, Camilo, 29
Comercio Exterior, 243
Commodity, 136, 245; and labor
    power, 164, 169; under capital-
    ism, 79, 115, 125; and value, 112–
    13, 116, 129, 131, 141, 156, 170

Commodity relations, 66–67, 84, 86,
    218; and money, 115–16, 128, 135;
    and New Economic Policy, 92–93;
    between state enterprises, 99–100,
    114, 122, 131, 137, 216–19; during
    transition to socialism, 118–25,
    164, 168. *See also* Law of value;
    Market economy mechanisms;
    Money
Communications, 75, 101, 226
Communism, 36–37, 52, 154, 168;
    and consciousness, 39, 44, 63–73,
    78–82, 103–4, 110, 115, 119, 131,
    171, 185–86, 195, 201, 214; and
    moral values, 111, 169, 212, 216,
    220; war communism, 83. *See
    also* Transition to socialism and
    communism
Communist and Workers' Parties,
    Conference of (1957), 61–62
Communist International, 15
Communist Party of Cuba, 13, 50,
    161; First Congress (December
    1975) of, 184, 185, 193
Communist Work, Certificates of,
    204–5
Competition, 91, 186; and emula-
    tion, 194, 195–96, 221; and law
    of value, 137–38; and state enter-
    prises, 99–100; under capitalism,
    104, 123, 144, 152, 156
Computer technology, 46–47, 50,
    102, 197, 215
Congo, 13
Consciousness: and budgetary fi-
    nance system, 119, 245–46; and
    building socialism, 39, 44, 59, 61,
    63–73, 212–13; and capitalist ves-
    tiges, 63, 72–73, 103–4, 186;
    Castro on, 15, 81–82, 185–86, 193,
    213; changes in, 63–65, 93, 111,
    121, 150, 171; and communism,
    78–82, 103–4, 110, 115, 119, 131,
    171–72; and economic planning,
    78, 212; Guevara on, 16–17, 39,
    44, 63–65, 69–73, 78–80, 103–4,
    115, 121, 122, 125, 150, 165, 167,

176, 179, 186–88, 193, 194–95, 196, 201, 205, 212–14, 217–18; 220–21; and incentives, 66, 186–89, 192–93, 194–95; Marx and Engels on, 63, 65, 67, 80, 212, 214; and relations of production, 168, 179, 186; and voluntary work, 165; and work norms, 66, 72, 80, 173, 175–76, 184, 190–91, 220–21. *See also* New man

"Considerations on the Costs of Production" (Guevara), 122

Consolidated Flour Enterprise, 241

Consolidated Petroleum Enterprise, 241

Construction, 40, 43, 46, 47; of day-care centers, 41, 49

Consumers and consumer goods, 64, 81, 120, 131, 185, 190, 192; and economic controls, 139–40, 184–85, 192; state role in, 121–22, 128, 138, 143, 218

Contribution to the Critique of Political Economy (Marx), 109

Controls, economic, 46, 111, 116, 119, 137, 144, 167, 171, 184, 213; and administration, 101, 104, 130–31, 139, 215, 218; and economic planning, 102, 197–201, 245; and finance, 130, 200–201; Guevara on, 46, 75, 105–7, 136, 179, 197–201, 221; and imperialist corporations, 75, 105, 170, 215, 218; and investment, 136. *See also* Accounting

Costs, 146–47, 190, 224; as performance index, 143–44, 198–200; and prices, 117, 118, 123, 138, 141, 142; of production, 75, 122–23, 133, 139, 169–70, 180, 225

Council of Local Industries (CILO), 228

Credit, 102, 131, 134–35, 137; and developing countries, 158–61; under socialism, 120, 134–35

Critique of the Gotha Programme (Marx), 18, 109, 189–90, 252

Day-care centers, 21, 41, 49

Debt, foreign, 160, 219

Defense, 228

Democratic centralism, 197

Depreciation, 145, 200

Determinism, 73

Development: economic and social, 42, 80, 173; scientific and technological, 48, 74–75, 139, 142, 144, 147, 197, 208, 225

Dictatorship of proletariat, 59–61, 68, 93, 109, 115

Distribution, 106, 121, 190; and market mechanisms, 131, 170; and socialism, 16, 63, 80, 85, 99, 116–17, 120, 121, 123, 138, 212

Eastern Europe, 10, 19, 22, 23

Economic Management and Planning System, 39, 41

Economic accounting system, 19, 20, 86, 103, 119, 136; and controls, 130, 135, 139, 144; and law of value, 119–22; money and banking under, 127–30, 132; and New Economic Policy, 93; and prices, 137–39, 144; in Yugoslavia, 99–100

Economic planning, 19, 75, 99–100, 109–25, 221, 223; aim of, 77, 213, 215–16; and banking system, 128–29, 135; and computerization, 46–47, 50, 102, 215; and consciousness, 63, 78, 212; and controls, 102, 197–201, 245; and efficiency, 71, 78, 111, 140–44, 167, 172; and law of value, 137–38, 171, 219; laws of, 61, 211; and market mechanisms, 86, 118–19, 217; and mass organizations, 139; political character of, 58–60, 68, 70, 110–11; and social rationality, 62, 65–66, 70, 78–80, 214; and social spending, 42, 191–92. *See also* Budgetary finance system; Central Planning Board; Economic accounting system

Education, 98, 208, 255; and consciousness, 78–79, 104, 121, 125,

171, 217; and material incentives, 44, 174, 176, 179, 186, 189
Emulation, 167, 194–96, 220, 224, 227; and competition, 221
Engels, Frederick, 17, 18, 55, 63, 67, 109, 124, 157, 198, 211, 238

Feudalism, 124, 168
Feuerbach, Ludwig, 233
Finance. *See* Accounting; Banks and banking system; Controls, economic
Financial self-management. *See* Economic accounting system
Free exchange, 91–92
French revolution, 15, 61
Fund for International Development, 161

German Ideology (Marx and Engels), 63, 67, 109, 242–43
Gómez, Máximo, 14
Granma (daily newspaper), 161
Granma (expedition), 27, 203
Great Depression of 1930s, 22
Guevara, Che, as combatant, 29, 97; death of, 10, 25, 31; as defender of Marxism, 55, 212; as economic leader, 38; example of, 33, 49–50, 51; incorrect interpretation of, 20, 39; as organizer of voluntary work, 18, 35, 205; positions of in revolution, 12–13, 18, 97, 99, 101, 198, 239; qualities of, 9, 12, 18–19, 27, 29–33, 37; study of Marxism by, 17, 57, 198

Health care, 47, 116
Housing, 41, 49, 116

Idealism, 39, 211
Imperialism, 10, 153, 160–61; attack on Russian revolution by, 83, 85; break of at weakest link, 103, 124, 241; struggle against, 9, 151–52, 154–55. *See also* United States, and Cuba; Blockade, U.S.

Incentives, material, 105, 114, 121, 169, 196, 197, 215, 220–22; abuse of, 35; and development of consciousness, 66, 187; gradual elimination of, 62, 186–87, 191–92, 212; as main lever, 67, 79, 93, 125; of a social character, 56, 106, 191; and transition to socialism, 37, 72. *See also* Bonuses and penalties
Incentives, moral, 56, 169, 188, 193
Industry, 40, 48, 74, 165, 194; state control of, 38, 97–98, 204, 240, 251
Inflation, 184, 190
Interest, 45, 75, 134–35, 215, 219, 246
Internationalism, 22, 24, 122, 149, 150–51, 158, 161; and Cuban volunteers, 21, 23, 48
Inventory control, 200, 225
Investment, 136, 143, 146, 225; in developing countries, 122, 150, 158; and social spending, 191

Job classifications, 173–75

Kolchak, Alexander V., 89, 90, 239
Kronstadt, 88

Labor: division of, 65, 147, 149, 158; socially necessary, 118, 143, 145; social surplus, 135, 169–70. *See also* Voluntary work
Labor law, 224
Labor power, 113–14, 116, 137, 164, 169–70; sale of, 172
La Cabaña fortress, 97
Land reform, 12, 97, 240
Lange, Oskar, 74
Las Villas, 29
Lassalle, Ferdinand, 190, 252
Law of value, 116–17, 137, 141, 219, 221; and international trade, 149, 150–51, 153, 156; and transition to socialism, 93, 110–11, 114–24, 143, 171, 216–17. *See also* Capitalist categories; Commodity relations; Market economy mechanisms; Value

Leadership, 203–10

Lenin, V.I., 15, 16, 17, 55, 57, 61, 124–25, 154, 198, 210, 236, 239; on imperialist breakup at weakest link, 103, 124, 241; on New Economic Policy, 71–72, 83–94, 234, 236; on politics as concentrated economics, 235

Liberalism, 224

Maceo, Antonio, 14

Manifesto of the Communist Party (Marx and Engels), 59, 109

Manual of Political Economy, 119–21, 243

Market economy mechanisms, 71, 75, 86, 114–15, 117–18, 121, 137, 214–15; Cuba's shift away from, 36–37, 41–42; Guevara on use of, 119, 186–87. *See also* Capitalist categories; Commodity relations; Law of value

Martí, José, 14, 52

Marx, Karl, 17, 18, 55, 57–58, 110, 124, 157, 198, 211, 216, 233–34, 238, 243, 244, 252–53; on consciousness, 63, 65, 67, 80, 212, 214; on interest-bearing capital, 134–35; on peasant war, 87, 238; on transition to socialism and communism, 93, 109, 124–25, 192; on unequal exchange, 155–56; on value, 111–14, 190, 249

Marxism, 55, 57–58, 60, 62, 67, 168, 215, 245–46; and "Castroism," 57; and internationalism, 149; revisionist theories of, 80; stagnation of, 56–57

Mass organizations, 139, 228

Massetti, Ricardo, 29

May Day, 187

Means of production, 115, 118, 169, 200; as social property, 16, 61, 66, 80, 94, 123, 137, 138, 221

Mensheviks, 86, 237–38

Minibrigades. *See* Voluntary work

Ministry of Domestic Trade, 106, 145, 146

Ministry of Finance, 136, 240

Ministry of Foreign Trade, 19, 106, 145

Ministry of Industry, 13, 19, 38, 48, 101, 103, 173, 193, 194, 198, 199, 221, 223, 225, 241, 248

Ministry of Labor, 173, 175, 220, 240

Moncada garrison, 14, 57, 232

Money, 86, 114, 120, 218, 244; as money of account, 128–31, 133, 142, 221; role of in transition to socialism, 127–47, 189

Mora, Alberto, 19, 243

National Bank, 13, 38, 99, 198, 239, 240

National Institute of Agrarian Reform (INRA), 13, 19, 38, 97, 98, 106, 239; Department of Industrialization of, 99, 198, 239

New Economic Policy (NEP), 71–72, 86; as tactical retreat, 83–85, 89–92, 93

New man, 32–33, 36, 63, 72, 110, 201, 216; and building socialism, 77, 79–80, 125

Newton, Isaac, 57

Nuestra Industria: Revista Económica, 123, 243

"On the Budgetary Finance System" (Guevara), 83, 103, 119, 127, 139, 144, 154, 236

"On the Law of Value" (Guevara), 123

"On the Slogan for a United States of Europe" (Lenin), 236

Organization of American States, 13

Outlines of the Critique of Political Economy (Marx), 155

Overstaffing, 51

Party, revolutionary, 39, 179, 188, 197, 201, 228, 233

Pasteur, Louis, 57

Pioneers, 32

"Planning and Consciousness in the Transition to Socialism." *See* "On the Budgetary Finance System"

Pragmatism, 66

Prensa Latina, 29

Prices, 117, 118, 123, 139–40, 197; under budgetary finance system, 137–47, 219; under economic accounting system, 137, 144–45; and trade with socialist countries, 141–42, 157–58; world market, 141–42, 145, 146–47

Production: and consciousness, 66, 72, 80, 175–76, 184, 190–91, 194–95, 220–21; costs of, 75, 122–23, 133, 139–40, 169–70, 179–80, 225; and prices, 139–40; quality in, 36, 47, 50–51, 78, 189, 226. *See also* Controls, economic; Work norms

Productivity, 74, 98–99, 224

Profit and profitability, 45, 46, 75, 79–81, 98, 115, 125, 135, 215, 245–46; and economic equilibrium, 116–17, 137, 138, 142–45, 219; and effectiveness of plan, 65, 216; and enterprise competition, 35–36; as incentive, 62–63, 212; and New Economic Policy, 92; and supply and demand, 45, 116, 137, 138, 139–40, 141, 145; and value, 155–56, 157

Proudhon, Pierre Joseph, 134

Rationing, 141

Raw materials, 141, 145, 146, 151, 153, 157–58, 159–60, 200; fall in price of, 152–53

Rebel Army, 14, 97, 239

Rectification process, 20–23, 34, 39–40

Religion, 233–34

Rent, 45, 59

Revolution, 60, 63

Revolutionary Offensive (1968), 183, 250–51

Rodríguez, Carlos Rafael, 19, 239

Russian revolution, 15–16, 61, 124, 154; early years of, 83, 86–93

Saint-Simon, Claude Henri, 134

Second International, 55, 87

Sierra Maestra, 97, 239

Sik, Ota, 117

Smena Vekh, 89–91, 238–39

Social democracy, 57

Socialism, 80, 150, 152, 200. *See also* Transition to socialism and communism

"Socialism and Man in Cuba," (Guevara), 124–25

Socialist countries: and Cuba, 61, 74–75, 122, 157; economic management systems in, 75–76, 105, 120–21, 215; trade between, 122, 142, 147; and unequal exchange, 149–62

Soviet Union, 10–11, 19, 22, 23, 105, 120, 154–55; and trade with Cuba, 11, 122, 150, 159–61

Spain, Cuban war of independence against, 14

Special Period, 22–23

Stalin, Joseph, 132

State and Revolution (Lenin), 124

State enterprises, 35–36, 39, 66–67, 118, 136, 197; measuring performance of, 130, 140, 143–44, 245–46; relations between, 99–100, 114, 122, 131, 136–37, 216

Statistics, 118, 197, 200, 226

Subsidies, 138, 145

Sugar, 154

Sukhanov, N.N., 87, 238

Surplus value, 60, 155, 170, 249

Taxes, 138, 246

Technical training, 197, 224, 226; for unemployed workers, 98–99; and promotions, 179, 183

"Theses on Feuerbach" (Marx), 109, 233

Trade: with colonial countries, 156; domestic, 116, 138; foreign, 116, 146; freedom of, 91–92; between socialist countries, 122, 142, 147; unequal terms of, 149–52

Trade unions, 139, 173, 178, 191, 200, 221, 228; and administration, 197; and economic controls, 201; and "historic wage," 181–82. *See also* Central Organization of Cuban Trade Unions (CTC)

Transition to socialism and communism, 55, 57–58, 61–62; and capitalist methods, 39; and incentives, 85–94, 220–22; and law of value, 113–25; Marx on, 93, 109, 124–25, 192; and money and banking, 27–37; production under, 170–72; published literature on, 56–57, 67, 69, 71, 111; role of consciousness in, 44, 62–63, 212; and sacrifices, 79, 125, 182, 205–6; setting prices under, 137–47; in underdeveloped countries, 83–85, 121, 124–25, 217; and voluntary work, 163–66; and wages, 167–84. *See also* Consciousness; Economic planning; New Economic Policy

Unemployment, 74, 97, 98, 116
Unequal exchange, 122, 49–62, 219
Union of Young Communists (UJC), 47, 81
United Nations, 13, 154, 160, 161
United States, 74, 101; and Cuba, 14, 154, 160–61. *See also* Blockade, U.S.
Ustryalov, N.V., 91

Value, 121, 144; Marx's theory of, 111–14; as measure of output/efficiency, 35–36, 40, 42–43, 189–90; money as a measure of, 128–31, 133, 142, 218; and prices, 116–17, 118, 123–24, 138, 141, 145. *See also* Law of value; Prices; Surplus value; Unequal exchange

Vanguard, 63, 69, 194, 204–6, 213. *See also* Party, revolutionary
Vanguard workers, 192, 195
Vilaseca, Salvador, 241
Voluntarism, 73, 211
Voluntary work, 21–22, 163–66, 227–28; bureaucratic opposition to, 35, 41; Castro on, 47; Guevara on, 163–66; and minibrigades, 40–42; participation by Guevara in, 204–5. *See also* Emulation

Wages, 21, 106, 146, 167–85, 220, 227; "historic wage," 180–82; and overtime pay, 183–84; and transition to socialism, 167–74. *See also* Bonuses and penalties; Incentives, material
War, 83, 85, 87, 88, 124–25, 228
Warsaw Pact, 100
Water conservation, 47
Wealth redistribution, 79, 125, 138
Women, 41–42, 51
Work: discipline, 163, 165–66, 183–84, 199, 224–25; and health and safety, 49, 175, 177–78, 207, 228; and length of workday, 36, 51; as necessity, 49, 65, 171–72, 176–77, 178–79, 190–91, 205, 206; social attitudes toward, 33, 46, 161; transformation of, 66, 99, 195–96. *See also* Voluntary work
Work norms, 169, 172, 173, 174, 191, 197, 227; and consciousness, 47, 107, 179; and incentives, 179–80, 183, 184, 186–87, 189; and low standards, 35, 36, 37; and quality, 37, 176–77, 178, 189; and voluntary work, 164–65
Working class: and administration, 78–79, 197

Yugoslavia, 99–100

The Cuban revolution

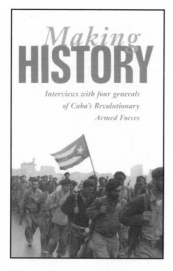

Making History

*Interviews with Four Generals of
Cuba's Revolutionary Armed Forces*
Through the stories of these four
outstanding Cuban generals, each
with close to half a century of
revolutionary activity, we can see
the class dynamics that have
shaped our entire epoch. We can
understand how the people of
Cuba, as they struggle to build a
new society, have for more than
forty years held Washington at bay.
With an introduction by Mary-Alice
Waters; preface by Juan Almeida.
$15.95

Dynamics of the Cuban Revolution

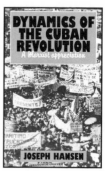

A Marxist Appreciation
Joseph Hansen
How did the Cuban revolution come about?
Why does it represent, as Hansen puts it, an
"unbearable challenge" to U.S. imperialism?
What political challenges has it confronted?
Written as the revolution advanced from its
earliest days. $20.95

In Defense of Socialism

Fidel Castro
*Four Speeches on the 30th Anniversary of the
Cuban Revolution, 1988–89*
Economic and social progress is possible without the dog-eat-dog
competition of capitalism, Castro argues, and socialism remains the
only way forward for humanity. Also discusses Cuba's role in the
struggle against the apartheid regime in southern Africa. $13.95

Celebrating the Homecoming of Ernesto Che Guevara's Reinforcement Brigade to Cuba

Articles from the *Militant* newspaper on the 30th anniversary of
the combat waged in Bolivia by Che and his comrades. $8.00

in today's world

To Speak the Truth
*Why Washington's 'Cold War'
against Cuba Doesn't End*
Fidel Castro and Che Guevara
In historic speeches before the
United Nations and UN bodies,
Guevara and Castro address the
workers of the world, explaining
why the U.S. government so hates
the example set by the socialist
revolution in Cuba and why
Washington's efforts to destroy it
will fail. $16.95

Che Guevara and the Imperialist Reality
Mary-Alice Waters
"The world of capitalist disorder—the
imperialist reality of the 21st century—would
not be strange to Che," Waters explains. "Far
from being dismayed by the odds we face, he
would have examined the world with scientific
precision and charted a course to win." Also
available in Spanish. Pamphlet. $3.00

Episodes of the Cuban Revolutionary War, 1956–58
Ernesto Che Guevara
A firsthand account of the military campaigns
and political events that culminated in the
January 1959 popular insurrection that
overthrew the Batista dictatorship. With
clarity and humor, Guevara describes his
own political education. He explains how the
struggle transformed the men and women of
the Rebel Army and July 26 Movement led by
Fidel Castro. Also available in a Spanish
edition by Editora Politica. $23.95

Che Guevara Talks to Young People

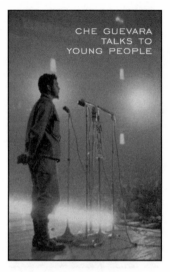

The legendary Argentine-born revolutionary challenges youth of Cuba and the world to work and become disciplined. To fearlessly join the front lines of struggles, small and large. To read and to study. To aspire to be revolutionary combatants. To politicize the organizations they are part of and in the process politicize themselves. To become a different kind of human being as they strive together with working people of all lands to transform the world. And, along this line of march; to renew and revel in the spontaneity and joy of being young. $14.95

The Second Declaration of Havana

With the *First Declaration of Havana*

Two manifestos of the Cuban people to the oppressed and exploited throughout the Americas. The first declaration, proclaimed September 1960, calls for "the right of the peasants to the land; the right of the workers to the fruit of their labor; and the right of nations to nationalize the imperialist monopolies." The second declaration, February 1962, calls for continent-wide revolutionary struggle. "What does the Cuban revolution teach?" it asks. "That revolution is possible." $4.50

Che Guevara: Economics and Politics in the Transition to Socialism

Carlos Tablada

Quoting extensively from Guevara's writings and speeches on building socialism, this book presents the interrelationship of the market, economic planning, material incentives, and voluntary work; and why profit and other capitalist categories cannot be yardsticks for measuring progress in the transition to socialism. Also available in Spanish and French. $18.95

by *KARL MARX* and
FREDERICK ENGELS

The Communist Manifesto *Karl Marx, Frederick Engels*

Founding document of the modern working-class movement, published in 1848. Explains why communism is derived not from preconceived principles but from facts, from proletarian movements springing from the actual class struggle. $3.95

Capital *Karl Marx*

Marx explains the workings of the capitalist system and how it produces the insoluble contradictions that breed class struggle. He demonstrates the inevitability of the revolutionary transformation of society into one ruled for the first time by the producing majority: the working class. Volume 1, $14.95; volume 2, $13.95; volume 3, $14.95

Anti-Dühring *Frederick Engels*

Modern socialism is not a doctrine, but a movement of the working class that arises as one of the social consequences of the establishment of large-scale capitalist industry. This defense of materialism and the fundamental ideas of scientific communism explains why. A "handbook for every class-conscious worker"—V.I. Lenin. In Marx and Engels *Collected Works*, vol. 25, $25.00

The Poverty of Philosophy *Karl Marx*

Written by the young Marx in collaboration with working-class fighters in the League of the Just, this polemic against Pierre-Joseph Proudhon's middle-class socialism gave Marx the opportunity to "develop the basic features of his new historical and economic outlook," Frederick Engels notes in his 1884 preface. $9.95

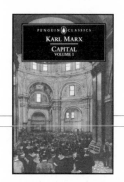

AVAILABLE FROM PATHFINDER

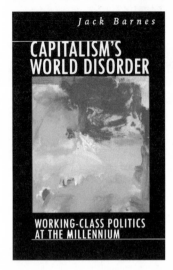

Capitalism's World Disorder

Working-class Politics at the Millennium

JACK BARNES

The social devastation, financial panic, political turmoil, police brutality, and acts of imperialist aggression accelerating around us are not chaos. They are the product of lawful—and understandable—forces unleashed by capitalism. But the future the propertied classes have in store for us is not inevitable. It can be changed by the timely solidarity, courageous action, and united struggle of workers and farmers conscious of their power to transform the world. Also available in Spanish and French. $23.95

The Changing Face of U.S. Politics

Working-Class Politics and the Trade Unions

JACK BARNES

A handbook for the new generations coming into the factories, mines, and mills, as they react to the uncertain life, ceaseless turmoil, and brutality of capitalism. It shows how millions of working people, as political resistance grows, will revolutionize themselves, their unions and other organizations, and their conditions of life and work. $19.95 Also available in Spanish and French

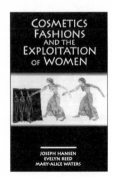

Cosmetics, Fashions, and the Exploitation of Women

JOSEPH HANSEN, EVELYN REED, AND MARY-ALICE WATERS

How big business promotes cosmetics to generate profits and perpetuate the inferior status of women. The introduction by Waters explains how the entry of millions of women into the workforce during and after World War II irreversibly changed U.S. society and laid the basis for a renewed rise of struggles for women's equality. $14.95

The Leninist Strategy of Party Building

The Debate on Guerrilla Warfare in Latin America

JOSEPH HANSEN

In the 1960s and '70s, revolutionists in the Americas and throughout the world debated how to apply the lessons of the Cuban revolution to struggles elsewhere. An analysis by the leading participant in that debate. $26.95

Teamster Rebellion

FARRELL DOBBS

The 1934 strikes that built the industrial union movement in Minneapolis and helped pave the way for the CIO, recounted by a central leader of that battle. The first in a four-volume series on the class-struggle leadership of the strikes and organizing drives that transformed the Teamsters union in much of the Midwest into a fighting social movement and pointed the road toward independent labor political action. $16.95

Lenin's Final Fight

Speeches and Writings, 1922–23

V. I. LENIN

In the early 1920s Lenin waged a political battle in the leadership of the Communist Party of the USSR to maintain the course that had enabled the workers and peasants to overthrow the tsarist empire, carry out the first successful socialist revolution, and begin building a world communist movement. The issues posed in Lenin's political fight remain at the heart of world politics today. Also available in Spanish. $19.95

The History of the Russian Revolution

LEON TROTSKY

The social, economic, and political dynamics of the first socialist revolution as told by one of its central leaders. Also available in Russian.
Unabridged edition, 3 vols. in one. $35.95

Malcolm X Speaks

"No, I'm not an American. I'm one of the 22 million Black people who are victims of Americanism." The best selection of speeches and statements from the last year of Malcolm's life. $17.95

U.S. Imperialism Has Lost the Cold War . . .

. . . That's what the Socialist Workers Party concluded a decade ago, in the wake of the collapse of regimes and parties across Eastern Europe and in the USSR that claimed to be Communist. Contrary to imperialism's hopes, the working class in those countries had not been crushed. It remains an intractable obstacle to reimposing and stabilizing capitalist relations, one that will have to be confronted by the exploiters in class battles—in a hot war.

Three issues of the Marxist magazine *New International* analyze the propertied rulers' failed expectations and chart a course for revolutionaries in response to the renewed rise of worker and farmer resistance to the economic and social instability, spreading wars, and rightist currents bred by the world market system. They explain why the historic odds in favor of the working class have increased, not diminished, at the opening of the 21st century.

New International no. 11

U.S. Imperialism Has Lost the Cold War *by Jack Barnes* ◆ Socialism: A Viable Option *by José Ramón Balaguer* ◆ Young Socialists Manifesto $14.00

New International no. 10

Imperialism's March toward Fascism and War *by Jack Barnes* ◆ What the 1987 Stock Market Crash Foretold ◆ Defending Cuba, Defending Cuba's Socialist Revolution *by Mary-Alice Waters* ◆ The Curve of Capitalist Development *by Leon Trotsky* $14.00

New International no. 7

Opening Guns of World War III: Washington's Assault on Iraq *by Jack Barnes* ◆ 1945: When U.S. Troops Said "No!" *by Mary-Alice Waters* ◆ Lessons from the Iran-Iraq War *by Samad Sharif* $12.00

Distributed by Pathfinder

These issues of **New International** are also available in the Spanish **Nueva Internacional**, the French **Nouvelle Internationale**, and the Swedish **Ny International**.

Revolution in Central America and the Caribbean

The Second Assassination of Maurice Bishop

by Steve Clark

The lead article in *New International* no. 6 reviews the accomplishments of the 1979–83 revolution in the Caribbean island of Grenada. Explains the roots of the 1983 coup that led to the murder of revolutionary leader Maurice Bishop, and to the destruction of the workers and farmers government by a Stalinist political faction within the governing New Jewel Movement.

Also in *New International* no. 6:
Washington's Domestic Contra Operation *by Larry Seigle* • Renewal or Death: Cuba's Rectification Process *two speeches by Fidel Castro* • Land, Labor, and the Canadian Revolution *by Michel Dugré*
$15.00

Che Guevara, Cuba, and the Road to Socialism

Articles by Ernesto Che Guevara, Carlos Rafael Rodríguez, Carlos Tablada, Mary-Alice Waters, Steve Clark, Jack Barnes

Exchanges from the early 1960s and today on the political perspectives defended by Guevara as he helped lead working people to advance the transformation of economic and social relations in Cuba. In *New International* no. 8.
$10.00

Distributed by Pathfinder